The United Nations System:
coordinating its economic and social work

The United Nations System:

coordinating its economic and social work

A study prepared under the auspices of the
United Nations Institute for Training and Research
(UNITAR)
by MARTIN HILL
*Former Assistant Secretary-General of the United Nations
for Inter-Agency Affairs*

CAMBRIDGE UNIVERSITY PRESS

CAMBRIDGE
LONDON · NEW YORK · MELBOURNE

CAMBRIDGE UNIVERSITY PRESS
Cambridge, New York, Melbourne, Madrid, Cape Town, Singapore, São Paulo

Cambridge University Press
The Edinburgh Building, Cambridge CB2 8RU, UK

Published in the United States of America by Cambridge University Press, New York

www.cambridge.org
Information on this title: www.cambridge.org/9780521216746

First published 1978
This digitally printed version 2008

A catalogue record for this publication is available from the British Library

Library of Congress Cataloguing in Publication data
Hill, Martin.
The United Nations system.
Includes index.
1. United Nations. 2. United Nations. Economic and Social Council. I. Title.
JX1977.H533   341.23   77–71410

ISBN 978-0-521-21674-6 hardback
ISBN 978-0-521-07298-4 paperback

Contents

Contents

Foreword

The author occupied a special place among international officials. In the first place, he was, so to speak, the doyen of the corps, having served without interruption since 1927 in the Secretariats of the League of Nations and the United Nations, and recently with the United Nations Institute for Training and Research (UNITAR) and the World Intellectual Property Organization (WIPO). In the second place, during almost his entire career he was concerned with building up the economic and social side of international work. He was, for example, Secretary of the Bruce Committee set up by the League in 1939, which prepared the ground for the United Nations Economic and Social Council; he was Dr Gunnar Myrdal's deputy during the earliest days of the Economic Commission for Europe; he was one of the top members of the staff of the San Francisco Conference and the Preparatory Commission of the United Nations that met in London in 1945; he was deputy-head of the United Nations Department of Economic and Social Affairs for 12 years, and, for more than 20, the personal representative of my predecessors Trygve Lie, Dag Hammarskjöld and U Thant to the Specialized Agencies; he was Rapporteur of the Administrative Committee on Coordination and Chairman of its Preparatory Committee; he held the newly created post of Assistant Secretary-General for Inter-Agency Affairs from 1967 until his retirement.

Mr Martin Hill wrote with the personal knowledge and authority which such experience affords. He had dealt with a broad spectrum of structural and organizational questions that have for some time been preoccupying the UN's intergovernmental organs as being of vital importance if the UN is to carry out effectively and comprehensively its enormous and rapidly expanding responsibilities. In the last few years, moreover, the General Assembly has been especially concerned to bring about such restructuring of the United Nations System as may be needed to make it fully responsive to the requirements of the new international order and the Charter of the Economic Rights and Duties of States. On some of the issues involved the views of Governments seem to have been moving closer together; on others the differences are still considerable.

The book owes its origin to an initiative of UNITAR, financially assisted by the Rockefeller Foundation that led to Mr Hill preparing, in the Spring of 1974, a study for UNITAR under the title 'Towards Greater Order, Coherence and Coordination in the United Nations System', which was made available to the Economic and Social Council that summer and since then to other organs concerned. That study has now been revised and enlarged and brought up to date. The views expressed in the paper that follows are the author's own; they do not necessarily correspond – and may even be at variance on specific points – with those of the responsible UN inter-governmental organs and myself. It represents, however, the most comprehensive treatment ever attempted of the burning issues with which it deals, and I cannot but think that it will long be found indispensable to students as well as to government officials concerned with international organization.

Preface

In his 'Introduction to the *Report of the Secretary-General on the Work of the Organization*', Dr Kurt Waldheim stated in August 1976 that '. . . in these last years I have learnt to appreciate the extraordinary range, variety and sometimes the unexpectedness, of the Organization's activities, the great possibilities as well as the obstacles which it confronts, and the wealth of human talent and dedication which is to be found among the national representatives and international civil servants who work in the United Nations System'. Martin Hill was one of these dedicated international civil servants, with an experience in addition which was unrivalled in international administration. He has brought to this study his unparalleled knowledge of the United Nations System, meticulous scholarship and much painstaking attention to the details of the relationship between various organizations.

The present work is an expanded version of an earlier study which was published by the United Nations Institute for Training and Research (UNITAR) in 1974, under the title, 'Towards Greater Order, Coherence and Coordination in the United Nations System'. That study exerted a significant influence on discussions and decisions on development and coordination within the United Nations System. The importance and value of this study was recognized by the United Nations Economic and Social Council, and was thus issued as one of its documents; the Council used it extensively in the rationalization of its structures and procedures and in preparation for what was to become the historic sixth Special Session of the General Assembly. This eventually culminated in the adoption of the momentous Declaration on the Establishment of a New Economic Order and a Programme of Action for Implementing the Declaration. I have no doubt that the present study by Martin Hill will assist not only the international community towards a greater understanding of the issues confronting the world, but also the United Nations System of organizations, through its better coordination of efforts, towards increasing its effectiveness as an agent for change and development.

Preface

The study begins with a lucid and brief introduction, which explains the concept and complex nature of the 'United Nations System', its purposes and objectives, and how it operates. While political and security questions engage a substantial part of the time and resources of the United Nations itself, the main preoccupation of the system of the UN Organizations and bodies is the promotion of economic and social development through global policies and operational programmes, which have increasing multi-sectoral implications. The introduction makes clear the role of substantive and administrative coordination and the machinery and mechanisms at the intergovernmental and secretariat levels.

Part I of the study deals with the problems of coordination and its setting. Chapter I sketches the difficulties inherent in the decentralized UN System, tracing its growth from the League of Nations through the tortuous path the United Nations took in its early years. Particular emphasis is given to the controversy over the extent and methods of decentralization. There is a broad view of the growth of the UN System on the basis of Charter provisions and the specific agreements concluded between the UN and its agencies. The problem of creating a common and integrated system, with a central role from the very beginning for the Economic and Social Council, assumes significance as new programmes and responsibilities are evolved. Questions of competing jurisdiction, conflicting patterns of intergovernmental participation and the absence of coordination at the national level soon came to bedevil the system.

The inter-agency relationships and coordination developed under the constraints of the above factors are fully illustrated in Chapter 2. The increase in operational activities, involving innumerable organs, called for coordination at all levels as the system was not built to resolve contentious issues thrown up at every stage. Piecemeal and expedient measures only helped to postpone a more radical and comprehensive restructuring and redefinition of roles and functions. We are still faced with this task and Chapter 2 provides a clear survey of issues involved in terms of programmes, organizations, procedures and above all basic principles.

Coordination is a much abused word in the national and international context. To understand the concept, one has to appreciate the full import of the matters susceptible to coordination. In the UN System these are more precise within its own policy objectives and built-in mechanisms. Chapter 3 gives us a very cogent account of the content of coordination activities. The straightforward aspect is administrative and budgetary coordination, based mainly on the

xii

formal powers of the Economic and Social Council and the concept
of the 'Common System' accepted by agencies in terms of the agreements entered into between them and the United Nations. The main
mechanism of administrative coordination is seen to be the Committee of Executive Heads (Administrative Committee on Coordination – ACC) established by the Economic and Social Council and its
many subcommittees and task forces; these are all functional groups
for implementing decisions and establishing inter-agency coordination at the inter-secretariat level. There is a broad legislative overview of specific matters, e.g. finance, by such intergovernmental
bodies as the Advisory Committee on Administrative and Budgetary
Questions, functioning primarily within the legislative framework of
the United Nations itself and serviced by the UN Secretariat, as contrasted with the ACC and its subgroups. But programme coordination, with its three-tier arrangement of central control, regional
distribution and country-level implementation, is a different and
more difficult operation, which continues to baffle all effective
attempts at understanding by intergovernmental bodies, special
UN Commissions and scholarly thinking. We are fortunate to
have a succinct statement of this fundamental subject in this
chapter.

Chapters 4, 5 and 6 give a detailed account of the powers, responsibilities and methods of operation of the intergovernmental and
inter-secretariat organs engaged in coordination. This is followed by
a brief statement, in Chapter 7, of the major constraints, and is
illustrated with typical examples of the confused situation. Thus we
find in Part I, a panoramic view of the purposes of coordination as
envisaged in the Charter, the many paths it has taken over the years,
the issues faced in carrying out the task, and the approaches and
instrumentalities used in actual practice.

Part II is, in a sense, more important and useful for solving the
problems of coordination, although on first reading, it might appear
very technical. However, the descriptive account of Part I, together
with the first chapter (Chapter 8) of Part II which provides the context and the perspective, adequately prepare the general reader for a
full understanding and appreciation of the sound prescriptive
measures proposed in Chapters 9 to 13.

The context and the perspective are updated in the light of the
comprehensive and concrete call for action embodied in the decisions
and recommendations of the Sixth and Seventh Special Sessions
which dealt with the theme of the New International Economic
Order. This new orientation requires considerable restructuring of

the UN System, a revitalized machinery for operational activities, and unavoidable coordination on a multi-sectoral basis.

The primary task in this context is the role and the functioning of the Economic and Social Council. Chapter 9 indicates how this can be achieved through strong leadership from the General Assembly and through rationalization of the procedures and methods of work by the Council itself. The wise suggestions for employing tact, persuasion and initiative over a widening circle of intergovernmental bodies and proliferating secretariats are timely and practical.

The elaboration of attitudes, practices and policies of intergovernmental organs and Governments, in Chapter 10, reflects Martin Hill's complete comprehension of the essential ingredients of the prevailing situation. This highly controversial and complicated situation is handled in this chapter with restraint, combined with bold imagination, and will be found extremely useful by national and international officials. The general reader is able to follow the intricacies of decision making and the challenging possibilities now available to the Secretary-General and other executive heads of agencies.

In logical sequence to the above, Chapter 11 provides the general guidelines governing the work of the Administrative Committee on Coordination, which is vested with the major responsibility for coordinating the work, both administrative and substantive, of the UN System.

While policies are set, centres of coordination established, and the correct procedures and mechanisms adopted, in the final analysis as Chapter 12 makes clear, the administrative and organizational arrangements, 'subject to the imponderable factor of the personalities, capacities and nationalities of the officials concerned' are the most crucial. This chapter advances a reasoned thesis for the central leadership of the Secretary-General in all matters of coordination. By analyzing the evolution of relationship between the United Nations Development Programme, with its new structures and procedures, and the UN Department of Economic and Social Affairs, with its pivotal role for policy coordination within the UN Secretariat on operational activities, we are able to see the need for changes at various levels based on the sound theory that 'the separation of policy and operations is of questionable validity'. The tasks performed by the Office of Inter-Agency Affairs and Coordination, functioning both as the secretariat for the inter-agency ACC and also the arm of the Secretary-General for these matters, are briefly indicated within the general context.

The last chapter (Chapter 13) of Part II of the study offers an

insight into the responsibilities of the General Assembly and the need
for a fresh and frank reappraisal of its functions if there is to be the
desired concentration of authority and administration. We are shown
the signposts of danger if the UN System does not move in this direction. Obviously the General Assembly will exercise its functions through
the Economic and Social Council, a principle which requires no change
but merely reaffirmation by 'streamlining policy making and management through a greater concentration of authority in the Council'.

We are made fully aware of the immediate task of bringing about
an increased measure of coherence and rationality to the United
Nations System as a whole, taking into account such factors as the
innumerable underlying issues of resource distribution, the allocation
of priorities for programmes among different agencies and sectors,
and the relationship of the system to non-UN organizations. While
not attempting to provide answers to such larger questions, the study
has, in my opinion, succeeded in unravelling the intricate and complex relationships that now exist at the intergovernmental and inter-
secretariat levels of policy making in operational activities within the
UN System, and the crucial function of coordination. This is no
small achievement and I have no doubt that with the greater understanding made possible by this study, those in the UN System can
undertake more effectively the gigantic task of reorganization before
them. The perception of possibilities in carrying out this task is a
tribute to the late Martin Hill's long years of hard work at the
United Nations in the area of coordination.

The special outlook of a scholar–administrator which was so
evident in Martin Hill, reached fulfillment in the last decade of his
life when he became one of the moving spirits behind the founding
and organization of the United Nations Institute for Training and
Research (UNITAR) and for a different purpose a few years later,
the United Nations University. I was privileged to have been associated with him during this period and admired him.

He became a Special Fellow of UNITAR under a Rockefeller
Foundation Grant during the period when most of this book was
written.

He was latterly the New York representative of the World Intellectual Property Organization until his death.

UNITAR is fortunate to have been a partner in the preparation
of this study and I commend it to a still larger audience.

Davidson Nicol
Executive Director, UNITAR
Under-Secretary-General,
United Nations

Introduction

The significance of coordination in the United Nations System
The term 'United Nations System' is used in this paper to denote all parts of the United Nations Organization itself which are concerned with promoting the economic and social goals set out in the United Nations Charter, as well as the specialized agencies and the International Atomic Energy Agency (IAEA), which are working with the United Nations towards the same ends. Coordination in the system is important in so far as it is a means towards those ends, but it should not be considered as an end in itself. As the then Director-General of the International Labour Office remarked a few years ago: 'In the final reckoning, the test of all our efforts is what we do for human freedom and human dignity, what we do to banish fear and want, what we do to promote greater economic security and greater equality of opportunity...We will not be judged by the perfection or imperfection of the institutional pattern but by the quality of human life which our work makes possible.'[1]

It may be argued that the contribution already made through the United Nations to economic development and social progress throughout the world has not been seriously affected by a touch, at least, of organizational incoherence. Indeed, some lack of coordination, including some duplication and overlapping of activities, disputes about competences, untidiness and discrepancies in administrative arrangements, occasional failures to cooperate, conceptual differences in regard to objectives – all of which are common phenomena in national administrations – is unavoidable in a dynamic, growing and pioneering international system. Furthermore, it is part of the price that will always have to be paid by the United Nations for the advantage of being able, through the international functional agencies, to mobilize the active participation and support of the relevant technical ministries and professional groups in each country. It would be easy, though tedious, to show how all parts of the decentralized system have learned to work together, on an ever-widening series of broad programmes in a way never envisaged in

1945, and, still more striking, how in major emergencies such as the Congo operation of 1960–1964,[2] the Biafra situation in 1969, the aftermath of the Bangladesh conflict of 1971–1972, and the Sudano–Sahelian drought from 1973, as well as in numerous operations for relief and reconstruction after sudden natural disasters, the specialized agencies and organizations such as the United Nations Children's Fund (UNICEF) and the Office of the High Commissioner for Refugees, have worked in concert under United Nations leadership.

While all this is true, there has been growing criticism, from different angles, of defects in the system, as well as doubt regarding the capacity of the system to cope successfully with the immense range and scope of new tasks requiring international action that each year brings forth. Part of this criticism and doubt has been concerned with issues connected with coordination which have been familiar for the past 25 years or more, such as the unresolved differences of view regarding the respective competences of different agencies in particular fields, and of the United Nations regional economic commissions and the specialized agencies in regard to action at the regional level; and there continue to be cases of duplication and overlapping, of lack of cooperation among organizations and their staffs, of failures to consult, and divergencies of objectives. But to a considerable extent the thrust of the criticism has been shifting. There has been wider recognition of the value of the practical, if often minor, results, reported on year by year, of the regular efforts to solve individual coordination problems, as they arise, through the machinery which has been built up under the Economic and Social Council (ECOSOC) and the Administrative Committee on Coordination (ACC). A broader set of problems moved to the centre of the picture, problems concerned with policy coordination as well as structure – and not incompatible with good coordination among officials, in the sense that they work smoothly together without duplication.

The very complexity of the system as well as the extraordinary diversity of, and often apparent lack of coherence in, its activities, are themselves sources of frustration, as is the sense, especially among the major contributors, that the regular budgets, and the programmes financed under those budgets by mandatory assessments, escape their control. Furthermore, frustration has been voiced, with different emphases by different groups of countries, because of the lack of cohesion within the United Nations itself and the various parts of its Secretariat; the proliferation of intergovernmental organs, many with overlapping mandates and almost all of unmanageable size; the proliferation of highly independent voluntary funds for purposes not necessarily corresponding to established priorities; the soaring budgets for tasks which may not always be well considered from the standpoint of cost/benefit or coordination; the quasi-impossibility of comparing and therefore of coordinating the future plans of different agencies; the involvement of so many agencies, including organs of the United Nations itself, in almost every undertaking; the independent public information and, in many cases, fund-raising activities of several agencies and most of the United Nations programmes; the 'jungle' of United Nations and agency regional and subregional structures which makes system-wide action at those levels so difficult; the over-frequent and uncoordinated visits by officials of different organizations to the capitals of developing countries, and last but not least, the unconscionable time and effort which the multifarious coordinating processes seem to require. Underlying such complaints – the list of which could easily be extended – but partly independent of them, is concern about the increasingly and seriously fragmented character of the system and the possibility of further fragmentation in very important fields such as raw materials and energy, and the resources of the sea-bed and ocean floor, if current trends are not arrested.

Such preoccupations and criticisms may not be altogether justified but they do have some substance and they combine to constitute a challenge to the reputation of the system that cannot be ignored. In some respects, the situation, especially within the UN itself, has been getting steadily worse. Future use of the UN machinery and support for its economic and social work may largely depend on the degree to which these shortcomings can be corrected. That was the justification for the United Nations Institute for Training and Research (UNITAR) paper, on which the present study is based; that paper was written in the belief that economic and social cooperation through the United Nations System has become essential and irreplaceable, that no effort must be spared to preserve and further it, and that considerable improvement can be brought about without insuperable difficulty.

The problems within the United Nations System represent, of course, only part of the problem of bringing greater order, coherence and coordination into international economic and social action as a whole, among United Nations and non-United Nations organizations, world-wide and regional, and between United Nations bodies and the bilateral aid activities of individual donor Governments. To separate the part from the whole has considerable disadvantages since the duplication and even conflict between United Nations and non-United Nations bodies are themselves among the most serious and conspicuous causes of criticism, and solutions may well affect the structure, functioning and programmes of organs within, no less than those outside, the United Nations System.[3] Nevertheless, enough has been said to indicate that, even with this restriction, the range of questions involved is enormous. It will be necessary indeed not only to confine discussion to broad issues, avoiding any attempt to consider detailed problems and methods of coordination, but also to exclude any but general references to the 'operational' problems and in particular those relating to technical cooperation – to which such close attention was given in the *Study of the Capacity of the United Nations Development System*[4] (hereafter referred to as 'the Capacity Study') and in the deliberations on it of the Governing Council of the United Nations Development Programme (UNDP) and the General Assembly.

Whatever the shortcomings of the United Nations' own structure, about which there will be a good deal to say later, the relationships between the United Nations and the specialized agencies have so far been the main object of official scrutiny. Government opinion in this regard seems to have shifted not a little from that which prevailed in 1945 at the San Francisco Conference (in which much less than half of the present membership of the United Nations and the agencies participated) and during the years immediately following, when most of the agreements between the United Nations and the agencies were concluded. Having shown at the beginning a perhaps excessive concern to protect the autonomy and independence of the specialized agencies and avoid any danger that the General Assembly or the Economic and Social Council might seek to control their policies and programmes, many Governments are now putting increased emphasis on the need for greater unity and leadership in the system.

Dag Hammarskjöld, as Secretary-General, sought the same thing more than 20 years ago. Using the theme 'Unity within Freedom', he envisaged the heads of agencies working with him to make ACC of greater service to the Council and the Governments through recommendations for action and priorities. He looked forward to the establishment of interorganizational relationships 'based on a spirit of mutual confidence directed towards common aims' which would 'in practice provide the Council with all the advantages of a closely unified system without any of the disadvantages of rigid centralization.'[5] This idea did not receive from the Council or agencies the support he had hoped for and he soon lost interest in pursuing it, believing that the absence of an 'organ which through majority decision can lay down a common line of action' represented a weakness in the system which a committee of the administrative heads functioning on the basis of unanimity (made necessary by the autonomy of the organizations) could do little to correct.[6]

But the need for greater unity of purpose and action in the system became more evident and was more strongly voiced year by year. It was, for example, a major preoccupation of the programme appraisals undertaken in 1959 and 1960 by a group of former officers of the Council,[7] and of the Enlarged Committee on Programme and Coordination which met from 1966–1969,[8] as well as of the Pearson Commission of the World Bank[9] and the Capacity Study issued in 1969.

Economic development and the growing need for greater unity of action and purpose

Discussion of organization and procedures in these and successive years must be viewed in the light of the growing intensity and scope of the demands presented in many UN organs but chiefly in the United Nations Conference on Trade and Development (UNCTAD) and the General Assembly, for UN policies and action to promote more actively and effectively the economic and social development of the Third World and particularly to redress the inequalities and injustices inherent in the existing pattern of international economic relations. The first UN Development Decade – of the 1960s – had not been without results, but it had represented an aspiration, not a programme of action, its achievements had been more than offset by adverse factors such as the continued fall in the terms of trade of the raw material-producing countries and the aid to be furnished by the industrialized countries fell, in most cases, far short of what had been accepted as the minimum required. A determined effort to develop an adequate international programme of action to meet the growing crises in the relations between the developed and the developing world – an effort in which UNCTAD took the lead and to which ECOSOC's Committee on Development Planning made a notable contribution – led to the unanimous adoption by the General Assembly in 1970 (Resolution 2626 (xxv)) of the International Development Strategy for the Second United Nations Development Decade. The Strategy, which represented a consensus built up after years of study and political discussion, called for a more complex and articulated programme than ever before of supporting action by the UN organizations. Concern among many Governments that the UN System was not adequately organized for this task soon found expression in the Council's Committee on Rationalization and in a resolution adopted at the Council's 54th (Spring 1973) Session that the existing Agreements between the UN and the specialized agencies should be reviewed 'with a view to strengthening the coherence of the system and its capacity to fulfil...the objectives of the International Development Strategy in an effective and coordinated manner'. (Resolution 1768 (LIV), para. 13.) At the opening of the Council's next session, its President, Ambassador Sergio Armando Frazao of Brazil, noted that the Council had:

failed to play its central role; as a consequence all the other organs had acted as if they were not part of the whole. The problem was to redress that situation in such a way that the respective duties and responsibilities were correctly discharged but with a deeper feeling of interdependence, conducive to a workable arrangement whereby the Council would contribute from the centre of the system to the objectives and purposes of the agencies. (E/SR. 1859.)

At the same session, the Secretary-General of the United Nations spoke in general terms of the 'danger of losing our way through excessive fragmentation' and of the need for 'over-all coherence and direction of the system'.

During the debate that followed, the representative of the United States of America, endorsing, as did several others, the view of the President and the Secretary-General, said that 'what is required... is for this Council to provide a greater degree of guidance, direction, integrated planning for the economic and social activities of the various United Nations agencies'. The point was considerably elaborated in the *Introduction to the Report of the Secretary-General on the Work of the Organization*, submitted to the General Assembly at its Twenty-eighth Session. To quote two sentences from that report:

...many of the problems we face require an integrated, disciplined and highly co-ordinated approach if the United Nations system is to operate with maximum effectiveness and if it is to be capable of clearly identifying degrees of urgency and of setting priorities in full knowledge of what is involved – in fact, of formulating a general policy...The reassertion of the constitutional authority of the Economic and Social Council within the system and its fulfilment of the function of providing the conceptual framework for the entire system of United Nations organizations would certainly be an important step in balancing the tendency to fragmentation. (A/9001/Add.1.)

Such thinking – which provided the context in which this study was begun – was accompanied by mounting concern about the world economic situation and particularly – to quote the cautious language of the General Assembly – 'the growing gap between the developed and the developing countries and the slow rate of progress in the implementation of the goals and objectives of the International Development Strategy'. At the Fourth Conference of Heads of State of Non-Aligned Countries, held at Algiers in September 1973, after extensive references to the evils of colonialism and exploitation, the Conference called upon the UN General Assembly to arrange for a Special Session devoted exclusively to development problems. This request was duly acceded to, the General Assembly deciding (Resolution 3172 (xxviii)) to hold a Special Session 'at a high political level' just before its Thirtieth (regular) Session (September 1975) 'for the purpose of examining the political and other implications of the state of world development and international economic cooperation, expanding the dimensions and concepts of world economic and developmental cooperation and giving the goal of development its rightful place in the United Nations system and on the international stage, and also decides that at the special session the Assembly will, in the light of the implementation of the International Development Strategy for the Second United Nations Development Decade:

(a) Consider new concepts and options with a view to promoting effectively the solution of world economic problems, in particular those of developing countries, and assist in the evolution of a system of world economic relations based on the equality and common interest of all countries;

(b) Initiate the necessary and appropriate structural changes to make the United Nations system a more effective instrument of world economic cooperation and for the implementation of the International Development Strategy'.

The Economic and Social Council was asked to take all necessary measures to organize the Special Session on Development and Economic Cooperation, including the final preparation of the documentation.

The world economic crisis and the demands for a new
international economic order

This action was taken in December 1973. Two months earlier, the world economy, already in serious difficulty, had been further shaken by the decision of the Organization of Petroleum Exporting Countries (OPEC) to increase approximately four-fold the price of crude oil. Among the measures proposed directly affecting countries, both industrialized and developing, that depended on oil imports, was a proposal by the French Government to convene an international meeting on energy problems. In a letter to the Secretary-General of 6 January 1974, the President of Algeria, in his capacity of President in office of the group of Non-Aligned Countries proposed, as an alternative to the French idea, a Special Session of the General Assembly to consider questions relating to development and all types of raw materials. The necessary support for this proposal under the General Assembly's Rules of Procedure was quickly obtained, and the Sixth Special Session on 'Raw Materials and Development' met from 9 April to 1 May.

Despite the language of Resolution 3172 of the Twenty-eighth General Assembly, earlier resolutions of UNCTAD and the Non-Aligned Countries, a message of the Shah of Iran envisaging a readjustment of the world economic order and a host of other indications, few observers foresaw the depth and universality of the demand by the Third World at the Special Session, or the support by many developed countries, for a profound change in international economic relations in the interest of justice and welfare; nor did they foresee the session's momentous consequences. The General Assembly drew up and adopted without vote (though with strong reservations by several developed countries) a Declaration on the Establishment of a New Economic Order and a Programme of Action for implementing that declaration. These documents have already exerted, and will inevitably continue to exert for many years to come, a major influence on international discussion and decision, as well as on national policies. While the central issues set forth below in Part I remain and the conclusions set forth in Part II have, in the author's view, lost none of their validity or priority, the new developments will affect – in ways so far only partially clarified – the tasks, the methods and the structure of the United Nations System and thus the context in which organization and coordination must be considered. It will be necessary, therefore, to devote a little time to reviewing the main reforms in international economic relations which are envisaged or have already occurred and to probing their implications. This will be attempted in the Postscript.

PART I

THE PROBLEM OF COORDINATION
AND ITS SETTING

1 Relationship problems inherent in the decentralized United Nations System

The organizational structure of the League of Nations' non-political work – on economic and financial matters, on communications and transit, on health, on narcotic drug control and certain other social problems – was essentially a centralized one, although each technical 'organization' enjoyed a considerable degree of independence. The Expert Committees in each organization reported to the League of Nations Council and were served by members of the League secretariat; and the work was financed from the budget of the League. That budget also financed the work of the International Labour Organization (ILO), which had been established, in accordance with Chapter 13 of the Treaty of Versailles, 'at the seat of the League of Nations as part of the organisation of the League'.

The proposals made in August 1939 by the Special Committee of the League of Nations on the Development of International Co-operation in Economic and Social Affairs (the Bruce Committee) would have replaced in this field the League Council – a body consisting largely of Ministers for Foreign Affairs and concerned primarily with political issues – by a Central Committee for Economic and Social Questions, composed in large part of ministers and high officials directly involved in such questions and in which non-Members of the League could participate on a basis of equality with Members. The Central Committee was to exercise, as the League Council had done, 'direction and control' over all the League's economic and social activities. The Bruce proposals – which did not affect or refer to the activities of the ILO – were endorsed by the League's General Assembly in December 1939; but, because of the World War, could not be carried into effect.

The ideas embodied in Chapters 9 and 10 of the UN Charter in regard to international organization in the economic and social fields, and, in particular, the establishment of the Economic and Social Council, drew heavily on the League's experience, including the proposed Bruce reforms. The new constitutional arrangements, however, were highly decentralized on a functional basis, autonomous international organizations being entrusted, under a some-what vague coordinating authority of the United Nations, with functions corresponding roughly to those of the traditional national government departments – finance, agriculture, labour, health, education, etc. The broad reasons for this change are not difficult to identify and understand. By the time the San Francisco Conference met, several essential parts of the new international economic and social organization already existed, or were in the process of being established, as autonomous international entities. The International Labour Organization which, throughout the inter-war years, had chafed under its – at least nominal – subordination to the League of Nations, emerged from the Second World War strengthened by the Philadelphia Declaration of 1944 and supported not only by Ministries of Labour but by organized labour and management throughout the world. One could scarcely imagine it being absorbed by the fledgeling United Nations Organization, even had Governments considered this desirable on general grounds. While it might have been just possible to bring the newly established Food and Agriculture Organization of the United Nations more closely within the United Nations framework, there had never been any question of more than a very loose relationship between the United Nations and the International Monetary Fund and the World Bank, which had likewise resulted from wartime decisions of the United Nations allies to create the elements of a new international system in time to act when peace returned.

Nor were many voices heard in favour of centralization.[1] Much was made of the argument that it would be safer to establish in each essential functional area international organizations which could stand on their own feet and survive if the United Nations Organization itself did not come into being, were torn by political conflicts, or were to be short-lived, like the League. Strong reasons of a longer-term character for a considerable measure of decentralization were also advanced, namely (a) that this was the only way the United Nations could cope with a task of the magnitude and scope envisaged in Chapter 9 of the Charter; and, (b) that successful international action in the various fields of economic and social policy depended on the active participation of, and complementary action by, the *national* authorities in each field which had close associations with their international counterparts. Such considerations could no doubt have been satisfied under varying degrees and forms of decentralization and, in the light of all that has since developed, one cannot but wonder why the most influential Governments, and in particular those of the USA and the UK, were at the time – and for many years – so unalterably opposed to any suggestion of central authority being exercised in respect of the United Nations System as a whole. This is one of the factors that differentiates the problem of coordination among international organizations from that in national administrations. It is true that in national administrations the ultimate authority of the Cabinet or Prime Minister is rarely invoked, but its very existence is not without importance. Furthermore, one lacks at the international level the influence of the Treasury or Ministry of Finance, and of the various groups of experts and task forces through which, in most countries, the draft budget has to pass.

One answer to the question just raised is no doubt that the looked-for expansion of international action in economic, social, humanitarian and related fields was envisaged largely in terms of what the League of Nations and the ILO had achieved. There would, it was thought, be more, much more, of the same. Some operational activities of the type carried out by the United Nations Relief and Rehabilitation Administration (UNRRA), of which there had also been examples in League days,[2] might continue to be needed in respect, for example, of refugees or particular devastated areas, but they were likely to be rather marginal. Essentially, the work would, as in the past, be concerned with the setting of standards, the conclusion of conventions, the interchange of experience, expert studies, consultations aimed at the harmonization of policies, and the development and refinement of statistical and other data required for the formulation of policy. Before the war, most of this work had been within sectors sufficiently self-contained to be handled by a single agency or organ. In the future, a rational division of work and arrangements for coordination[3] would, it seemed, be needed rather than unified action or central direction. The bringing into relationship with the United Nations of 'the various specialized agencies, established by intergovernmental agreement and having wide international responsibilities...in economic, social, cultural, educational, health and related fields' was provided for in Article 57 of the Charter; coordination was directly provided for in Articles 58 and 63[4] and implicit in the broad responsibility for the promotion of the economic and social objectives of the United Nations given to the Council, under the authority of the General Assembly, in Article 60; it was implicit, furthermore, in the specific authorization given to the Council by Articles 62 and 68 to initiate studies and reports, make recommendations, call international conferences and set up commissions on matters within its competence.[5] The United Nations was, in effect, given a central role and a universal competence in the field of economic and social cooperation. At the same time – as is clear not only from the Charter provisions and the relationship agreements subsequently concluded, but also from the texts of the constituent instruments of many of the agencies – it was intended that the agencies should participate, and consider themselves as participating, in promoting the purposes of the Charter as a whole.

Relationship agreements were negotiated by the Council between 1946 and 1951 with the major existing intergovernmental institutions (ILO, FAO, the United Nations Educational, Scientific and Cultural Organization (UNESCO), the International Bank for Reconstruction and Development (IBRD), the International Monetary Fund (IMF) and the International Civil Aviation Organization (ICAO)), certain smaller agencies (the Universal Postal Union (UPU), the International Telecommunication Union (ITU) and the World Meteorological Organization (WMO) (all three dating from the nineteenth century, the two first as international bureaux, the third as a non-governmental organization of meteorological services)), and three organizations which were created through the instrumentality of the United Nations itself (the World Health Organization (WHO), the International Relief Organization (IRO) and the Inter-Governmental Maritime Consultative Organization (IMCO)). The Charter of a fourth agency with a very wide mandate (the International Trade Organization (ITO), drawn up at the Havana Conference of 1947–1948 called by the United Nations, never came into force, the convention not having been ratified by the USA. This failure had a big effect on the later development of international organization – more particularly, the conclusion of the General Agreement on Tariffs and Trade in 1948 among many of the major trading countries and ultimately the establishment of the UN Conference on Trade and Development (UNCTAD) in 1964 (see Chapter 2.) Some of the other proposed functions for ITO were taken on by UNIDO in 1966.

The first agreement was concluded between the United Nations and the ILO and constituted the model on which most of the others were based, subject to considerable modification in the case of IMF and the Bank Group and simplification in the case of the smallest agencies. It was also the model for the agreement concluded by the General Assembly in 1957 with the International Atomic Energy Agency (IAEA),[6] which because of the nature of its responsibilities and its obligation to report directly to the General Assembly, was established as an agency 'under the aegis of the United Nations' and not as a 'specialized agency' under the terms of Article 57 of the Charter. Agreements, usually of a more limited character, have been concluded by a number of specialized agencies and IAEA with one another.

Apart from extensions of the United Nations–IBRD agreement in 1957 to include the International Finance Corporation (IFC) and in 1961 the International Development Association (IDA) (now known collectively as the Bank Group), no move to increase the number of specialized agencies was taken by the Council between 1951, when WMO entered the fold, and 1973, when the Council decided that it was desirable that the World Intellectual Property Organization, which had recently been restructured and expanded and was cooperating actively with several United Nations bodies, be 'brought into relationship with the United Nations and that the Council should enter into negotiations with a view to achieving that end, in accordance with Articles 57 and 63 of the Charter of the United Nations'.[7] In the intervening years, many new and important institutions including the United Nations Development Programme (UNDP), the United Nations Conference on Trade and Development (UNCTAD), the United Nations Industrial Development Organization (UNIDO) and the United Nations Environment Programme (UNEP) were created as subsidiary organs of the General Assembly; different degrees and forms of relationship, including reciprocal representation at meetings, were established with non-United Nations regional and other organizations, while working agreements providing for cooperation and coordination, but not conferring specialized agency status, were concluded with a number of organizations such as the International Union of Official Travel Organizations (IUOTO) (in anticipation of its being transformed into the World Tourism Organization) and the International Criminal Police Organization (INTERPOL).

To return to the United Nations agreements with the specialized agencies, the system of weighted voting adopted by the Bretton Woods institutions always distinguished them sharply from the others and the relationship the United Nations established with them, after considerable difficulty, was much less close and was hedged about by reservations to prevent possible interference by the United Nations that they might find embarrassing or prejudicial. The first article of the agreement with each of these organizations contains the statement 'by reason of the nature of its international responsibilities and the terms of its Articles of Agreement, the Bank (Fund) is, and is required to function as, an independent international organization. Both agreements also contain the following statement: 'the United Nations agrees that, in the interpretation of paragraph 3 of Article 17 of the United Nations Charter it will take into consideration that the Bank (Fund) does not rely for its annual budget upon contributions from its members, and that the appropriate authorities of the Bank (Fund) enjoy full autonomy in deciding the form and content of such budget'.[8]

About the content of the other United Nations–specialized agency agreements, not a great deal need be said here. They generally begin with the United Nations' recognition of the agency's authority in its field and proceed to provide for reciprocal representation at meetings, reciprocal right to propose items for the agenda of the main organs, the treatment to be given by the agency to formal recommendations of the United Nations, the exchange of information and documents, assistance to United Nations organs, and cooperation in regard to personnel arrangements, statistical services, administrative and technical services and budgetary and financial arrangements.

Certain features may, however, be mentioned because of their bearing on the purposes of this paper. First, importance was attached to defining the status and the scope of the representation of the United Nations and the agencies at one another's meetings, and to ensuring that reciprocity should be complete within the limits of relevant fields of interest. In the agreements with all the specialized agencies except the Bank Group and IMF, United Nations representatives were to be 'invited to attend' all agency meetings, in effect, and to participate without vote in them; agency representatives were to be invited to attend meetings of the Council and its commissions and committees, as well as meetings of the main committees of the General Assembly and to participate 'without vote in respect to matters of interest to them' (the language varying from case to case). The scope of these provisions has not always been understood in United Nations organs.

Secondly, the agreements with all the agencies, except IMF and the Bank Group (which have, however, provided such cooperation in practice), contain the following clause which authorized agency participation in ACC as well as other bodies such as the Committee on Programme Appraisals and the Committee for Programme and Coordination, as they were established:

The [specialized agency] affirms its intention of co-operating in whatever further measures may be necessary to make co-ordination of the activities of specialized agencies and those of the United Nations fully effective. In particular, it agrees to participate in and to co-operate with any body or bodies which the Council may establish for the purpose of facilitating such co-ordination.

Thirdly, the article on 'Budgetary and financial arrangements' in the United Nations agreements with the ILO, FAO, UNESCO, WHO, ICAO and WMO begins by recognizing

The desirability of establishing close budgetary and financial relationships with the United Nations in order that the administrative operations of the United Nations and of the specialized agencies shall be carried out in the most efficient and economical manner possible, and that the maximum measure of co-ordination and uniformity with respect to these operations shall be secured.

It proceeds to an undertaking by both parties to consult together concerning appropriate arrangements (FAO and UNESCO), or the desirability of making appropriate arrangements (ILO), for the inclusion of the budget of the Organization within a general budget of the United Nations. A similar clause appears in the other three agreements. After extensive study and consultations, the idea of a consolidated budget, or even of approval of agency budgets by the General Assembly, was found to raise such difficulties of a policy,[9] constitutional and procedural order that it was dropped and efforts were concentrated instead on developing standard or comparable budgetary and financial practices. The above agreements also provided for consultations between the Secretary-General of the United Nations and the Director-General of the agency in connexion with the preparation of the agency's budget, and authorized the General Assembly to make recommendations to the agency concerning any item or items in its budget or proposed budget.

Fourthly, agreements between the United Nations and the major 'programme' agencies recognized 'that the eventual development of a single unified international civil service is desirable', and with this end in view, the parties agreed to develop common personnel standards, methods and arrangements and, *inter alia*, to consult concerning the establishment of an International Civil Service Commission to advise on the means by which common standards of recruitment in the secretariats of the United Nations and the specialized agencies might be ensured. The agreements with IMF, IBRD and several of the smaller agencies provide in more general terms for consultations concerning personnel with a view to securing as much uniformity as practicable.

One cannot but be struck by the relative lack of importance attached, in those early days, as well as later, to the effects in terms of efficiency, costs and difficulties of coordination inherent in the geographical separation of the different organizations. It is true that a strong bid was made in 1950 to locate FAO – which had started in Washington – with the United Nations in New York, but it was lost by a narrow margin to Rome, the seat of the old International Institute of Agriculture, whose assets and liabilities had passed to FAO. Among the factors influencing the choice were the very tempting terms, including a fine headquarters office building and diplomatic privileges for the entire non-Italian staff, offered by the Italian Government. There was never any question that ILO would leave its permanent headquarters in Geneva, to which it had returned after its sojourn in Montreal during the war, that the Bank and the Fund would be elsewhere than Washington, or, for that matter, that UNESCO would be elsewhere than in Paris. Ministries of Health showed no desire to place WHO's headquarters in New York, while available accommodation in the Palais des Nations and the existence of the archives and a few remaining officials of the League's Health Service provided sufficient arguments in favour of Geneva. Among the old international bureaux originally located in Berne, the Universal Postal Union (UPU) stayed where it was, while the International Telecommunication Union (ITU) moved to Geneva in 1948, and the United International Bureaux for the Protection of Intellectual Property (BIRPI) (later transformed into the World Intellectual Property Organization) in 1961. IAEA was located in Vienna in 1957 as part of the arrangement among the principal nuclear powers, while Vienna, with the help of strong pressure from the Austrian Government, became the seat of the United Nations Industrial Development Organization (UNIDO) in 1966, after a hot contest with Paris, which had been generally favoured on professional and administrative grounds.

Many other general problems of coordination that have since faced the system were apparent at an early stage. Even in 1949, the General Assembly in Resolution 310 (IV), complained of 'the proliferation of activities and the multiplicity of programmes', and went on to observe that 'the resulting excessive numbers of sessions and meetings as well as the creation of subsidiary organs' were placing a severe burden on the technical and personnel resources of member states. It drew attention to a resolution adopted earlier the same year by the Council (Resolution 259 (IX)) calling for 'a greater concentration of efforts and available resources'. It was already a major problem how to reconcile respect for the autonomy and technical competence of the agencies with the more general responsibilities of the United Nations. Another was how to reconcile the Council's dual role of (a) coordinator and (b) governing organ for a broad sector of activities that needed to be coordinated with those of other organizations. The first problem has arisen again and again and indeed has been responsible for many of the coordinating difficulties encountered. But it has lost some of its importance as a result of a growing recognition that only the United Nations itself can (a) provide *policy* coordination within the entire system – that is, a framework to ensure that policy decisions of different agencies in different sectors are, if related, consistent and mutually supporting; and (b) mobilize the political will and take the political decisions necessary to enable the agencies to contribute effectively to the solution of major (and many-sided) world problems. For such reasons, it gradually became customary for Governments to launch major programmes (e.g. on the application of science and technology to development in 1963, or the preservation of the human environment in 1969), call world conferences (e.g. on the peaceful uses of atomic energy in 1955, 1958 and 1964; on world population and world food in 1974) or consolidate and intensify existing activities (e.g. on problems of the 'protein gap' through the United Nations rather than the technically concerned specialized agencies, and expect the United Nations to retain some degree of supervision and responsibility.

From an early stage, a limiting factor has been the difficulty of getting the Economic and Social Council, on which the whole system hinges, to work as it should. More than 20 years ago, its then President was complaining that 'the Council must exercise a high degree of leadership, and I submit that few can be fully satisfied with the role it has thus far played'.[10] At that time, a perceptive commentator remarked of the Council: 'the best proof that it is not fulfilling the role of leader lies in the facts that on the one hand it has constantly found its agenda overcharged, and on the other it is not being used for problems of major importance'.[11]

Another 'built-in' problem, the full significance of which was only gradually realized, was how to bring about – even assuming much consultation and cooperation – a coherent international programme, or to obtain something approaching an agreed conceptual framework, from a variety of independently conceived programmes, each with its own objectives and administration. A further set of problems has resulted from the absence, noted above, of any central authority in respect of the United Nations System as a whole to which, in the last resort, disputed issues could be referred for decision. Such issues have tended to be settled through compromise, based usually on a sort of 'distributive justice' among agencies, some of which (the outstanding example being the International Atomic Energy Agency (IAEA) in the energy field) are professionally disposed towards particular types of solutions.

Of fundamental importance have, of course, been the overlaps in the range of activities of different organizations sanctioned by their respective constitutions and desired by their national counterparts – a problem compounded by difference in structure (more particularly, the tripartite structure of the ILO) and membership. The ILO provides a host of illustrations. Its main fields of activity are employment promotion, vocational guidance, social security, safety and health, labour laws and labour relations, labour administration, workers' education, cooperatives, rural and related institutions. Most of these fields contain 'grey areas' where other agencies are also much concerned. Furthermore, the ILO is empowered by the Philadelphia Declaration of 1944, which is incorporated in its revised Constitution, to undertake, if it wishes, a considerably broader range of international economic and social responsibilities. Small wonder then that not a few cases of overlap and proliferation of machinery have occurred. For example, the improvement of living conditions has involved the ILO in aspects of rural development generally, including land reform (FAO) and the conditions of indigenous populations;[12] training is closely linked to education (UNESCO); manpower to questions of small industries (FAO and UNIDO); workers' health standards with health standards generally (WHO). Such situations are of course met so far as possible by an appropriate division of tasks or by various coordinating devices, while some major ILO programmes (for example, the World Employment Programme) involve cooperation with all or most members of the United Nations family.

The United Nations Educational, Scientific and Cultural Organization (UNESCO) provides illustrations no less striking. UNESCO has a general responsibility in matters of science, education and culture which entitles it to contribute to almost every field of international endeavour. To take the field of science, UNESCO has a direct responsibility for the development, dissemination and teaching of science in general, the establishment of scientific cadres in developing countries, etc. It follows and cooperates in the scientific activities of other organizations such as the United Nations itself, WHO, WMO, ITU, IMCO, IAEA, which, however, retain responsibility for scientific work in their own spheres. Since UNESCO interprets the term 'science' to include social as well as natural sciences, it has been concerned from time to time with such subjects of major concern to the United Nations as development theory, the peaceful settlement of disputes, and the reduction of 'tensions'. On the basis of its scientific mandate, it has established an International Oceanographic Commission, while FAO (Fishery), IMCO (Marine Pollution), IAEA (Pollution through Atomic Wastes) and, of course, the United Nations itself have all developed their own machinery and programmes in closely related aspects of oceanography. In the field of science in general, the United Nations has had the task of mobilizing the efforts of all concerned agencies in connexion with the application of science and technology to development and the peaceful uses of atomic energy. Reporting to the Economic and Social Council, there is a 54-member intergovernmental committee on Science and Technology, and the expert Advisory Committee on the Application of Science and Technology. A Scientific Advisory Committee (SAC) consisting of eminent nuclear physicists was set up under a decision of the General Assembly in 1954; it remains formally in being but has not met for some years.

Few agencies are free from some situations of overlapping jurisdiction, or parallel activity, with others – situations which, although partly responsible for the proliferation of machinery that is so evident in certain fields, are usually prevented, through the exercise of sheer common sense, from adversely affecting the thrust of common action or otherwise doing much damage. One important source of parallel activity, incidentally, is an organization without a prescribed area of substantive responsibility, namely the World Bank, the impact of which will be referred to later.

When a new field of activities emerges, or when new institutional arrangements are made to give existing problems a new focus and priority, conflicting decisions touching on competence are apt to be taken in the organizations concerned with different aspects of the same question. For example, some of the functions assigned to IAEA under paragraph 6 of Article III of the Statute of the agency were already performed, mainly by FAO and WHO, under provisions of their Constitutions relating to the establishment of international standards in their own fields. The built-in overlap, due partly to differences of opinion in many countries on the distribution of work between medical or agricultural scientists on the one hand, and atomic energy authorities on the other, could not be resolved by agreement between the secretariats concerned, and is one indeed which it is difficult to resolve in general terms. A Resolution adopted by the Council in 1963 (986 (xxxvi)) recognizes 'the primary responsibility' of IAEA 'for work in the field of atomic energy, without prejudice to the constitutional responsibilities of the specialized agencies each in its own particular field', and the dividing line is drawn in the following paragraph which assigns to IAEA primary sponsorship of activities 'in which atomic energy or research relating thereto forms the major part of the subject matter'. It would thus seem that the competence of the other agencies is recognized to the extent that atomic energy is only instrumental to the achievement of purposes outside the atomic field. The resolution also provided that no proposal in which more than one agency may have an interest be approved by the governing organ of one of them without a clear statement of the steps taken to collaborate at the formative stage with other interested agencies. A disagreement between the United Nations and IAEA Secretariats as to responsibility for the conduct of mineral surveys led to the adoption of another resolution in 1970 by the Council which reaffirms the 'primary role and responsibility' of the United Nations in both multimineral and single mineral surveys, but recognizes the 'special competence and responsibility' of IAEA to conduct surveys for nuclear metals and the need for it to continue to cooperate with the United Nations in multimineral surveys by making available to the United Nations, on request, experts for such surveys.

An underlying and pervasive problem is, of course, the absence of coordination at the national level in regard to international policies and programmes. The weakness and rareness of such policy coordination in many Governments has led not only to divergent positions being taken by the representatives of the same country in different organizations but also not infrequently – as we shall see in the case of UNCTAD and GATT as well as of UNIDO and the ILO – to divergent decisions actually being reached. Despite repeated resolutions of the General Assembly and the Council urging better coordination of policies at the national level, as well as studies by the United Nations Secretariat and by UNESCO of measures taken in some countries to this end,[13] little overall improvement in the situation appears to have occurred. It is a devastating fact that most countries still lack systematic arrangements even for keeping the activities of international organizations under central review, let alone for developing coordinated positions on issues coming before them. One cannot expect anything approaching full coherence and coordination in the United Nations System so long as this situation prevails. At the same time, differences of view among delegates from the same country are influenced by differences within the international organizations they participate in, so every step towards harmonizing the attitude of those organizations should improve the situation. Another hope lies in the coordinating role that the secretariats, individually or collectively through ACC,[14] are able – and are desired by most Governments [15] discreetly to play.

Difficulties of coordination in respect of international activities in certain fields – one of which has been the application of science and technology – usually reflect difficulties of coordination on those subjects at the national level. Again, proliferation and overlapping of programme activities – which is even more obvious at the country and regional levels than at the global level – arise because in so many broad fields different ministries and divisions are involved in different countries and initiatives varying slightly in approach but having very similar objectives can well be launched and carried through simultaneously in two or more international agencies. For example, the United Nations regional and community development programme is closely related to UNESCO's work on functional literacy, FAO's agricultural extension work, aspects of the public health work of WHO and aspects of the ILO programme on handicrafts and cottage industries. UNESCO's early work on fundamental education and that of the United Nations on community development, each with its separate antecedents, were found to be so similar in aim and content that they were eventually merged under arrangements proposed by the secretariats concerned.

This chapter cannot be concluded without reference to a further result of functional decentralization, with the wide freedom of action it allows the individual organizations in their respective fields. Decentralization has been a source of great strength and vitality to the United Nations System; this very vitality has inevitably led to some of the coordination difficulties, as well as to some of the proliferation of activities and machinery that have been encountered. However dedicated they may be to the ends and purposes of the United Nations Charter, the leading agency officials and experts as well as Government representatives tend to feel a special loyalty towards their own organization and a sense of mission, which grows only more intense with time, to advance its particular purposes and its prestige.

2 Developments that have affected inter-agency relationships and coordination

Increase in scope and interdependence of international activities

All the problems just discussed are still with us, but big changes in the context and dimensions of many of them have occurred since the general structure of international organization was determined in the 1940s. Of these changes, and their effects on the coordination issue, one may note, first, the vast increases in the scope of international economic and social activities since the mid-1940s, an increase that has naturally been accompanied by a constant broadening of the programmes and an ever-greater interdependence of the activities of different agencies.[1] The task of the UN has been increasingly to promote and to help organize and guide the use of the skills and thinking of the agencies, and of its own subbodies and services, in the solution of world problems which straddle the competence of numerous national departments and international organizations. Except in a few cases, such as the campaign against illiteracy (UNESCO), and the World Employment Programme (the ILO), the broad inter-agency programmes – for example, the International Development Strategy, the World Plan of Action in the field of science and technology, the United Nations Environment Programme, community and rural development – have been led by the United Nations itself. Some of these programmes have underlined the problem, referred to in the last chapter, of reconciling the role of the Council as coordinator and initiator with its role as a governing body responsible for a sector of the United Nations System's substantive work and properly subject to coordination as much as any specialized agency. It has been a recurring complaint of some of the specialized agencies that the Council sometimes overlooks the dual character of its role, to their disadvantage.

Development of operational activities

The second change, no less fundamental, was the advent and rapid growth of field activities, especially technical assistance, through the international organizations, which have become the disbursers of considerable public funds and the purveyors of extensive advisory services direct to their member Governments. This development called for major changes in the internal structure and staffing of most of the organizations concerned, which, with the notable exception of the WHO, were geared to non-operational activities, as the League of Nations and the pre-war ILO had been. Different organizations experimented – in some cases for years – with different solutions. The UN Secretariat, on the basis of League experience, originally had separate Departments for Economic and for Social Affairs, while the new emphasis on technical assistance led to the creation of a separate Technical Assistance Administration (TAA) to handle operations for both. As time went on, the disadvantages of maintaining these three entities entirely separate and distinct became increasingly obvious: How, for example, could social development in general and problems in such fields as population, housing and community development in particular, be dealt with in isolation from general economic development? How could the Organization provide maximum substantive assistance to developing countries in the subjects within its competence if the substantive services and the Administration dealing with technical assistance were under separate commands? The two departments were brought under a single head and then merged between 1953 and 1955 and the TAA became a Bureau of the combined Department of Economic and Social Affairs (ESA) early in 1959.

The most difficult and overt inter-agency problems of coordination, at the centre and in the field, resulted from the new emphasis on field operations, the impact of which was heightened by the Council's early decision that, contrary to the view of the Secretary-General,[2] the funds available for the Expanded Programme of Technical Assistance (EPTA) should be distributed among the United Nations and the various specialized agencies, first on a basis somewhat arbitrarily determined by itself, then in accordance with decisions reached through the inter-agency Technical Assistance Board. It is true that EPTA worked under the authority of the Council and ACC, both the Technical Assistance Committee and the Technical Assistance Board reporting to the Council (the second through ACC). The position was altered, however, in the cases of the Special Fund, which was added to the armoury in 1958, and the United Nations Development Programme (UNDP), which resulted from the merger of EPTA and the Special Fund as from January 1966. For UNDP, following the pattern of the Special Fund, special coordinating arrangements were made by the Council and the General Assembly, providing at the staff level for a coordinating body (the Inter-Agency Consultative Board (IACB), advisory to the Administrator and having no formal contacts with ACC, and, at the intergovernmental level for a Governing Council which reports to the Economic and Social Council. Until recently, the Council has shown little sign of asserting itself in respect of this large and vital part of the work of the United Nations. In 1967, the Governing Council of UNDP called for a study of the capacity of the United Nations development system which led to the remarkable report under that title published towards the end of 1969. A Consensus on certain steps to be taken in the light of that study was reached in the Governing Council in 1970 and endorsed by the Council and the General Assembly. Neither the Capacity Study itself, nor the implications of the Consensus for the United Nations System as a whole has ever been considered by ACC – or, for that matter, except in the most general terms, by the Council.

Some progress has been made, mainly through the 'country programming' procedures instituted under the Consensus, in correcting or containing certain weaknesses that had formerly been prominent, e.g. the competition for requests for assistance by different agencies, disputes as to which agency should handle particular projects, and the absence of coherence in total UNDP assistance in individual countries, but these weaknesses have by no means disappeared.

Action at the regional level

A third development affecting United Nations–agency relations has been the growth of activities at the regional level. Problems, which were enlarged and aggravated in later years, began to appear with the creation by the United Nations in 1947 – primarily for the purpose of helping to meet reconstruction problems of war devastated areas – of two regional economic commissions, the Economic Commission for Europe (ECE) and the Economic Commission for Asia and the Far East (ECAFE). These and the regional economic commissions subsequently established[3] have, like the General Assembly and the Council, a broad responsibility for economic and (since the 1950s) social development, and this responsibility covers the sectoral areas of many specialized agencies, to which, as well as to Governments, they are authorized to make recommendations direct. From the outset, the attitude of some of the agencies, with their global responsibilities in specific sectoral fields, towards the regional commissions has been somewhat guarded because of the danger of over-lapping, and several of the major agencies have set up their own regional networks. The guarded attitude has tended to be recipro-cated by the regional commissions, which have often been critical of the agencies' sectoral approach to the problems of their region and its individual countries. Nor has the work of the commissions' staffs and of the Department of Economic and Social Affairs (ESA) at Headquarters, which is concerned with so many common issues, always been easy to coordinate, despite the special arrangements for liaison and consultation referred to below. Year by year, for example, regional economic surveys are published by the commissions' economists, with the minimum of consultation with the staff res-ponsible for preparing the annual World Economic Survey at UN Headquarters.

In 1948, ACC made clear its view that effective coordination of regional activities depends upon adherence to the principle that the agreements between the United Nations and the specialized agencies apply fully to such activities.[4] Some years later, the Council con-firmed its acceptance of that position, which implied, among other things, that the United Nations regional economic commissions recognize the competence and responsibilities of the agencies within their respective fields, and vice versa.[5] Elaborate measures – includ-ing the establishment of joint divisions of certain agencies and the commissions, the posting of agency representatives at the commis-sions' headquarters, and frequent arrangements for jointly sponsored meetings and conferences – have been taken to forestall difficulties between the commissions and the agencies and promote coopera-tion.[6] Such measures have proved useful though by no means fully effective, and the price may, in some cases, have been rather high in terms of staff and budget.

The commissions have no explicit coordinating authority, but their broad terms of reference have tended to give them a position of considerable influence vis-à-vis the agencies. This has not often been stated, since the subject is a delicate one, but the Council at its Fifty-fourth Session in the Spring of 1973 reaffirmed that 'the regional economic commissions, in their respective regions, are the main general economic and social development centres within the United Nations system', and called up 'all the organizations and agencies in the system to work closely with [them] to achieve the over-all economic and social development objectives at the regional level'.[7]

In accordance with its Constitution, WHO at an early stage established a highly decentralized regional structure. UNICEF, working closely with WHO, followed suit. Some years later, FAO and UNESCO developed extensive regional activities and still later the ILO initiated the same process. While the seats of the regional economic commissions have attracted a number of agency offices, the agency centres and subcentres are spread over every region; and in the case of each agency the powers and functions of these offices differ. The resultant 'jungle' – in the words of the Capacity Study – has naturally been a further cause of coordination difficulties both for international organizations and for Governments.

New members and new interests

Fourthly, no less important has been the effect on the structure, efficiency and coordination of international organizations of the increase in their membership and the determination of the new members, mostly poor developing countries, to maximize the development assistance provided to them through those organizations. The new members, furthermore, have wished to exercise maximum influence in, and control over, the central policy organs concerned with economic and social development. Until quite recently, when it began to be realized that good coordination might result in more and more effective assistance and that the lack of it might contribute to drying up the source of funds, coordination had little appeal for such countries. This attitude was strengthened by the attempt which appeared to be made by a number of donor countries, especially as the financial stringency in the United Nations became acute following the Congo intervention, to use the organs concerned with administrative and budgetary coordination to check or delay the expansion of United Nations and agency budgets for economic and social programmes.

The absence of a clear mandate for the Council vis-à-vis the General Assembly also became a factor of importance. It was natural and fully understood that the General Assembly should take the lead in securing action or consideration by the different organizations in respect of questions of a political character such as decolonization, or on questions extending beyond the Council's normal sphere, such as the establishment in 1966 of the Enlarged Committee for Programme and Coordination for the purpose of enhancing the contribution of the United Nations System to economic and social development. But it became more and more common for the Council to be bypassed in respect of initiatives which the developing countries wanted to be launched or supported by the superior and more prestigious body, and – the Council's membership no longer reflecting the political balance in the Organization[8] – for developing countries to appeal to the General Assembly, and to appeal successfully, from decisions taken in the Council.

Institutional fragmentation

The failure of the Council to reflect the changed political balance in the United Nations or the new concepts of justice and economic cooperation that were emerging in the Third World contributed much to the fragmentation of the United Nations economic machinery – an amputation from the viewpoint of the Council and the Department of Economic and Social Affairs, or even a revision of the Charter system of international organization – that occurred in the mid-1960s: namely, the establishment by the General Assembly, under strong pressure from the developing and 'non-aligned' countries[9] (and despite resistance from some of the developed countries), of important new organizations within the United Nations in the fields of trade and development (UNCTAD)[10] and industrial development (UNIDO). These organizations were not placed under the Economic and Social Council and their secretariats were made independent of ESA. The form they were given – that of 'an organ of the General Assembly' (UNCTAD) or an 'autonomous organization within the United Nations' (UNIDO), and not of specialized agencies – was influenced largely by the General Assembly's desire to exercise control, but also by considerations of economy and doubts as to the efficacy of the arrangements between the United Nations and the specialized agencies for ensuring coordination.

The new organizations, whose creation represented a significant reorientation of United Nations action, as well as an enlargement of its scale and scope, were given certain coordinating functions in their respective fields; UNCTAD was 'to review and facilitate the co-ordination of activities of other institutions within the United Nations system', but to 'co-operate with the General Assembly and the Economic and Social Council with respect to the performance of their responsibilities for coordination under the Charter of the United Nations'.[11] UNIDO was to 'play the central role in and be responsible for reviewing and promoting the coordination of all activities of the United Nations system in the field of industrial development'.[12] Both organizations were to report to the General Assembly through the Council; this meant, in effect, that the Council could comment, but that decisions could only be taken by the General Assembly: as in the case of UNDP, it has been the Council's practice to send on their reports without significant comments. Given the circumstances in which they were established, considerations of good administrative order were perhaps bound to be secondary, but the then Secretary-General felt it necessary to observe that

> The creation of autonomous units within the Secretariat, and therefore under my jurisdiction as Chief Administrative Officer, raises serious questions of organizational authority and responsibility. Moreover, such a trend is not altogether consistent with the concept of a unified secretariat working as a team towards the accomplishment of the main goals of the Organization. On the contrary, it may tend to have the adverse effect of pitting one segment of the Secretariat against another in competition for the necessary financial and political support for its own work programmes.[13]

The creation of UNCTAD and UNIDO, as was predicted, involved considerable uncertainty as to competences, as well as overlapping with ESA, the regional commissions and the agencies. The position was complicated, in the case of UNCTAD and the Council, by the absence of a clear conceptual distinction between their respective roles as regards development. Arrangements on a pragmatic basis for the distribution of Secretariat responsibilities were in most cases eventually worked out, while a series of decisions at the intergovernmental level have further eased the position. For example, the Council at its Fifty-fifth Session (1973) decided to transfer to UNCTAD for consideration documents relating to the transfer of operative technology, while an annual ESA publication on financial flows to developing countries has been discontinued and replaced by an annual UNCTAD publication dealing with the same subject. A *modus vivendi*, but no firm agreement, exists between UNCTAD and FAO as regards trade in agricultural commodities and between UNIDO and FAO as regards the pulp and paper industry, with which FAO continues to deal.[14] In a number of other areas also, including shipping, uncertainties as to competence have by no means been completely overcome.

One early case of duplication is particularly interesting in relation to the respective roles of governmental bodies and secretariats: the case of UNCTAD and GATT, which was then regarded in most of the 'Third World' as a bastion of the great trading countries. UNCTAD represented a direct challenge to GATT, which, apart from its traditional work on tariffs, quickly embarked on a number of the activities which were assigned to UNCTAD by the General Assembly after the first UN Conference on Trade and Development in December 1964. In February 1965, the Contracting Parties to GATT added a Fourth Part, on Trade and Development to the General Agreement, giving GATT a mandate – as well as subsidiary bodies – on subjects falling directly within UNCTAD's domain. Two great intergovernmental institutions with largely overlapping membership were thus, by deliberate decision of their governing organs, engaged in open duplication. Despite representations by their chief executive officers – Mr Raul Prebisch for UNCTAD and Mr (later Sir) Eric Wyndham White for GATT – neither the new GATT Committee nor the UNCTAD Trade and Development Board (37 of whose 55 members were also Parties to, or associated with, GATT), nor even the New Delhi Conference of UNCTAD in 1967, would discuss the overlap, let alone take any decision to correct it, but confined themselves to calling for intersecretariat coordination and for the Governments to be kept informed 'so that they may give such directives as may appear necessary'. Cooperation in several areas (for example, the establishment in 1967 of the Joint UNCTAD–GATT Trade Centre) and a provisional *modus vivendi* have been worked out between the staffs of the two organizations. Such arrangements are, however, no substitute for intergovernmental decisions and no solution for structural shortcomings. As the present Secretary-General of UNCTAD has stated,[15] 'the consequences of this omission to provide intergovernmental guidance ... include the negation of an integrated approach to trade and development problems, the duplication of efforts by governments as well as by the secretariats concerned, and the prospect of inconsistent or conflicting actions in the two bodies which work in separate compartments without adequate co-operation or coordination'.

When the tasks of UNIDO were being defined, a wide range of functions were assigned to the new organization in the training field, most of which were – or had been – within the competence of the ILO. The matter was extensively discussed by the Governing Body of the ILO at its 165th Session and at the 50th Session of the International Labour Conference, which put its position on record in a formal resolution concerning the role of the ILO in the industrialization of developing countries. The matter was similarly discussed at the July 1966 joint meetings of ACC and CPC, at the 41st Session of the Council and at the Twenty-first Session of the General Assembly, which had before them the views of the ILO that were submitted both in writing (E/4229 and Add.1), and orally by the Director-General, accompanied by a delegation of the Governing Body. This eventually led to the adoption of a revised version of the original text, which became paragraph 2(a)(ix) of Resolution 2152 (xxi) setting out the functions of UNIDO. The revision did not in itself resolve all difficulties, and it was necessary to accompany it with an agreed interpretation (A/6508, para. 8(b), p. 13) which itself provided for a future modification of the definition of competence by mutual agreement between the ILO and UNIDO. The respective roles of the two organizations was further dealt with in a Memorandum of Guidelines for Cooperation between ILO and UNIDO, signed by the Director-General and the Executive Director on 3 April 1968, and a joint inter-secretariat working party established under that memorandum meets regularly to apply to concrete activities the principles governing the delineation of competence of the two organizations. This procedure seems to have worked reasonably well, but no one could deny that it is a heavy and time-consuming one.

The fragmentation of major intergovernmental institutions has naturally contributed to an ever-growing proliferation of suborgans and much uncertainty and confusion as to their respective functions. If this uncertainty is due partly to overlapping of competences among the parent institutions, other factors have also contributed. One such factor is the geographical dispersal of the decision-making organs and the differing attitudes that develop at different headquarters. Another is the fact that, in recent years, decisions as to which organization or organ should be given a particular task have often been affected by political considerations. From this development, UNCTAD, as the preferred instrument of the developing countries in a wide area of development questions, has been a notable beneficiary.

The process of institutional fragmentation, including in some cases the assignment of coordinating authority to new organs, did not, of course, begin or end with the creation of UNCTAD and UNIDO. While those organizations were financed by the regular budget of the United Nations, the process had become increasingly associated with reliance on voluntary contributions rather than assessed contributions to finance new economic and social activities. As early as 1946 the General Assembly had decided that the then United Nations International Children's Emergency Fund (UNICEF), which it set up for the purpose of meeting in part some of the most pressing emergency needs which the wartime United Nations Refugee and Rehabilitation Administration (UNRRA) had covered, should be financed entirely from extra-budgetary sources. The Expanded Programme of Technical Assistance (EPTA) created in 1949 under the influence of President Truman's Point Four, was likewise financed by voluntary contributions. After years of pressure in the General Assembly for a Special United Nations Fund for Economic Development (SUNFED), the voluntarily financed Special Fund for assistance to developing countries in pre-investment projects appeared in 1958. The Joint UN–FAO World Food Programme, whose primary aim was to use voluntarily donated food surpluses for economic and social development as well as for emergency relief, was established in 1962; UNITAR – also financed exclusively by voluntary contributions – came into being in 1963. The movement has, of course, not always been in this direction. For example, when the International Relief Organization (IRO), an independent specialized agency, was wound up in 1952, some of its principal functions were taken over by the office of the High Commissioner for Refugees, which was within the United Nations structure and financed, so far as administrative expenditure was concerned, by the UN regular budget. In 1965, the General Assembly merged EPTA with the Special Fund to form a single United Nations Development Programme (UNDP), and for many years pressure to give UNIDO administrative and financial autonomy was successfully resisted.[16] But the general trend has been towards fragmentation and voluntary financing continued. In 1967 the General Assembly created a United Nations Capital Development Fund, with its own Managing Director and 24-Nation Executive Board, which, for lack of adequate financial support, remained inactive for several years but has recently been attracting fresh interest. The UN Fund for Population Activities (UNFPA) began as a very independent Trust Fund under the Secretary-General in 1967 and still retains a great measure of autonomy. One might mention, lastly, the United Nations Environment Programme (UNEP), set up by the United Nations General Assembly in 1972, following the Stockholm Conference. While UNEP's administrative expenses were to be borne by the regular budget of the United Nations, a voluntary fund was established to provide for additional financing of environmental programmes.

UNEP offers other features of interest to a study of coordination. Great emphasis is placed on its coordinating and promotional role. The General Assembly decided among other things that the Executive Director shall 'coordinate, under the guidance of the Governing Council, environmental programmes within the United Nations system,...keep their implementation under review and...assess their effectiveness', and that an Environment Coordination Board under the chairmanship of the Executive Director should be established under the auspices and within the framework of the Administrative Committee on Coordination. The language used to protect the overall coordinating role of the Council is more specific than in the case of UNCTAD and UNIDO. The Governing Council 'shall report annually to the General Assembly through the Economic and Social Council, which will transmit to the Assembly such comments on the report as it may deem necessary, particularly with regard to questions of coordination and to the relationship of environment policies and programmes within the United Nations system to overall economic and social policies and priorities'. Many organizations have direct responsibilities relating to the environment, and dangers of overlaps and costly additional procedures for coordination have already appeared. The General Assembly, when deciding at its Twenty-eighth Session on the recommendation of the UNEP Council to call a Conference–Exposition on Human Settlements in 1976, decided to set up, in addition to a large intergovernmental preparatory committee, a special secretariat under a Conference Secretary-General.

It is interesting to note that special problems of readjustment for the UN System are posed by UNEP. At the outset, each part of the United Nations System was conceived of as covering one or more economic or social sectors – for example, food and agriculture; health; education; science and culture; labour. UNCTAD and UNIDO, likewise, each covered a broad economic sector. Some organs and agencies, however, have been created on the basis of other criteria: for example, UNICEF and UNHCR deal with special groups, UNRWA with a special group in a particular area, while UNEP, like the Council itself, is largely concerned with the pursuit of objectives that are within the functional competence of other organizations.

Budgetary fragmentation

The trend towards the establishment of semi-independent organs to undertake new activities has – as indicated above – been associated with rapid growth in the number and size of the 'voluntary funds'.[17] Over half of the economic and social (including humanitarian) activities of the United Nations is now financed not by the regular budget approved by the General Assembly and assessed on Member States, but out of extra-budgetary resources – consisting mainly of voluntary government contributions for a variety of purposes and administered in a variety of ways. The proportion in the United

Nations itself stood at 56 % (35 % for UNDP Project expenditures and 21 % for other expenditures) – in 1973 and this proportion has since been rising. The purposes vary from development and humanitarian assistance of a short- as well as long-term character, e.g. UNDP, UNICEF, the Refugee Fund, the Capital Development Fund, the Funds for Relief in Bangladesh, in Zambia and elsewhere, to the financing of the Programme of Drug Abuse Control, much of the work on development programming, the revolving fund for Natural Resources Exploration and numerous small funds in respect of particular projects, either global or in favour of particular countries. The activities financed are not subject to the same central programme or administrative and budgetary controls as are exercised in respect of regular budget activities, nor are they subject to approval through the normal budgetary processes.

The device of trust funds is strongly defended in many quarters and on many grounds. It is useful both for countries which wish to choose the programmes they support financially and for countries which wish to hold down their assessed contributions. The relative speed and flexibility with which they can be used gives them a further advantage and they facilitate the increasing use of multi-lateral programming and coordination by bilateral aid programmes. Most important, without this device much valuable work of world-wide scope – for example on population, on narcotics control, on economic and social programming as well as on particular projects in developing countries – could not be pursued. But the trust funds have also given rise to much criticism. In so far as they are semi-autonomous and their activities are not closely integrated with those financed by the regular budgets, they tend to be wasteful administratively, a cause for duplication and an impediment to integrated UN action. As regards the effect of the proliferation of such funds on United Nations operational work, the opinion of the Administrator of UNDP is categorical: 'whether or not such proliferation results in an absolute increase in the resources available for development assistance, the continual establishment of additional secretariats and reviewing bodies to deal with special purpose trust funds is costly in terms of time, effort and brains, and is an unproductive use of scarce resources.' (A/8840/Add.1.)

New regulations in regard to the trust funds have recently been issued and further changes in policy are under study.[18] Some consolidation and greater integration may result, though the conflict between the positions referred to above does not seem to have been overcome.

The impact of the United Nations Development Programme (UNDP)

The United Nations Development Programme is a potent unifying force in the United Nations System, since it carries out the key task of coordinating operational activities not only through the headquarters of the agencies concerned but also at the country level. It has the means, and it has been able, to achieve a degree of inter-organizational coordination in such activities far greater than is normally possible through ACC procedures. Its network of resident representatives, of which there are now about 100, many of them with deputies and sizable offices, is among the greatest assets of the UN System. It is responsible for the administration not only of its own funds, amounting now to approximately $400 million per year but also those of UNFPA, the Capital Development Fund and the funds for the United Nations Volunteers programme. It has developed cooperative relations with UNICEF and – of a different order – with the International Bank for Reconstruction and Development (IBRD), as will be discussed in the next section.

At the same time, UNDP has presented some special problems in the total coordination picture, reflecting in part the differences in respect of membership and (in the case of some common members) representatives on the Governing Council and the Economic and Social Council, in part a lack of contact that prevailed for many years between the headquarters staff of UNDP and both ESA and ACC, but also in part UNDP's special needs and circumstances. UNDP has, quite independently of ACC, built up its own contacts and coordination arrangements with the agencies, including an annual review of projects with each of them, and has its inter-agency Programme Working Group and Working Group on Administration and Finance Matters. It is able, even after the introduction of country programming, to exercise considerable influence as to which organization undertakes a particular project. There have in the past been dangers, and cases, of its thwarting the efforts made at the global level, through the ACC machinery, to promote an agreed division of tasks among different organizations. There was for years little contact between the management of UNDP and ACC, and a certain reluctance on the part of the former to have discussion in ACC of matters affecting the development programme. The decision of ACC in 1969, endorsed by the Council, that the executive heads of the main United Nations programmes, who were previously 'observers', should be full participants in ACC, was motivated largely by the widely felt need to bring the UNDP Administration and ACC more closely together.

Developments that have affected relationships and coordination

Such a *rapprochement* has begun. UNDP officials now attend meetings of the consultative ACC machinery more frequently, and the Council staff as well as the Office for Inter-Agency Affairs and Coordination attend the meetings of the Governing Council and the Inter-Agency Consultative Board (IACB). If cooperation is still incomplete, country programming seems to be exerting a twofold influence in the desired direction. First, since the country programme is now determined at the country level, the Administrator need no longer fear pressure from high-powered members of ACC in a forum where he is not in control and where consensus is so highly prized. Secondly, since the position of the resident representative has been so much strengthened, inter-agency coordination at the country level has tended to be facilitated; and the advantages have been widely recognized of using more fully the ACC consultative machinery for purposes of operational coordination.

There remain, however, some anomalies. One of these concerns the resident representatives of UNDP, about whose functions a few general observations may first be useful.[19] The resident representatives are expected to exercise overall responsibility for the United Nations development programme in their respective country or countries and, in relation to the representatives of other United Nations organizations, to act as team leaders and coordinators; they constitute a natural link and harmonizing influence between those programmes and the policies enunciated in the intergovernmental organs of the United Nations and the agencies. They act, furthermore, as country representatives of the United Nations itself, including UNCTAD and UNIDO, and of some of the smaller specialized agencies; they are country agents for WFP and act as local coordinators for United Nations action and as contact points with the government authorities in connexion with natural disasters. Close relations have been established between them and the UNICEF representatives in the field. FAO and UNIDO have in a number of countries appointed advisers to them, UNDP paying for the advisers in full (UNIDO) or in part (FAO), while the question of other ways in which sectoral support to the resident representatives by these and other agencies can be maximized is under constant discussion. The anomaly lies in the fact that despite their heavy responsibilities for coordination at the country level and their unique contacts with the planning and other central authorities of Governments, the resident representatives are largely outside the system-wide coordinating arrangements; they do not take part in the work of the Council's coordinating organs or the mechanism of ACC, and their direct contacts with the Office of Inter-Agency Affairs and Coordination are still sparse. Above all, their indoctrination in the International Development Strategy, and the processes of Review and Appraisal that are central to it, must come mainly from documents sent from Headquarters. There is an increasing awareness of the need to ensure that there is better feedback between the field and Headquarters;[20] furthermore, UNDP Headquarters and the Office of Inter-Agency Affairs and Coordination, through newsletters and the use of opportunities for contact that may arise, for example at the Administrator's periodic meetings of resident representatives, have been trying to keep the latter abreast of Headquarters developments and thinking. While such measures ease, they do not solve the problem.

The second anomaly concerns the top-level coordination arrangements, and in particular the complete separation from ACC of the Inter-Agency Consultative Board (IACB), chaired by the Administrator. According to the decision establishing UNDP, in order to provide the participating organizations with the opportunity to take part fully in the process of decision and policy making in a consultative capacity, IACB was to be 'consulted on all significant aspects' of the programme and among other specific tasks, it was to 'advise the management on the programmes and projects...with a view to ensuring more effective coordination'.[21] Owing to the recent changes in UNDP's approach to and procedures for programming and project approval, IACB is no longer concerned with the review of programmes and projects and emphasis is placed instead on 'broad policy issues and on operational matters of system-wide interest'.[22] Broad policy issues used to be considered in ACC, with which IACB has no organic relationship although its membership is practically the same (except that the Secretary-General himself does not attend the meetings of IACB) and for reasons of convenience the two bodies synchronize their meetings. The Capacity Study proposed that IACB should be discontinued and its functions divided, consultations about overall inter-agency coordination and development policy to revert to ACC while a new Technical Advisory Panel would provide 'sectoral advice on the various aspects of operational programmes and projects'. The discussions in the IACB, whose twice-yearly sessions have recently been very brief, do not in fact duplicate those in ACC. But the Capacity Study proposal had – and has – much to commend it from the angle of good organization and the streamlining of work. That proposal was, not unexpectedly, opposed by the Administrator and by the majority of the agency heads, who attached importance to their statutory role in the UNDP structure, nor was it supported by the then Secretary-General who wanted to leave as much as possible in the Administrator's hands. In the light of these attitudes, the Governing Council, followed by the Council and the General Assembly, confirmed IACB in its existing role.

Another Capacity Study proposal for UNDP was that a United Nations development service should be established on a career basis, with its own salary structure and conditions of service, more attractive to field staff than those now in force under the common system of salaries and allowances. This proposal has for some time been under consideration in UNDP. It has encountered criticism because of the danger of causing a breach in the 'common system'; it may also have been affected by uncertainties as to the future scope and character of UNDP's work and also perhaps because UNDP's existing top staff structure is already considerably more generous than that of other United Nations programmes or ESA.[23] UNDP and its executing agencies, on the other hand, must be enabled to attract top-level people for development work under conditions that sometimes offer little attraction and often involve hardship. Efforts are being made through the newly established International Civil Service Commission (ICSC) and Consultative Committee on Administrative Questions (CCAQ), to reconcile these considerations through a general improvement in field conditions under the common system.

The Council and the Committee on Programme and Coordination, as well as the General Assembly's Fifth Committee and ACABQ, have traditionally avoided any thorough consideration of UNDP and other United Nations activities financed by voluntary funds. Moreover, one searches in vain for any real discussion of the coordination of the activities with those of the regular programmes of the United Nations and the specialized agencies, or of the effects of administrative arrangements for the voluntary programmes on those of the United Nations as a whole. Divergencies and anomalies have indeed been tending to increase.[24] There are signs, however, that, on the administrative, as well as the programme, side serious efforts to improve the position are now being taken.

The impact of the International Bank for Reconstruction and Development (IBRD)

The economic and social activities of the United Nations and those of the major programme agencies (the ILO, FAO, UNESCO and WHO) have been expanding at a roughly comparable rate and the percentage allocations of UNDP funds to those organizations, despite annual variations, has not shown striking changes. On the other hand, there has been a dramatic increase in the activities of, and the funds available to, the World Bank, with its affiliates, the International Finance Corporation (IFC) and the International Development Association (IDA). The Bank Group has become a great international development agency, enjoying the immense advantage over the other members of the United Nations family of being able to provide funds for investment, not just for expertise and advice. It lent or made investment commitments of upwards of $6·1 billion in the past financial year (1974) for development programmes or projects in the Third World and vastly expanded its technical assistance for the purpose; it organized consortia and consultative groups of major donors and particular recipients of Bank or IDA aid to review those countries' development progress, policies and problems; it sent economic survey missions for much the same purpose to some 60 of its developing member countries and major sector survey missions to about half that number also in the course of the past financial year. It has formed cooperative programmes with FAO, UNESCO, WHO and UNIDO. In each case, the Bank and its partner agency help Governments to identify and prepare projects for Bank financing and to provide support for Bank economic sector studies and economic survey and project missions. In Washington and through its training courses in the field, for example, in Belgrade, Ibadan, Bombay, Brasilia and Bucharest, the Bank's Economic Development Institute trained a total of some 700 participants in the past year.

These growing activities of the Bank Group, which is not, as other specialized agencies are, limited to particular sectors, represent an incalculable contribution to the work of the United Nations as a whole. They naturally have an important bearing on the responsibilities of the UNDP and the central organs of the United Nations, for which the promotion of the economic and social development of the developing world is an 'overriding priority' and the Development Decade and the International Development Strategy are of such major concern. The Centre for Planning, Projections and Policies at United Nations Headquarters, in most cases with UNDP financial support, has some 350 experts on development programming in some 70 developing countries, and, in association with the regional commissions and individual agencies, has organized multinational interdisciplinary development advisory teams in certain subregions.[25]

The UNDP's leading role in the 'pre-investment' field is recognized, in principle at least, by the Bank, which recommends to it such projects in areas it feels may eventually qualify for financing. But the process leading to financing is essentially continuous and the Bank does a great deal of its own preparatory work and feasibility studies; as an executing agency, for UNDP 'pre-investment' projects, it can show a good record of follow-up financing, though its services tend to be relatively expensive, particularly because it can and does offer higher emoluments than other members of the United Nations System.

It must be stressed, however, that the Bank Group represents a vehicle for development aid distinct from the United Nations and UNDP, and not necessarily inspired by identical priorities; indeed these priorities are normally enumerated at the annual Governors' meeting with little, if any, reference to United Nations decisions. The Group is another source within the 'United Nations family' from which Governments can obtain advice and assistance in the programming and execution of development plans. Its distinctness reflects at once the line that customarily divides Ministries of finance and Economic Development and the constraint imposed on the Bank, in its relations with the United Nations, so often expressed during the negotiations of the relationship agreement in 1947. The gist of that constraint has been that the Bank must be free from political pressures or associations that might make it more difficult to raise funds for the developing world from the world's money markets at the lowest possible terms.

Efforts are, of course, made to forestall, or overcome as far as possible, overlaps or conflicts. The related development of Bank and United Nations activities has been accompanied by extensive consultation and exchange of information. The President of the Bank has been assiduous in maintaining contacts with the Secretary-General personally on matters of policy and common interest; he has participated, though not regularly, in ACC and IACB and attends meetings of the Council at least once a year in person for the presentation and discussion of the Bank's annual report to the United Nations. There are permanent liaison officers of the Bank (and IMF) with the United Nations and fairly frequent exchanges of visits between Washington and New York by United Nations and Bank officials. The resident representatives of UNDP sit on each of the Bank's consortia and consultative groups, and the Bank's missions are under instruction to consult them.

As part of the 1961 relationship agreement between the United Nations and IDA, a Liaison Committee was created, to meet not less than four times a year, 'composed of the Secretary-General of the

United Nations and the President of the Bank and of the [International Development] Association, or their representatives, which the Executive Chairman of the United Nations Technical Assistance Board (UNTAB), the Managing Director of the United Nations Special Fund or their representatives, shall be invited to join as full participants'. This Committee has not met for some time but it is worth considering whether somewhat more regular meetings of corresponding officials might not be helpful for the purpose of ensuring maximum agreement on broad priorities and issues of development policy (see Chapter 13 and the Postscript).

3 The content of coordination activities

It is a tribute to the resilience of the United Nations System that it has continued to work reasonably smoothly despite the drastic transformations that have occurred in its whole context. Without dealing historically with the corresponding changes that have occurred in the coordination problems to be faced, it may be well at this point to outline very briefly the nature of those problems, administrative, substantive and others. The next chapters will discuss the instrumentalities and procedures, intergovernmental and inter-secretariat, that have been developed to deal with coordination and to facilitate the functioning of the system.

Let it be stressed that while the total activities of the system are to be seen as a whole and in perspective, only a part – and probably a minor part – need coordination, in the narrow sense of the term, the remainder being self-contained and not impinging on the activity of other agencies. This is especially true of the work of WHO and some of the highly technical agencies such as the International Telecommunication Union (ITU) and the Universal Postal Union (UPU); it is least true of the United Nations itself, almost all of whose activities have a bearing on, or require support from, the agencies. Furthermore, the greater part of the coordination takes place informally among the officials directly concerned. What remains and constitutes the substance of the inter-agency arrangements for coordination is, of course, still sizable.

Administrative and budgetary coordination

For the discharge of its duty under Article 17 (3) of the Charter, to examine the administrative budgets of the specialized agencies with a view to making recommendations to the agencies concerned, the General Assembly has always relied first and foremost on its Advisory Committee on Administrative and Budgetary Questions. The ACABQ has sought to help the agencies rather than to impose its views on them, and its procedures are designed to this end. On the basis of the agencies' draft estimates (or in the case of agencies such as the ILO and WHO, whose Conferences meet in early summer before ACABQ can look at the estimates, their approved budgets), ACABQ consults personally each executive head, or his head of administration, before formulating its draft comments (or draft recommendations for adoption by the General Assembly), which are then sent to him for scrutiny and possible suggestions for revision. Its consolidated report on agency budgets is issued when this procedure has been completed, usually in November during the session of the General Assembly; the gist of its contents will be made known by the executive head, with his own comments, to the agency organs which meet at that time of the year. The degree of thoroughness with which the agency budgets are examined varies greatly. Generally, however, the ACABQ's reports have been essentially descriptive and little attempt has been made to go into the details of the agency's budget or to make specific recommendations. A few years ago, the General Assembly asked ACABQ to undertake on-the-spot 'in-depth' studies each year of two or three agencies, but it is doubtful that the results of these exercises justified the special effort and expense involved.

In its 1975 report on 'Administrative and Budgetary Coordination of the UN with the specialized agencies and the IAEA' (A/10360), the ACABQ questions the continued usefulness of its annual reports, noting that it is impossible for the General Assembly to make detailed recommendations about agency budgets and that the introduction of programme budgeting has blurred the lines between programme and administrative coordination. It makes the points that coordination problems can usefully be considered only in the context of specific substantive items and that new techniques such as programme budgeting do not necessarily lead to better coordination. It points out that there are a number of questions of broad application which agencies are tending to deal with piecemeal and on which central guidance would be useful and suggests a tentative list of such questions including the interaction between activities financed under the regular budgets and those financed from voluntary funds; improvements in administration and management; greater assimilation in important aspects of personnel policy, e.g. the grading and classification patterns; and improvements in budgetary methods – noting for example that the budgets of most jointly financed operations have hitherto escaped the scrutiny of any intergovernmental body.

In the United Nations System, coordination attempted in administrative and budgetary matters has generally been different in purpose and nature from coordination of substantive work. While it has included efforts to ensure a pooling of resources and other direct economies, the task has been largely, indeed mainly, the tedious and time-consuming one of securing agreement to adopt common methods and standards and common forms of presentation, or promoting an assimilation of them. Such, at any rate, has been a major concern of the General Assembly, ACABQ and the Consultative Committee on Administrative Questions (CCAQ), whose biggest achievement, however, has been the common system of salaries and allowances for the professional grades and above. For almost 20 years the common system has been in force in the United Nations, the ILO, FAO, UNESCO, ICAO, WMO, ITU and UPU; it is also applied in IMCO, WIPO and IAEA as well as other agencies such as GATT. It has not necessarily been a means of securing economies – indeed at the outset the salaries in Europe were substantially increased in order to bring them up to the New York level – and the assimilation of conditions of service has been far from complete.[1] It would, however, be difficult to imagine that the concept of the United Nations family, and still less, the United Nations Development Programme, as a combined undertaking of the United Nations System, could have thrived or even survived without it.

Complementing the common system has been the work of encouraging the adoption of common standards and methods of recruitment and common conditions of employment, in the interest of developing something approaching an international civil service. The role of the International Civil Service Advisory Board (ICSAB), an organ created by ACC in 1948 at the behest of the General Assembly, in this endeavour was originally limited in effect to responding to specific requests of ACC or one of the participating agencies for advice on methods and standards. But in the early 1960s, following a crisis regarding remuneration of general service staff in Geneva (which the heads of the Geneva-based agencies were unable to resolve), ACC agreed to broaden ICSAB's terms of reference so that it was allowed, on its own initiative, to review and advise on conditions of service and divergencies between organizations in the application of the common system; it was furthermore provided with a small permanent staff. ICSAB has now been replaced by the International Civil Service Commission (ICSC), a body with wider powers and more time and staff, and with Headquarters in New York, the Statute of which was formally adopted by the General Assembly in 1974 (Resolution 3357 (XXIX)), and it has been or is being accepted by all the agencies participating in the 'common system'. The Commission reports and is responsible to the General

Assembly, which appoints its chairman and members on the proposal of the Secretary-General, acting as Chairman of ACC, and in
consultation with ACABQ. This development represents an important step towards fulfilling one of the objectives incorporated in most
of the United Nations–agency agreements, namely, 'the eventual
development of a single unified international civil service'. While the
covering resolution asks the Commission to review the UN salary
system as a matter of priority (and a report on the subject was
promised for 1976), the Statute gives it a wide range of advisory functions, from which much improvement in administrative coordination
is hoped over the coming years in relation to such matters as job
classifications, standards of recruitment, career training, staff development and staff evaluation. It also gives the Commission powers of
decision in respect of a few matters, including the establishment of
some categories of allowances and benefits and the classification of
duty stations for the purpose of post adjustments, which had hitherto
been decided by the executive heads (or in some cases their executive
boards). While emphasis is laid in the Statute on consultation between
the Commission and the executive heads (as well as staff representatives), and arrangements have been made for regular meetings of the
Commission and ACC, there is at least a theoretical possibility of a
conflict of view developing, a possibility which, it is already clear,
every effort will be made to avoid.

The General Assembly itself has tended to devote little time to
administrative and budgetary coordination of the United Nations
with the specialized agencies and IAEA, the annual agenda item
under this heading being usually dealt with in a few moments, and
to devolve responsibilities in administrative matters wherever possible to subordinate expert bodies. An important instance of the
latter tendency was the setting up by the General Assembly in 1965
of the *Ad Hoc* Committee of Experts to Examine the Finances of the
United Nations and the Specialized Agencies, generally known as
the Committee of 14. This high-powered body, which owed its origin
largely to the special financial difficulties prevailing in the years
following the Congo operation, produced a massive series of recommendations covering such questions as the budget cycle, the methods
of budget preparation and budget presentation and performance,
which were adopted by the General Assembly and laid the basis for
inter-agency work in these fields for many years. Furthermore, on
the recommendation of the *Ad Hoc* Committee, the General Assembly,
in Resolution 2150 (xxi), established the Joint Inspection Unit
(JIU), and simultaneously enlarged the terms of reference of the

Joint Panel of Auditors to include consideration of methods of administration and management.[2] The JIU, set up in agreement with the specialized agencies, other than the Fund and Bank Group, was given 'the broadest powers of investigation in all matters having a bearing on the efficiency of the services and the proper use of funds'.

The Council, with its Committee for Programme and Coordination, has devoted much time to supporting the General Assembly and ACABQ in regard to administrative and budgetary coordination and to implementing the recommendations of the Committee of 14. It was, for example, the Council that arranged for the common classification of activities and the annual presentation by ACC of a consolidated statement of expenditures by the United Nations and the agencies on the basis of that classification; it is the Council and CPC which have taken the lead in regard to programme budgeting and medium-term planning. Interorganizational coordination in regard to public information, particularly on economic and social activities and problems, has always been a close concern of the Council; and the Council is at least as much concerned as ACABQ with the question of information systems and computers and with the reports of JIU, so many of which deal with general matters affecting all or most organizations, such as publications and documentation, conference schedules, official travel and trust funds.

The two-year budget cycle which has been adopted by the United Nations and several agencies is intended, among other things, to help Governments plan their contributions and to allow organizations to plan their work further ahead than the old annual budget would allow. However, inflation and the rapid changes in priority demands for international action have been making the two-year forecasts increasingly unrealistic. The situation is worst in the case of agencies with a 3-year (WMO and WIPO) or 4-year (ITU) budget cycle respectively. Several organizations including UNDP and UNICEF have decided not to give up annual budgeting.

If the recent measures taken in the United Nations itself and several of the agencies towards medium-term planning and programme budgeting owe their origin to the Committee of 14, they have been much influenced not only by the Council and CPC, but also by the Joint Inspection Unit,[3] and the secretariats themselves. These steps have had the further aim of facilitating programme coordination among the United Nations organizations and enabling the Governments to exercise greater control over programmes from the earliest stages of planning. It must be borne in mind, of course, that control over programmes, in so far as it means an attempt to curtail, is more difficult to exercise than control over budgets, since every programme and every project has its supporters, and usually its ardent supporters. Furthermore, some flexibility will inevitably be lost – a point not to be overlooked in the case of the United Nations, which should be in a position to respond at short notice to changing and emergency needs. A warning to the effect that sufficient flexibility must be consciously safeguarded was sounded by ACABQ in 1971.[4] Flexibility has also been lost in the United Nations itself as a result of the recent abandonment of the 'consolidated manning table' (under which the Secretary-General had considerable freedom, within the total of funds available for staff costs, to adjust the level and distribution of posts) in connexion with the introduction of programme budgeting. It may be added that the Administrative Management Service, a secretariat unit created in 1968, has made a useful contribution not only towards improving international organization and methods but also towards uncovering areas of duplication and overlap in the programmes being carried out by ESA, UNCTAD and UNIDO, as well as the regional economic commissions.

In coordination matters, the General Assembly with its subsidiaries and the Council thus normally complement and support one another. Sometimes the General Assembly duplicates and even contradicts the Council – though actual contradictions (e.g. restoration of meetings disallowed by the Council) are rare on administrative and economic issues. The blurring – and indeed the overlapping – of the functions of the two principal organs of the United Nations has however presented less of a problem than the demarcation itself. Programmes and budgets cannot be considered and determined in isolation from one another: they are two sides of the same coin and some form of joint consideration is essential. In the early years of the United Nations, from 1947–1952, an attempt was made to meet the problem within the General Assembly itself by organizing joint meetings of the Second (Economic Questions), Third (Social Questions, including Human Rights) and Fifth (Budget and Finance) Committees to consider the report of the Council on coordination and relations with the specialized agencies. This procedure was abandoned because it was unsatisfactory on several counts: the joint meetings suffered from the absence of any preparatory body; they were marked by diffuse discussions, great differences of approach and opinion, and consequent difficulty in reaching a consensus; they presented a problem of internal coordination for many delegations in deciding which of their members should sit and what line should be followed; and, by immobilizing three committees, they made heavy demands on the time of the General Assembly. In recent years, a number of alternative methods of meeting the problem, at least in part, have been developed. These include referral by the General Assembly of the Council's programme proposals – many of which involve the agencies – and the Council's report on inter-agency coordination matters, simultaneously to its Fifth Committee for comments, and to the Second and Third Committees; the somewhat closer association of the budgetary authorities, both in the Secretariat and ACABQ mainly on an informal basis and through its Chairman and Secretary with the programme-formulating process has been helpful. There have been some signs of progress towards greater coherence, stability and soundness of programmes and closer conformity of programmes to budgetary possibilities, resulting from the efforts of the United Nations and other organizations to achieve an integrated programme and budget on a long-term basis – efforts in which, in the case of the United Nations, the Committee for Programme and Coordination (CPC) has been making an essential contribution. But the situation is fundamentally unsound and is becoming more serious, owing to differences, which are impossible to avoid altogether, in the approaches of different legislative organs and the not infrequent failure – because of perfectly worthy endeavours to keep expenses down and to prevent the total budget level from rising above what Governments seem willing to pay – to provide the minimum necessary to carry out even the priority work decided upon.

The balance-sheet in respect of administrative and budgetary coordination of the United Nations, the specialized agencies and International Atomic Energy Agency (IAEA) is on the whole, frankly, not impressive. It is true that in recent years, the cooperation of the agencies in the various General Assembly initiatives – some of which, like the establishment of an International Civil Service Commission, had been resisted in an earlier period – has been quite noteworthy. There have also been noteworthy failures. One, which has been referred to earlier, has been the failure to apply to the United Nations programmes financed by voluntary contributions, and the budgets and administration of those programmes, the same criteria and standards as are applicable to the programmes financed from the regular budget. This omission – which efforts are being made to overcome[5] – has not contributed to order and coherence in the system nor has the disparity in the classification of professional jobs from one organization to another. There have long been difficulties in the way of reaching inter-agency agreement regarding computerized information systems. In the top staff structures of the major agencies and the United Nations, striking differences have developed which have not been without effect on United Nations–agency relationships, but this question has never been accepted as appropriate for inter-agency discussion.[6]

As regards administrative arrangements of the different organizations and programmes 'in the field', there is a long history of efforts by the United Nations to encourage the establishment of agency offices in the same cities and the same buildings, for the purpose of facilitating the establishment of common services and local coordination and of emphasizing the unity of the United Nations System. While some successes have been registered, especially where Governments have put up special buildings for the United Nations family, much of this effort has been fruitless, among the reasons being that different ministries so often put accommodation free, or at a nominal cost, at the disposal of the corresponding international organizations and that certain agencies (essentially the Bank Group), while prepared to cooperate with others and the United Nations, have preferred to be separate.

Other aspects of coordination in the field, likewise unsettled, have been curiously neglected. First, it is still standard practice in the capitals of developing countries for each agency office to have its own car, and for each car, when transporting the agency's Chief of Mission, to fly the United Nations flag. Secondly, while the pre-eminence of the resident representative of UNDP in development matters has been established and confirmed by the Consensus of 1970, and a particular official – usually the resident representative but sometimes the director of the United Nations information centre – has on occasion been designated by the Secretary-General, in consultation with the heads of agencies and programmes, to represent the United Nations family in times of political emergency, not only is there no rule as to which official represents the United Nations family and takes precedence but no procedure has been laid down for making such a designation, case by case. Such authority could be – indeed, could only be – exercised by the Secretary-General, but the matter has never been raised at ACC or between the Secretary-General and the heads of individual agencies.

There are wide variations in the privileges and immunities granted to staff of the United Nations organizations by Governments. No blame in the matter is imputed to the organizations concerned, but the fact must be noted that such variations, especially between organizations at the same duty stations, are apt to have a divisive effect on staff and to affect the equitable application of the common salary system.

Before closing this section it may not be inappropriate to mention a lack of coordination of a quite different order, which might nevertheless be considered as 'administrative'. Most of the numerous programmes of the United Nations and the agencies that are financed by voluntary contributions need constant replenishment, and a major responsibility for fund-raising falls in many cases on the executive heads of the mother agency or of the programmes themselves. Apart from consultations with interested delegations in New York, Geneva or wherever the fund is based, this fund-raising often requires direct contacts with national Ministries of Finance and even heads of Governments. It happens quite frequently that several high officials are for such purposes on the road simultaneously – and for weeks at a stretch – each working independently for the financing of his side of United Nations activity and sometimes – even when efforts are made to coordinate visits – unaware of the plans and movements of the others. Various devices (notably, in the United Nations itself, arrangements for governmental pledging conferences) have been adopted to lessen the need for competitive personal approaches for funds, which, however effective they may sometimes be, inevitably arouse criticism in the countries concerned, not to mention their administrative effects at home. But under present conditions such approaches are still often essential if the work is to be maintained.

Programme coordination

Here we reach the area where the need for order, coherence, coordination and clarity has always been most conspicuous and which has from the earliest years of the United Nations been a principal concern of the Council as well as ACC and the staff of the different organizations.

The first aim was negative: to avoid duplication and overlapping, sins which were fatally easy to commit because of the multiple aspects, each falling within the sphere of some agency, of so many economic and social problems. Proliferation of activities, also much complained of, was largely due to the same reasons. The General Assembly and the Council exhorted, but could not easily deal with cases: that task fell to the secretariats and occupied – indeed still occupies – much of the time of ACC machinery. It has involved a search for agreement on concepts, a sorting out of functions, and the establishment of criteria and guidelines in respect of closely related activities of different organizations. The magnitude of the task can be judged by the extent and growth of the network of interdependent activities to be carried out by organizations with such broad and overlapping mandates, a network outlined in a 274-page United Nations document of 1969, usually referred to under the disarming title, 'The clear and comprehensive picture'.[7] This document shows in detail how, on literally hundreds of subjects in each of several broad fields,[8] divisions and bureaux of from six to ten agencies and the United Nations Department of Economic and Social Affairs, plus a varying number of United Nations programmes and regional commissions, all have parts to play – parts that often need to be closely defined and interpreted in consultation with other agencies and programmes and then carefully orchestrated. A vivid illustration is provided in the 1972/73 report of ACC to the Council (E/5289 (part I)), which contains a list, which does not attempt to be exhaustive, of 48 separate activities within a single medium-sized subgroup, namely, marine science and its applications, in which two or more organizations are cooperating or trying to coordinate their efforts.[9]

As a general rule – indeed in the overwhelming majority of cases – reasonably satisfactory and economical arrangements are worked out among the respective staffs (personalities sometimes playing a helpful, sometimes an unhelpful role), aided, as necessary, by more formal inter-secretariat consultative arrangements, and are eventually endorsed by the intergovernmental organs. But in a few cases in some areas the problems of jurisdiction have been difficult to overcome. For example, the problems of how the three organizations concerned – UNESCO, FAO and, to a lesser extent, ILO – should divide or coordinate their responsibilities in regard to agricultural education reappeared constantly on the agenda of ACC for years. It was eventually settled through ACC, under strong pressure from the Council, on the cumbersome basis of a joint and complementary approach and the setting up of a joint advisory committee on policy.

Still more intractable differences, reflecting as in the case just cited, differences in the allocation of responsibilities within different national administrations, long existed between United Nations Headquarters and some agencies concerning aspects of the development and utilization of water resources. The United Nations position, put very briefly, has been that the United Nations itself, with its comprehensive outlook and broad responsibilities for development – rather than an agency whose interests are primarily scientific or related to some particular 'end use' such as irrigation, pure drinking water or water for industrial purposes – should have the primary role in advising Governments on general water policy, on water management administration and law, and be the executing agency for relevant UNDP-financed projects. Without denying that the United Nations should have a say, the agencies have tended to reply that most water projects primarily serve particular objectives, such as agricultural development, environmental, health or industrial development, and would therefore be best carried out by the organizations having know-how and expertise in those fields. The controversy, which has accounted for weeks of inter-agency discussion and scores of documents over the years, was recently taken in hand by the United Nations Committee on Natural Resources. That Committee has taken no sweeping decisions of principle, preferring to look into individual cases, on a pragmatic basis, with the help of ACC, and there are some prospects that the issue will soon cease to be troublesome.

From the earliest days, stress has been laid on two aspects of early consultation as essential ingredients of programme coordination and cooperation. The first is consultation with other agencies before an intergovernmental organ takes a decision that might closely affect them. The obligation so to consult was, at the urging of ACC, accepted at an early stage by the Council and incorporated in its rules of procedure (Rule 80) and those of its functional commissions (Rule 74); it was thereafter accepted by the governing organs of a number of agencies. It has not, however, been formally accepted by the General Assembly or, pending such action, by the International Labour Conference or the legislative organs of other major agencies. The required consultations usually take place in practice, but there have been cases in the General Assembly when this had not happened. One instance was the General Assembly's decision in 1959 to award prizes for successful cancer research, a decision much resented by WHO even though it was given the task of designating the prize winners. The renewal of the credit for the awards was to have been considered in 1964, but this was the year when the General Assembly was not functioning because of the dispute over the right of the USSR and France to participate in the voting owing to their failure to contribute their share of the Congo expenses. The cancer award question was shelved and thereafter forgotten – the best solution that could have been devised.

The second aspect of consultation relates to the draft work programmes drawn up by the secretariats. The initiative in sending regularly draft programmes to other agencies' secretariats for comment was taken by UNESCO in the 1950s. Consultations through this and other means, despite exhortations that they be undertaken at the earliest stage of planning, have usually been undertaken too late to avoid a good deal of unnecessary duplication and misunderstanding; but recently, with the new emphasis on programme budgeting and medium-term planning, the problem has begun to be tackled more purposefully.

The search for priorities, how best and in which order to use the limited resources available, represents another aspect of programme coordination which has long claimed attention. The Council, in 1950, for example, laid down fairly elaborate criteria and procedures for the establishment of programme priorities and, in 1952, in the course of a very lengthy session, drew up six major programme priorities for the guidance of all United Nations organs concerned as well as the specialized agencies. These programme priorities, which represent a rather different frame of thinking from that of today, were as follows: increased food production and distribution; increased production in fields other than food; measures for promoting domestic full employment and economic stability within an expanding economy; acceleration of welfare, social security and basic public health programmes; development of education and science; promotion of wider observance of human rights. The difficulties in the way of establishing priorities between broad areas of work – for example, public health, agricultural development, education – are, of course, enormous, and even within each group there are many different criteria that could be used – the activities aimed at meeting the most urgent needs, those most widely and authoritatively recommended, those ripe for positive action, those which the international organizations are best equipped to handle, those aimed at current major objectives such as the development of the least developed countries, the promotion of world food supplies, the protection of the environment. In the background lies the problem of the relationship between priorities centrally determined and those of individual Governments. That the issue has still found no full solution can be inferred from the resolution adopted by the General Assembly in 1973 (3199 (xxvii)), calling on the Council to indicate clearly the priorities that should govern the Secretary-General's medium-term plan for 1976–1979 and his programme and budget for 1976–1977 and the Council's inconclusive discussion of the Secretary-General's report on the matter in 1974.

The secretariats of the United Nations and the specialized agencies have devoted a good deal of effort for many years past both on concerted planning and on the modalities of programme cooperation.

Work programmes blessed by intergovernmental bodies are normally fashioned through processes of cooperative planning and constantly adjusted in response to questions such as: How in detail can the different organizations contribute most effectively? How should work be adjusted or modified in the light of experience? How should particular problems that arise in the course of executing a programme be faced? Are special measures (e.g. budgetary) needed to enable one or more of the cooperating agencies to contribute more fully? This sort of positive coordination is not new; it began years ago with programmes on housing and on fundamental education, which were later merged with other initiatives under 'rural and community development'. But it has grown immensely in range and scope and is now applied to the Programme of Action for a new economic order and to work under the Development Strategy, as well as in more specific fields such as the human environment, natural resources, the protein problem, marine science and its applications, statistics, education and training, population activities, action against drug abuse, and natural disasters. The success of such positive coordination depends, first, on the degree to which each programme has been planned in concert with the other organizations concerned and related from the earliest stage, financially as well as substantively to the whole body of their work, and, secondly, on the adoption by each organization of work programmes and longer-term plans on a reasonably comparable basis. Programme budgeting and a biennial budget cycle have been developed in the big programme agencies over a period of some years and were adopted by the United Nations itself in 1972. A first biennial programme and budget for the United Nations, together with a medium-term plan for 1973–1978, was submitted in 1973. To achieve really comparable plans and programmes among organizations with such varying traditions and interests bristles with difficulties but, without such comparability, the contribution of these programming exercises to greater coherence and coordination of programmes may be disappointingly modest. Efforts are therefore now being directed, in inter-agency discussion and with the help of the Joint Inspection Unit[10], to improve the presentation of, and bring about greater uniformity among, the programmes and budgets, and especially in respect of the medium-term plan. There is still little to show for these efforts, but meetings of the Senior Programming Officers of the United Nations and the major programming agencies for the above purpose were begun in 1974.

What are the prospects of success in this whole venture? There is little doubt that they depend above all on the willingness of all the organizations concerned to devote much staff time and effort to an exercise which, however rewarding it is likely to be in the end to the system as a whole, may not offer much early advantage to individual agencies. They will also depend in large measure on the ability of the United Nations Secretariat itself to develop some form of central decision making in programme matters. There can only be inter-agency anarchy if the United Nations Secretariat has not settled its own policy and distribution of work; and there are far too many areas – for example, as between the regional commissions and Head-quarters staff, and between UNCTAD and ESA – in which this situation exists. The prospects will inevitably depend in part on the success of a central programming group, of which there is already a nucleus, and an official in charge of sufficient authority throughout the Secretariat and with the intergovernmental organs concerned to make the groups' findings stick.

Regional coordination

Many questions of programme coordination, referred to so far in the global context of the Council and ACC, reappear at the regional level, sometimes complicated by factors such as the conflicting authority of regional organs, uncertainty as to the respective roles of Headquarters and regional staffs, ignorance of agreements reached at Headquarters, and sometimes by arrangements relating to opera-tions, made through the processes of the development programme, that cut across those agreements.

Such difficulties, usually soluble only on a pragmatic rather than a logical or constitutional basis, are likely to increase despite the recent confirmation by the Council of the central role of the executive secretaries of the United Nations regional commissions, because of the continued trend towards regional devolution of programme res-ponsibilities in many organizations. One of the most intractable problems is that of the place of the regional commissions and regional arms of the agencies in the development system. If the commissions are mainly concerned with problems affecting the region as a whole for a number of countries, they also seek to provide development advice and assistance to individual countries. But UNDP deals direct, through its resident representatives, with the development authori-ties of each country and until recently there was scarcely any con-tact – and no direct contact – between it and the commissions or their secretariats except in so far as 'regional' projects were concerned. The Capacity Study called attention to the seriousness of this problem but felt unable to make recommendations regarding the best means of utilizing regional organs in the development process until greater order had been introduced in the regional structures of the United Nations System. An extensive inquiry requested by the Council in Resolution 1553 (XLIX), among Governments, specialized agencies and the commissions themselves, led to a report and recommendations on regional structures being submitted by the Secretary-General to the Council at its Fifty-fourth Session (E/5127). The Council then asked for a further report for its Fifty-eighth Session on regional structures 'aimed at their gradual simplification and adjustment to the realities, needs and aspirations of each region',[11] which is where the matter stands. Meanwhile, UNDP has created at Headquarters four regional bureaux, each under an assistant administrator which, although their 'regions' do not all correspond to those of the United Nations regional commissions, are to maintain contact with the regional commissions' secretariats; and, as an experiment, a special resident representative of UNDP has been appointed at Addis Ababa for the purpose of coordination and cooperation with the Economic Commission for Africa (ECA). By various other means – for example, the United Nations Development Advisory Teams (UNDATS)[12] – efforts are being made to use the commissions' development expertise to a greater extent than in the past.

Most of the executive secretaries of the regional commissions, men of authority in their own right, have exercised an influence far beyond the letter of any texts. Some of them have made a practice of calling from time to time informal meetings at the commissions' Headquarters of regional representatives of specialized agencies and United Nations programmes, such as UNCTAD, UNIDO and UNDP, for purposes of mutual exchange of information and consultation on matters of common concern. The Secretary-General has recommended that he be authorized,[13] in cooperation with the heads of other United Nations organizations, to arrange for such meetings on a regular basis. The discussion of this proposal in the Council raised some of the old questions: How would the agencies react to such a 'leadership' role for the United Nations commissions? Should the commissions' staffs assume responsibilities for promoting coordination? How closely should the secretariats act under the supervision of their intergovernmental bodies? How could the Council exercise due control? Some of these considerations found expression in the Resolution adopted by the Council (1757 (LIV)) which, while basically accepting the proposal, both restricts and formalizes it by stipulating that the meetings should be 'under the authority of the intergovernmental bodies of the regional economic commissions', and that the purpose should be to improve 'at the regional level, co-operation and co-ordination in the implementation of economic and social activities approved by the respective policy-making organs concerned'.

A strong tendency towards autonomy and fragmentation is to be found rather generally in the regional bodies of the various United Nations organizations. Illustrations are provided by the unanimous 'commemorative' resolutions adopted by ECA in 1969[14] and the recent decision of ECAFE (Resolution 137 (XXIX)), because of crop failures and other agricultural problems, to set up an Agricultural Committee that would tend to deal – if from a somewhat different angle – with much the same problems as the biennial FAO Regional Conference for Asia and the Far East. The classical case, however, has been provided by FAO. In 1968, its newly elected Director-General, Mr Boerma, supported by the Secretary-General of the United Nations, was anxious to bring about closer integration between the regional policies and programmes of FAO and the United Nations regional economic commissions in matters relating to agriculture. Mr Boerma proposed, as a first step, to appoint the Executive Secretary of ECA as FAO Regional Director for Africa and to transfer the FAO regional office from Accra to the seat of ECA at Addis Ababa. The proposal was decisively rejected at the Kampala session of the African Regional Conference of FAO, consisting, of course, mainly of representatives of African Ministries of Agriculture, who inveighed against the danger of FAO losing its independence. The FAO Council then endorsed the Kampala decision. In view of this reception, the whole initiative was dropped and other more costly means had to be explored for improving coordination in regional agriculture work of the United Nations.

The moral of that failure is certainly not that coordination on major issues within Governments is impossible, but rather that it needs much staff work and time, case by case, since positions are usually left to the technical ministries (or their representatives) to determine, unless some particular issue is flagged for consideration at the top level. Had it been possible for Mr Boerma's proposal to be first discussed fully with the missions at United Nations and FAO Headquarters and at Addis Ababa, and perhaps in the CPC and the Council, the outcome might have been very different.

The episode also brings out the degree to which cooperation has developed among the top officials of the United Nations organizations in the interest of greater order and coherence in the United

Nations System. If it is no longer quite true to say, as the then Secretary-General said in a 1948 report, that good general coordinated action is the aggregate of hundreds of points of contact between the United Nations and the agencies and between the agencies themselves, such contacts, maintained informally by telephone and mail, plus possibly an occasional visit, are in general – and certainly as regards coordination of programmes – more important than any formal arrangements. Coordination is not something to be pursued only in and through coordinating units which can do little more than help and stimulate; it is, on the one hand, a function and responsibility of all management, and, on the other, an objective which all senior officers should pursue and a discipline to which they should subject themselves. To help develop such attitudes and practices in the international staffs has been a major purpose of ACC and one which it has gone some way towards achieving.

Before concluding this section, a word must be said about the United Nations regional development institutes and the regional development banks. ECLA, ECAFE and ECA have been instrumental in setting up, with financial assistance from UNDP, regional economic development institutes which provide training, research and, in the case of the ILPES (the institute attached to ECLA in Santiago, Chile) some advisory services to Governments. The contacts between the institutes and the commissions vary considerably. Until recently they have been very close in Latin America and somewhat remote in Africa. In general, they are not very close with United Nations Headquarters, and still less so with the specialized agencies.

The institute directors do, however, have certain regular contacts with one another and Headquarters, e.g. through the United Nations Research Institute for Social Development in Geneva on whose board they sit, and through UNITAR, whose Executive Director chairs an annual meeting of directors of all institutes in the United Nations System, global and regional (which cover a very wide range of subjects including educational planning, social defence, and higher vocational training). These annual meetings provide for an exchange of information and views concerning work programmes and a limited number of matters of particular common concern (such as, recently, relationships with the United Nations University).

Of the regional development banks, two (the Asian and the African) were established on the initiative of United Nations regional economic commissions, which are represented on the Banks' Boards. Their relations with the regional commissions are, however, rather tenuous, as are also the relations between the Inter-American Development Bank with ECLA. The regional banks which, like the World Bank, have their cadres of economic and other experts, maintain close contacts with one another as well as with the World Bank Group and IMF.

Coordination at the country level

Allusions have been made earlier in this chapter to administrative situations that needed coordination between the staffs of different organizations in individual countries; of even greater importance for the public image of the United Nations, no less than in the interests of the developing countries themselves, is programme and project coordination, country by country, among the various United Nations organizations concerned with technical cooperation. The subject has been discussed at length in United Nations documents,[15] and only a brief note on it will be given here. It was a subject of constant concern to the Technical Assistance Board in the 1950s because of the reluctance of some agencies to accept any control over their representatives by non-specialists or restriction on their direct relations with the technical ministries concerned. But in 1961, in consultation with the Board, ACC drew up a list of 10 principles, agreed to by all organizations participating in the Expanded Programme of Technical Assistance (EPTA), governing the status, powers and functions of the resident representatives, who had become the key figures in inter-agency coordination in each developing country. These principles, which were endorsed by the Economic and Social Council, were elaborated by ACC in 1967. The missions to evaluate the impact and effectiveness of the technical cooperation programmes of the United Nations System, undertaken in several developing countries in 1967 and 1968[16] and a report by the Joint Inspection Unit in 1968 on coordination and cooperation at the country level[17] brought out the need to strengthen the position of the resident representatives vis-à-vis the country representatives of the specialized agencies, and a Resolution (1453 (XLVII)) with this end in view was adopted by the Council in 1969.

The whole problem took on a new dimension with the introduction of 'country programming' and the establishment of indicative planning figures (IPF) which, though not to be construed as representing a commitment, have in practice come close to being such. The Consensus adopted by the Governing Council of UNDP in the summer of 1970 and later in the year by the General Assembly enlarges and further strengthens the role of the resident representatives. Two sentences of the relevant provision deserve to be quoted in full:

The resident director[18] should have ultimate authority on behalf of the Administrator for all aspects of the programme at the country level and should, subject to the agreement of the organizations concerned, be the central co-ordinating authority on their behalf for the other development assistance programmes of the United Nations system. In this connexion, the organizations in the United Nations system are requested to ensure that the resident directors of the Programme are consulted on the planning and formulation of development projects with which those organizations are concerned and that they are supplied with reports on the execution of those projects, as requested by the Economic and Social Council in resolution 1453 (XLVII) of 8 August 1969.[19]

If country programming has raised new problems for the resident representatives, the local authority of the latter has been increased; new possibilities have been opened up for a constructive dialogue and cooperation between them, on behalf of the United Nations System, and the Government planners; and a new aspect of coordination in which they may have an important and delicate part to play, namely, between the objectives and priorities determined by the United Nations intergovernmental organs and those of the individual countries, has asserted itself.[20] The main responsibility in this area lies with UNDP, a fact which reinforces the argument for closer association between UNDP and the organs of the system concerned with general economic, and more especially economic development, policy.

4 Intergovernmental organs responsible for coordination

Coordination is naturally fostered by knowledge, and hampered by ignorance, of what others in the international field – Governments, organs and staff – are doing and thinking. The obligation to take account of what others are doing which rests on Governments and intergovernmental organs, as well as on individual staff members, is fundamental. In a very real sense, coordination is also exercised, willy-nilly, by every expert group or person or organ whose views carry authority. There is certainly a need for international institutions and procedures especially concerned with coordination and we shall now discuss briefly the roles of the General Assembly and the Economic and Social Council in this connexion, while bearing in mind that the importance and the usefulness of institutionalized coordination have tended to be exaggerated – with resultant loss of time and effort. Whatever the effect on the General Assembly's authority and effectiveness of the confrontations on economic policy that have occurred in recent years, it is well to bear in mind that in this period both the General Assembly and the Council have been making a serious attempt to address themselves to the task of increasing not only efficiency but also coherence and coordination in the United Nations System.

The General Assembly

Under the Charter, the General Assembly is the highest authority in matters of coordination within the system. Article 13 empowers it to 'initiate studies and make recommendations for the purpose of... promoting international co-operation in the economic, social, cultural, educational and health fields, and assisting in the realization of human rights and fundamental freedoms for all...'; Article 15 empowers it to receive and consider reports 'from the various organs of the United Nations'; under Article 17(e) it is to consider and approve financial and budgetary arrangements with specialized agencies and examine 'the administrative budgets of such specialized agencies with a view to making recommendations to the agencies concerned'; under Article 22, it may 'establish such subsidiary organs as it deems necessary for the performance of its functions'; Article 58 provides that the Organization shall coordinate the activities of the specialized agencies; and Article 60 vests in the General Assembly and under its authority in the Economic and Social Council 'responsibility for the discharge of the functions of the Organization in regard to economic and social co-operation as a whole'.

As the supreme political organ of the United Nations System, as the organ that takes most of the big initiatives that are elaborated and followed up by the system's component parts, it is true that the General Assembly has always played a big part in leading and, in a broad sense, in coordinating the policies and the activities of the system. But for many years after it abandoned the attempt to deal with programme and administrative coordination together through joint meetings of the Second, Third and Fifth Committees, the General Assembly left the specifics of programme and general coordination almost entirely to the Economic and Social Council and, as regards agency budgets and administrative matters, to its ACABQ. Those parts of the reports of the Council that dealt with coordination and relations with specialized agencies went not to any committee of the Assembly for consideration but direct to a plenary session, where they rarely evoked more than a passing comment; and the annual discussion of ACABQ's reports on agency budgets and 'general coordination matters' normally took up only a few minutes of the Fifth Committee's time.

Recently, there has, in some respects, been a change. For several years, the Second, Third and Fifth Committees of the General Assembly have had before them the chapter in the Council's annual report on 'Coordination of and Relations with the Specialized Agencies', and since 1972 the chapter has been given the new title of 'Programme and Coordination' to mark the new approach. There has been considerable discussion of the formulation, review and approval of programmes and budgets, and their significance for coordination in the United Nations System, with special reference to the introduction of programme budgeting. In 1973, the General Assembly went so far as to request the Economic and Social Council to indicate clearly 'the order of priorities in the economic, social and human rights fields to be reflected by the Secretary-General in his medium-term plan for 1976–1979 and the proposed programme and budget for 1976–1977'[1] – a request that the Council has since referred to CPC for study and advice.[2] The same year, as mentioned in the Introduction, the General Assembly decided to hold a special session itself in 1975

for the purpose of examining the political and other implications of the state of world development and international economic co-operation, expanding the dimensions and concepts of world economic and developmental co-operation, and giving the goal of development its rightful place in the United Nations system and on the international stage.[3]

The preparations for that special session, the developments in policy and ideas that preceded it and the results of the session itself, as well as the results of the Conferences, are described in the Postscript.

A turning-point as regards General Assembly involvement in matters affecting organization and coordination in the United Nations System had, in fact, come in 1965 with its establishment of the Committee of 14.[4] At that, Twenty-first Session, the General Assembly requested the Council to enlarge the membership and terms of reference of the Committee for Programme Coordination (CPC) for three years for the purpose of carrying out a full review of the activities of the United Nations family and to make 'recommendations on modifications in activities, procedures and administrative arrangements' in order to ensure:

(i) The maximum concentration of resources, at present and increasing levels, on programmes of direct relevance to Member States;
(ii) A flexible prompt and effective response to the specific needs of individual countries and regions, as determined by them, within the limits of available resources;
(iii) The minimum burden on the administrative resources of Member States and of members of the United Nations family of organizations;
(iv) The evolution of an integrated system of long-term planning on a programme basis;
(v) The institution of systematic procedures for evaluating the effectiveness of operational and research activities.[5]

This admirable statement reflected views that were also preoccupying the Governing Council of UNDP, which in 1968 made arrangements for a study to be undertaken of the capacity of the United Nations development system. That study and the final report of the Enlarged Committee on Programme and Coordination appeared almost simultaneously in the autumn of 1969. The Capacity Study has had a far-reaching influence on the organization and coordination of the United Nations' development work, and some of its recommendations which were not acted upon at the time are still highly relevant.

The report of ECPC (E/4748) represented in part an elaboration of and a follow-up to the recommendations of the Committee of 14, but went further. It recommended among other things that the functions of CPC should be permanently expanded in order to allow it to carry out the broad reviewing functions given to the Enlarged Committee. More specifically, CPC was to have close working relationships with the United Nations Secretariat, especially the Office of Inter-Agency Affairs (OIAA) and ESA, as well as with ACC and ACABQ. The Inspectors were to participate in its work as appropriate. It was 'to advise and assist the Council on discharging its co-ordination functions' and 'keep under review the activities of the United Nations and its related agencies and programmes, study the present procedures for co-ordination and co-operation and submit its conclusions to the Council on issues and problems arising thereon'. It was also to be 'concerned with the review of programme planning, implementation of programmes, their evaluation and the effectiveness of co-ordination machinery'. It should develop, in consultation with the Secretary-General, its own process for carrying out the system of long-term planning and programme formulation envisaged by the General Assembly and 'consider further steps required to implement within the United Nations the recommendations (of the Committee of 14) concerning the development of an integrated system of long-term planning, programming and budgeting'. The proposals in the chapter of the report of ECPC from which these provisions are taken, together with the recommendation of the Committee of 14, have since constituted the framework for most of the intensive activities of the Council and CPC, ACABQ and ACC relating to coordination.

The General Assembly has no direct relations with ACC or, except on administrative and budgetary matters and particular issues that may arise, with the specialized agencies. On one occasion the then Secretary-General, Mr Trygve Lie, presented the executive heads of the specialized agencies to the General Assembly at a Plenary Session, but the presentation evoked no particular interest and was not repeated. An item to celebrate ILO's Fiftieth Anniversary was included in the General Assembly's agenda in 1969, the year the ILO had received the Nobel Peace Prize. The Secretary-General and the then Director-General of ILO, Mr David Morse, were among those who, under this item, addressed a Plenary Meeting, which alas! was almost empty.

The Economic and Social Council

The Council's general responsibilities for coordination are linked to those of the General Assembly in Articles 58 and 60; it has been given specific authority in regard to the negotiation of relationships, agreements with, and coordination of the activities of the specialized agencies in Articles 57 and 63; Article 64 authorizes it to obtain reports from the specialized agencies; and Article 70 to arrange for representatives of the specialized agencies to participate without vote in its deliberations.

For the Council, unlike the General Assembly, 'coordination' has from the outset been a constant and central preoccupation. Negotiation of agreements with the specialized agencies figured prominently in its early agendas and before the end of 1946 it had provided for the establishment of an inter-agency coordinating committee under the Secretary-General's chairmanship which somewhat later was named the Administrative Committee on Coordination (ACC). Since 1948, it has had at its summer session a Committee of the whole on Coordination (known in recent years as its Policy and Programme Coordination Committee) to consider the annual agency reports, the annual reports of ACC and the ever-increasing range of subjects on the Council's agenda that affect or call for action of the specialized agencies. The Coordination Committee, for more than 20 years, enjoyed the great advantage of continuity, at a high level, in the representation of the important Member that was most interested and active in promoting coordination in the system, namely the USA.

But the Council as a whole has never been fully reconciled to the autonomous status of the agencies or been satisfied with its own performance as a coordinator. This dissatisfaction has been largely responsible for the repeated reviews it has undertaken of its functioning and machinery. Admittedly, it cannot claim great success for its efforts so far to deal with either the structural developments that have led to serious coordination problems or the practical coordination problems themselves. Reasons for its somewhat unimpressive record in this regard are not hard to identify if one reflects on the character of the system, the Council's lack of financial powers and the history both of the erosion of its authority and the narrowing of its areas of responsibility. But they also include its own failure fully to grasp two essential truths: firstly, that in international organizations, coordination requires persuasion and cannot easily be imposed; secondly, that, if intergovernmental bodies can lay down policies, give directions and evaluate performance, no such body – let alone one meeting only for short periods from time to time – *can* coordinate, in a transitive, active sense of the term, the actual substantive work and administration of the United Nations System which is planned and executed by the secretariats. It can only carry out its coordinating job if the secretariats of the United Nations and the specialized agencies do the spade-work. The Council's long-held doctrine that it must somehow do all the coordinating (ACC merely assisting and making suggestions). combined with its traditionally critical and defensive attitude towards ACC, has been a constant handicap, preventing it from more fully mobilizing the resources of the United Nations System. The secretariats have had much experience in working out – usually through ACC but also bilaterally – reasonably satisfactory institutional arrangements within the framework of decisions taken by intergovernmental organs, and where those decisions are a source of confusion, the secretariats can likewise exert a powerful influence in having them adjusted or rescinded. If more coherent, purposeful and better coordinated arrangements are to be achieved and maintained in the United Nations System, the UN secretariat's contribution in providing guidance to the General Assembly as well as to the Council itself will be essential.

More about this will be said in the sections that follow. In part, however, the Council's dissatisfaction with its performance as coordinator has been exaggerated. It has done more than is generally recognized in keeping the United Nations System in step. In some degree, to adapt an over-used quotation, it has been coordinating all its life without knowing it, its Charter status being a unique asset. By its very insistence on the need for cooperation, for advance consultation, for constant inter-agency consideration of priorities, it has kept the United Nations and the agencies – all of which wish to seem, and so far as possible to be, cooperative – up to the mark. It has focused the attention of ACC and individual agencies on measures that needed to be taken in the interest of coordination by launching broad programmes involving the competence of several organizations, it has made cooperation among those organizations essential; and, as a world policy forum, it has clearly exercised an influence on the policies and activities of the entire United Nations System.[6]

There are signs of a resurgence and revitalization of the Council. Among these, the decisions of the General Assembly in 1973–1975, which are discussed in the Postscript, are clearly of paramount importance. But there were not a few earlier indications, including the way in which the Council had been approaching the problem of rationa-

67

lizing its procedures and structure, the preoccupation with its role vis-à-vis the specialized agencies, its approach to coordination in the context of programming and medium-term planning; and the possibility of a strengthened body emerging to assist the Council in this programme and coordination work. Finally, the threefold increase in the membership of the Council has in itself been a new source of strength.

As in the case of the General Assembly, turning points in the history of the Council's handling of coordination matters can be identified. The very major one which has just occurred was preceded by one in 1957 when, despite reservations on the part of certain specialized agencies,[7] the Council arranged for appraisals to be made by a group of its former officers of the scope, trend and costs of programmes of the United Nations, the ILO, FAO, UNESCO, WHO, WMO and IAEA. A consolidated report, entitled *Five-year Perspective, 1960–1964,*[8] was completed in 1960.

The appraisals were regarded by the Council – and rightly so – as a step towards 'the development of co-ordination, through which the respective programmes of the United Nations organizations have gained, over the years, in purpose, depth and strength'.[9] It was also hoped that the consolidated report would bring into focus the relationship between the work of the different organizations and thereby facilitate closer cooperation and, wherever feasible, concerted action. The Committee on Programme Appraisals found, among other things, that the Council needed much more help than the Coordination Committee of the whole, which it was wont to set up at each summer session, could provide. A small *ad hoc* working group was accordingly established[10] to study before the next summer session the reports of ACC and of the agencies and come up with a statement of issues in the field of coordination calling for special attention by the Council. In the following years this group went through a series of reorganizations and reorientations, and became the Special Committee on Coordination. One year emphasis was laid on the contribution it could make to the first United Nations Development Decade[11] and an expansion of concerted action among United Nations organizations. In 1966, the Special Committee became a 16-member Committee for Programme and Coordination whose time was to be divided between coordination and examining the programmes of the United Nations itself. The same year, the Enlarged Committee for Programme and Coordination was formed, as mentioned above; and when it reported in 1969, its functions, by and large, were duly passed on to CPC.

One important series of coordinating steps taken by the Council has still to be mentioned. At its behest, a meeting between ACC and the officers of the Council, together with the Chairman of the Council's sessional Coordination Committee, was arranged in 1964, 'to discuss practical and effective means to bring about a closer relationship between the two bodies'.[12] It proved quite a success and a similar meeting was arranged for 1965. That summer, the Council asked that meetings be continued and that ACC and the Special Committee should together:

(a) Examine the provisional agenda of the Council's sessions, and draw attention whenever necessary or desirable to the major questions that require the Council's urgent action;
(b) Keep under review the activities of the United Nations and its related agencies in the economic, social, human rights and related fields, particularly in respect of the United Nations Development Decade;
(c) Submit conclusions and recommendations to the Council on those questions as well as on problems in the field of co-ordination which call for special attention by the Council.[13]

For the joint meetings, which last two or three days, agendas are worked out, on the basis of suggestions from the two committees, by the Secretary-General and the Chairman of the CPC, who preside in turn, usually on alternate days. The CPC countries have been encouraged to be represented by the heads of their delegations, but this has by no means always happened and there has sometimes been difficulty in ensuring reasonable equality in the level of representation. This has perhaps been one reason for what the Council in Resolution 1771 (LIV) has called the formal group dialogue which has characterized the joint meetings and which the Council wishes to see changed into 'a more active working discussion of questions currently on the agenda of the Council, particularly those with system-wide implications'. Some participants have tended to regard the past joint meetings as a waste of time since little, if any, enlightenment or agreement has emerged from the usually rather discursive discussions of broad items such as the Development Decade, the possible restructuring of the machinery for coordination, multilateral food aid or institutional arrangements in respect of science and technology; and underlying sources of tension have seldom been removed. For others, however, the procedure represents a not unimportant part of an essential educational process; it has provided the only regular and reasonably informal contacts that exist between the officers and some of the representatives on the Council and the heads of the agencies and United Nations programmes. The meetings have probably contributed – even if marginally – to bringing the thinking of the Council and ACC closer together; if it did not exist, such an arrangement would, without doubt, have now to be established, as part of a process that has still a long way to go.

The resolution just referred to called also for fuller participation by 'the agencies and organizations' in policy-determining discussions in the intergovernmental organizations of the United Nations, stressing the need for the agencies' contributions to be action-oriented and to be made at a sufficiently early stage in the policy elaboration process. It must be admitted that recent practice has not been altogether consistent with the first of these aims. Decisions tend, more and more, to be hammered out not just at private meetings of the 77 and other groups but then at private or 'informal' meetings or 'consultations' of the entire membership of the international organs concerned; and only in rare and exceptional cases are representatives of the specialised agencies admitted to these meetings. While frequent recourse to informal and private consultations (that is to say, without the presence of the Press and the public) is becoming well nigh essential because of the great expansion of the membership of the United Nations central organs and of negotiations between the different groups, it is difficult to justify the exclusion of the agencies from such meetings as a general rule, the reciprocal right to be represented laid down in the UN–agency agreements not being limited to regular or formal meetings.[14] Not unnaturally, the agencies have been concerned. What has mattered most, however, is the attitude of the UN organs and the Secretariat. Sometimes, this attitude has been less than fully cooperative; sometimes on the contrary, a real effort has been made to keep the agencies informally advised on developments at private consultations, to make their views known to delegations, and to ensure that no decisions of direct importance to them are finally adopted, except at regular meetings in which they can take part.

Three issues recently facing the Council of special relevance for this study are the streamlining of parts of the highly complex and partially overlapping structure of intergovernmental organs reporting to the Council or through it to the General Assembly, the future character and functions of CPC or its successor (referred to in the Resolution as the 'Council organ delegated the functions of programming and co-ordination') and the nature and scope of the Council's cooperation with the specialized agencies and the United Nations programmes not under its direct jurisdiction, including improvement of the relationship between the Council and ACC.

The last paragraph refers to one aspect of the third of these issues; it can best be discussed further in the light of the character and potentialities of the ACC which form the subject of Chapter 5. Regarding the two other issues which have been discussed exhaustively in the Working Group on Rationalization[15] and in CPC itself,[16] it should be emphasized, first, that the proliferation and overlapping of intergovernmental machinery is one of the main problems in the search for greater order and coherence, and that the suggestions concerning staff and internal organization made in Part II, Chapters 11 and 12, are aimed at facilitating and contributing to a simplification of that machinery in certain fields; secondly, that the transformation and strengthening of CPC now proposed[17] reflects not the Committee's shortcomings but rather its success in dealing with the first United Nations work programmes and budgets and the possibilities which the procedure revealed.

Other intergovernmental bodies

The way the responsibilities of other bodies in regard to coordination – and UNCTAD, UNIDO and UNEP are especially in mind – relate to those of the Council depends to a peculiar extent upon perspective and context. Seen as competitive, as challenges to a Council striving to carry out its responsibilities under the Charter, they pose a problem, which could in some cases be a serious one. But they can also be seen as, on the one hand, complementary, fulfilling part of a task in which numbers of bodies must participate, and, on the other, as responsibilities which except in matters of overall policy or disputes as to jurisdiction, naturally fall to the organ or organization having primary competence in the field. This is the kind of relationship which was envisaged at the beginning of this chapter and which, within the United Nations' own structure prevails, in the case of UNCTAD and UNIDO – the position of UNEP being more complicated, for reasons already stated.

Nor is the demarcation between the roles of the Governing Council of UNDP and the Council too difficult to observe in matters affecting coordination of operations,[18] especially since many of the same delegates are involved, a condition of coherent relationship being that the overall Charter authority of the Economic and Social Council is recognized and safeguarded.

The steps taken to facilitate coordination among United Nations organizations at the regional level and the usefulness, as a complement to the Council's actions and subject to Headquarters' general surveillance, of the informal coordinating activities of the executive secretaries of the regional economic commissions in the regions has been brought out in Chapter 3. While the commissions themselves are natural coordinating centres, it would seem premature at least to attribute to them any part of the formal coordinating authority vested exclusively in the Council and the General Assembly.[19]

5 The Administrative Committee on Coordination

Organizations get together for coordination purposes or joint actions in many ways. There are hundreds of arrangements for informal and occasional consultations among 'opposite numbers' and quite a network of official committees linking two, three or even more members of the United Nations System (and in some cases outside agencies) on particular subjects, such as nutrition (FAO, WHO, UNICEF), protein (FAO, WHO) or occupational health (ILO, WHO). The World Food Programme works under the joint sponsorship of the United Nations and FAO, the International Centre for Theoretical Physics under that of UNESCO and IAEA. As mentioned earlier, joint divisions are maintained by some agencies with most of the regional economic commissions; there has also been some outposting of staff, as well as the establishment of liaison offices, between one organization and another.

While all such standing arrangements for specific purposes – and many more could be cited – are of interest in the context of the present study, central importance must be attached to the Administrative Committee on Coordination (ACC), composed of the executive heads[1] of all organizations and programmes under the Secretary-General's chairmanship, which supervises the entire range of intersecretariat coordination and cooperation and plays a big part in the smooth and efficient functioning of the UN System. It is through ACC and its subsidiary bodies that most cooperative arrangements involving more than three or four agencies, and all system-wide arrangements for such purposes, on the immense variety of subjects on which cooperation or assimilation among several organizations is needed are worked out and supervized. The importance has been underlined of cooperation being established between ACC and the Council if the latter is to fulfill its task. It may be well to consider for a moment the character of ACC and of its relations with the Council hitherto, the kind of contribution it might be in a position to make should the Council so desire and some modifications in its structure and *modus operandi* that may be desirable and feasible.

The problem of coordination in the United Nations System

The paramount need for a standing committee of the executive heads of specialized agencies under the chairmanship of the Secretary-General of the United Nations was brought out in the 1945 Report of the Preparatory Commission of the United Nations.[2] A Resolution in the following terms[3] to give effect to this recommendation was adopted by the Council at its Third Session in 1946:

The Economic and Social Council, being desirous of discharging effectively its responsibilities under the Charter of the UN to coordinate the activities of the specialized agencies –

1. Undertakes, after reference, if necessary, to an appropriate committee or to an *ad hoc* committee, to consider and to make recommendations or decisions, as may be suitable, regarding matters referred to the Secretary-General from the committee established under paragraph 2 below, and matters arising outside the scope of the agreements between the United Nations and specialized agencies which are or may become the subject of difference of view between the specialized agencies of the United Nations or between the specialized agencies and committees or other subsidiary organs of the Council:

2. Requests the Secretary-General to establish a standing committee of administrative officers consisting of himself, as chairman, and the corresponding officers of the specialized agencies brought into relationship with the United Nations, for the purpose of taking all appropriate steps, under the leadership of the Secretary-General, to ensure the fullest and most effective implementation of the agreements entered into between the United Nations and the specialized agencies.

The committee was first called simply the Coordination Committee, but this title had to be changed when the Council began to set up its own Sessional Coordination Committee in 1948. The alternative title of Secretary-General's Coordination Committee was suggested but was not liked by the agencies because of the role the committee was expected to play vis-à-vis their governing organs. The title of Administrative Committee on Coordination (ACC) was a compromise which has survived, although it has never been considered satisfactory, since it suggests that administrative matters are the committee's main concern.

It will be noted that the Council did not ask for reports from this committee, but expected the Secretary-General to refer to it from the committee for consideration and recommendation or decision, matters on which there were or might be differences of view. Things worked out differently. The ACC reports have, from the beginning, been agreed documents submitted in the name of ACC itself rather than the Secretary-General. It was not, in fact, realistic to imagine that the ACC could function except as a club, or that the Secretary-General could appeal from it to the Council and yet retain its confidence and his leadership, or again that the kind of issues with which the ACC would be mainly concerned were such as could be settled by the Council.

This is not to imply that the Secretary-General's influence in ACC is not of prime importance: on the contrary, his personality, the degree of his personal involvement in the substance of the issues considered and his personal relations with his colleagues have contributed much to determine the ACC's role and accomplishments at different periods. Mr Trygve Lie carried out his duties conscientiously, used his position constructively to promote system-wide projects such as the Expanded Programme of Technical Assistance and the Joint Staff Pension Fund and defended the interests of the United Nations itself vis-à-vis the agencies when he felt it was necessary; but he was essentially a political man and inter-agency issues or the concept of the United Nations System for economic and social cooperation never greatly interested him.

As mentioned in the Introduction, Mr Hammarskjöld, in the early years of his secretary-generalship, devoted much thought and effort to giving ACC the positive role of adviser to the Council on the tasks the UN System should and could undertake and the priorities to be observed. He gradually lost interest in this objective partly no doubt because of his growing involvement in urgent political issues before the UN, but partly for reasons which have been mentioned earlier. His relations with the heads of some of the agencies became strained, and he came to doubt whether it was possible, in view of the agencies' autonomy, for the system to work.[4]

U Thant, who presided over ACC for the ten years following Hammarskjöld's death, was no innovator. He never attempted to impose his views or to exercise personal leadership, nor was he particularly interested in international economic and social action unless directly related to the development of the developing countries, other than that of an urgent humanitarian character or closely associated with problems of peace. At the same time, he was convinced of the importance of 'the UN family of organizations' working together in a coherent and coordinated way to achieve the economic and social purposes of the Charter; he conceived his role in ACC as that of an impartial moderator and was anxious not to favour UN units against the specialized agencies. He quickly achieved something quite essential to the successful working of the ACC, namely relations of warmth and mutual confidence

between himself and all the heads of the agencies and UN programmes.

The Council and the General Assembly, by innumerable resolutions, have enormously expanded the mandate of ACC to touch on
almost every aspect of the activities and organization of the United
Nations System; they have, however, never specifically assigned to
ACC coordinating responsibilities as such, which, no doubt, they
have felt belonged to themselves alone. On the other hand, many of
the questions dealt with in ACC fall within the responsibilities of its
members individually, as executive heads of organizations, who
believe that by reaching decisions through ACC they are helping to
carry out a share of the responsibilities for coordination laid on the
United Nations central organs. The ACC has become indeed more
than just an organ of the United Nations. Its members participate in
it under mandates from their respective governing bodies, which
receive and consider its reports. It constitutes a direct link between
the organizations in the United Nations System and unquestionably
plays a big role in promoting coherent action by the system as a whole.

Except as regards possible budgetary consolidation, the kind and
degree of United Nations–agency cooperation that was developed in
ACC from an early stage went far beyond what the agreements had
envisaged. The longest section of ACC's first report (January 1948)
was devoted to cooperation on substantive questions, while its latest
reports are almost exclusively concerned with these and other
matters to which the agreements are only indirectly relevant.

When it first met in 1947, ACC was of quite manageable size; it
brought together the Secretary-General, the heads or representatives
of six or seven agencies or prospective agencies, together with two or
three high-level United Nations officials and the secretary. It now
includes, in addition to the Secretary-General, 13 executive heads
of agencies, together with the Administrator of UNDP, the Secretary-General of UNCTAD, the Executive Directors of UNICEF,
UNIDO, UNEP, the World Food Programme and UNITAR, the
High Commissioner for Refugees, the Commissioner General of
UNRWA and the Director-General of GATT (sitting as the Executive Secretary of the Interim Committee for the World Trade
Organization, which has never been formally dissolved). Officials
other than heads of specialized agencies and IAEA used to attend and
participate as observers, but ACC decided in 1969 that the executive
heads of UNDP, UNICEF, UNCTAD and UNIDO should henceforth be considered as full participants, and this was welcomed and
endorsed by the Council. One aim of this decision was to maximize

the opportunities for consultation; another that the heads of these programmes should become, and feel themselves to be, parties to consensuses reached in the Committee.

The Under-Secretary-General for Economic and Social Affairs,[5] always present, and the Under-Secretary-General for Administration and Management, present when needed, take part and handle the briefs on programme and administrative matters; while the Under-Secretary-General for Inter-Agency Affairs and Coordination, who is Chairman of ACC's Preparatory Committee and ACC's Rapporteur to the Council, the General Assembly and their appropriate organs, always plays a leading role. As noted below, various other high officials – including the Chairman of ACABQ and representatives of JIU – attend some sessions, as do senior United Nations officials concerned, e.g. with legal questions, with public information, and with colonial questions, when items they are concerned with come up for discussion. The Council has recently asked that arrangements should also be made for the executive secretaries of the regional economic commissions to attend from time to time. At a regular closed meeting of ACC, more than 60 people, including advisers, are likely to be present, and at the strictly private meetings without records, with which the sessions begin and which are only for principals, together with the Rapporteur and one or two Under-Secretaries-General, between 25 and 30. A major organizational problem facing the Committee is that it has become not only too heterogeneous but too large.

At this point, a passage from an earlier study by the present writer bearing on the character and functioning of ACC may be quoted.

An unwritten convention was established at the outset that meetings of the Committee would continue to be attended by the Secretary-General and the executive heads of the specialized agencies themselves, and that it would meet in private. These practices, which reflect primarily the importance attached by its members to having a centre for contacts and the confidential exchange of information and views at the highest level, have had a decisive influence in building up the authority of the Committee and in determining its character. In particular, it made it inevitable that the Committee would (a) take initiatives and propose solutions and not merely carry out the requests of the Council or other intergovernmental bodies; (b) concern itself with broad issues of policy, and any matters affecting the United Nations system as a whole, and (c) be able to meet at most two or three times a year and for very short periods, relying on subordinate bodies to dispose of routine matters and to prepare the ground for its consideration of other matters up to the point where policy decisions were needed.[6]

ACC's principal subordinate body is its Preparatory Committee of Deputies, of which more below. In addition, the network of subsidiary bodies of ACC, in many of which only officials of organizations closely concerned participate, currently comprises the Consultative Committee on Administrative Questions (CCAQ); the Joint United Nations Information Committee (formerly CCPI and CESI Programme Committee); the Inter-Organization Board for Information Systems and Related Activities; the Sub-Committees on Education and Training, Science and Technology, Water Resources Development, Marine Science and its Applications, Statistical Activities, the United Nations Development Decade, Population; then there are 'working groups' or study groups on Outer Space, on Youth and on Housing and Urbanization.

Most of these bodies meet annually, two or three more frequently, and the last three irregularly, as required. Consultations on other subjects are, of course, arranged as necessary.

'Functional groups' consisting only of members of ACC directly interested in a particular problem area and chaired by the head of the agency most concerned, have in recent years been formed, and have reported through ACC. The subjects covered have been the 'green revolution' (FAO taking the lead), the human environment (WMO taking the lead – the group having met before the establishment of the United Nations Environment Programme) and the world employment programme (ILO), emphasis being laid on the implications for the work of different members of the United Nations System. One aim of this experiment, which, for different reasons in each case, has not so far been completely successful, has been to contribute to government thinking about emerging problems. The Environment Coordination Board, which reports to the Governing Council of UNEP and has been set up to promote the coordination of environmental programmes at the secretariat level, is the latest, and certainly a significant, innovation. This body operates 'within the framework of ACC'; it is advisory to, and is chaired by, the Executive Director of the United Nations Environment Programme, who keeps ACC informed of its proceedings.

On the Preparatory Committee, which dates from early 1948, ACC depends very greatly, especially because of the short time the executive heads themselves are able to meet. There have been frequent and usually inconclusive discussions in ACC about its composition and functioning. Some heads of agencies have felt that their actual deputies, others that a senior official enjoying their confidence and dealing with inter-agency affairs, should serve. Its membership has indeed been uneven, but among those who have served for long periods on it may be mentioned the late Mr Wilfred Jenks (who became Director-General of the ILO and who served regularly for 20 years), Mr Addeke Boerma and the late Mr René Maheu, recently Directors-General of FAO and UNESCO respectively. There have been complaints that its work takes up too much of high officials' time and effort. There have also been complaints from high-level administrative and financial members of the ACC's Consultative Committee on Administrative Questions (CCAQ) – complaints echoed by the staff office CCAQ still maintains at Geneva as a strictly inter-agency institution – that the 'generalists' in the Preparatory Committee should not touch or comment on CCAQ's findings. An attempt to decide some of these questions was made in ACC's Thirty-fifth Report of May 1969[7] which caused such repercussions in other areas. But arrangements in regard to such matters are based on realities which are difficult to alter. It has not, in fact, proved possible to reduce significantly the length of the Preparatory Committee's sessions; CCAQ has remained almost as independent as before; nor has there been much change in the level of representation on the Preparatory Committee in the years that have intervened.

In order to keep the picture in perspective, four factors may usefully be borne in mind: firstly, the work of the Preparatory Committee on behalf of ACC, including the drafting of much of ACC's reports, is itself carefully prepared by the Office for Inter-Agency Affairs and Coordination and is complemented by continuing efforts of its Chairman and staff throughout the year; the evolution and functioning of this central inter-agency staff are discussed below. Secondly, several members have served the Preparatory Committee for 10 years or more and the continuity of membership in some subsidiary bodies like CCAQ is comparable. While this makes for conservatism, it is also a source of strength. Thirdly, while ACC's reports are always approved by the whole Membership, it has long been understood that the views on specific issues expressed in the reports are those of concerned organizations alone. Thus, for example, views expressed on social policy are not considered as engaging the responsibility of the executive heads of, say, IMF, ICAO, ITU or UPU. Fourthly, it is quite clear that so long as the constitutions of the specialized agencies and IAEA are not radically changed and so long as it is desired that these organizations should cooperate and concert their efforts with the United Nations itself, something very like ACC in composition and character – though not necessarily without changes in procedures and organization – will be essential.

This is so because, through such an instrumentality, the central United Nations organs can obtain most easily the cooperation needed from the agencies, and the agencies can maintain, without compromising their independence, the cooperation with the United Nations and with one another which is required for the achievement of their own purposes.

The relationship between ACC and the Council has been ambivalent; each body relying on but suspicious of the other, and jealously maintaining its own prerogatives. The Council has more than once complained of ACC's bland reporting which tends to conceal inter-organizational differences of which the Council feels it should be aware.[8] The ACC's reports have been somewhat modified to meet this and other criticism, but there are limits beyond which it would be difficult to go without affecting the whole nature of ACC[9] and there is no doubt that most of its members still feel that 'there would not be advantage in making public...differences of views that might arise in the course of inter-agency discussion leading ultimately to agreements in ACC'.[10]

The relationship between the Council and ACC has also varied greatly, being sometimes reasonably harmonious, sometimes tense, depending largely on the state of relationships between the major programme agencies and the UN Secretariat. In the Spring of 1969, there was considerable tension in ACC, the culmination of resentment felt in those agencies, and others including WMO and IAEA, at what they considered to be unjustified encroachments, especially by the Advisory Committee on the Application of Science and Technology to Development and the failure by the United Nations Secretariat Office serving that committee to consult duly with them. At the same session, the following statement on the functioning of inter-secretariat machinery for coordination was included in ACC's Thirty-fifth Report to the Council:

The main task of the ACC is to identify, for the benefit of the Council and the governing bodies of the organizations concerned, the major problems that confront the United Nations system of organizations, and collectively to tender advice on the manner in which its resources should be used to resolve such problems in a constructive manner.[11]

This statement, which was followed by another to the effect that 'the secretariat of ACC should function under the direct authority of the Secretary-General, reporting directly to him', produced a lively reaction in CPC. That reaction seems to have been based partly on misunderstanding,[12] but members also asked why ACC's other tasks, including that of helping the Council to coordinate, were not mentioned and how ACC could 'agree' on structural changes in the United Nations Secretariat?

At a joint meeting of CPC and ACC later in the year, the Secretary-General defended the ACC position, explaining that

By 'policy issues' it naturally did not mean 'political issues' nor did it mean to impinge in any way on the authority of Governments – which would not only be contrary to the duty of the members of ACC, but clearly impossible. What the ACC was referring to were the factors within the purview of member organizations that all Governments had to take into account in order to devise feasible solutions. That was the essential staff-work which was expected of the ACC and which it was attempting to provide.[13]

Despite strong resistance from one quarter,[14] the organizational changes the agencies had asked for were approved and were brought into force at the beginning of 1970, but the clock was set back, the 'inner unity' on which ACC's strength is based was temporarily shaken and suspicions of ACC on the part of the United Nations governmental organs were rekindled.

The next summer the Council somewhat stiffly reaffirmed that the policy-making role in the United Nations System is the prerogative of Member States in the competent organs of the system, and instructed CPC to review the sphere of activities and competence of ACC.[15] That review led to a lengthy Council resolution the following year, which, while requesting ACC to undertake a number of specific tasks and its assistance in others, decided 'that all members of the Council and of the Committee on Programme and Coordination should receive notification of the meetings of the Administrative Committee on Coordination, its Preparatory Committee and other subsidiary bodies, together with an indication of the agendas of those meetings'.[16] It was the clear intention to relegate ACC to a more subordinate position.

The inherent limitations of ACC are, of course, important and must be well understood. Some of them have been summarized elsewhere by this writer:

Because of its composition, it cannot easily take a position detrimental to the interest of any agency or in opposition to the wishes of its executive head: it can be used as an instrument for economizing staff and other resources but not as an instrument of budgetary stabilization; it has no authority to decide on the distribution of international resources as between different purposes, or to settle jurisdictional disputes (though it has usually been able to find practical solutions in cases of overlapping competences). It cannot establish, though it may influence, the policy decisions which are fashioned through the intergovernmental organs of the United Nations, the specialized agencies and the IAEA...Towards the coordination of overall policy, indeed, it cannot be claimed that the ACC has made more than a minor and intermittent contribution.[17]

But ACC has great sources of strength. One of these lies in its preparing the ground for, and ensuring smooth implementation of, almost the entire range of concerted programmes as well as system-wide administrative decisions. To quote again the late Mr Jenks:

> The ACC is simply a device, but an immensely valuable one, enabling its members to exercise their executive authority more responsibly, after consultation with each other and in the light of a wider range of considerations than they are in a position to assess individually. They are enabled to take uniform action in matters calling for uniformity, synchronize parallel action, avoid conflicting action, and take mutually complementary action whenever appropriate and possible.[18]

This is, of course, only one of ACC's principal tasks, another being to act as a mechanism for helping to ensure system-wide implementation of decisions of the General Assembly and the Council and for tendering, when so desired, collective advice to the Council and other governing organs on issues within the competence of its members. Mr Jenks also wrote that ACC 'is one of the real political inventions of the present pattern of world organization and that its potentialities are only beginning to be tapped.'[19] Is it likely or even possible that this optimistic assessment of ACC's potentialities can be realized? The answer will depend on a number of factors which have already been discussed, including the attitudes, on the one hand, of the Council and, on the other, of the ACC's own members.

It will also greatly depend on some far-reaching measures of reorganization by ACC itself, including measures, firstly, that will enable questions relating to central economic policy to be discussed by a group restricted to the heads of the organizations directly concerned, and, secondly, make it possible for the innumerable matters that could finally be dealt with at a lower level to be kept off the agenda for the heads of agencies.

6   The Secretary-General and the secretariats of the United Nations and the agencies

Two crucial factors in any consideration of improvement in the internal functioning of the United Nations System have still to be mentioned. The first is the immense influence exercised by most heads of agencies and their close associates, all of whom are likely to be involved in one capacity or another in the work of ACC, on their respective intergovernmental organs. The basis of this influence is not only personal but constitutional, since, in most agencies, the executive head is responsible for preparing, submitting and executing the programme, as well as submitting the budget and administering the funds. Because of this factor, a strengthening of the relations between the agencies and the Council depends to a large extent on the active support and participation of the heads of agencies and their senior staff. Such support and participation, it is true, are being given fully in numerous programmes, but it is needed more purposefully, more intensively and on a broader scale; furthermore, its importance needs to be more widely recognized by the Council.

A similar influence is enjoyed by the top staff of most of the United Nations programmes and, even though the constitutional position differs somewhat, by those at United Nations Headquarters and the regional secretariats. With the extension and development in the United Nations of programme planning and budgeting, in consultation with ACABQ and such a body as CPC, this influence should grow. As it is, the claim could be sustained that the great majority of successful United Nations projects have been launched, or put into acceptable form, by the Secretariat, supported by the agencies and in close contact with some interested national delegations as well as intergovernmental voting groups. Such a claim would not apply to proposals, whether of a programme or an organizational character, having strong political implications or adversely affecting some country or 'constituency'. A warning is provided by the fate of the 1968 initiative by the Director-General of FAO already referred to. (See Chapter 3.)

The second factor, complementing the one just mentioned, is the importance of active United Nations leadership and organization. This is indeed a condition for the functioning of the whole ACC system. At least 90 % of the ACC's business arises out of United Nations decisions, for the implementation of which the Secretary-General has a central responsibility; so, however important may be the discussion with and among the agencies, the adjustments to which such discussions lead, and the contribution the agencies may furnish, it is in most cases true that the United Nations Secretariat alone can 'carry the ball' and make this inter-agency cooperation meaningful.

In some cases, the Secretary-General has endeavoured to use his personal influence with Governments and intergovernmental bodies in the interest of the United Nations System as a whole. For example, in his 1963 *Report to the Gegeral Assembly on the Work of the Organization*, U Thant urged that political issues such as *apartheid* or possible action against South Africa and Portugal should be left to the General Assembly and not allowed to interfere with the technical work of the specialized agencies. His representatives intervened in this sense – and not without temporary success – in the conferences and governing bodies of several agencies; but it was a lost cause, the countries taking the lead in such issues arguing – and in the end gaining their point – that it was for each autonomous agency and each sovereign Member to decide on the action to be taken within that agency.

By and large, however, the Secretary-General's responsibilities on behalf of the system as a whole have been such as could only be exercised with strong staff support. How to organize that support was in the early years the subject of frequent debate, partly because of the sharply contrasted views held by the then heads of the two United Nations departments mainly concerned regarding the desirable relationships between the United Nations and the agencies – the then Assistant Secretary-General for Economic Affairs, Mr David Owen, being a partisan of what may be called the ACC approach, the Assistant Secretary-General for Social Affairs, Professor Henri Laugier, on the other hand, insisting that the central organs of the United Nations, and in particular the Economic and Social Council, assisted by the Secretary-General must assert their coordinating authority and make recommendations concerning priorities for each organization.[1] Partly because of these differences, responsibility for inter-agency coordination and relations was early placed not with either of the above departments but in a special office directly under the Secretary-General. The author was both Deputy Executive Assistant to the Secretary-General, with responsibility for internal coordination in economic and social matters, and Director of the above office, working in consultation with the heads and senior officials of all interested departments, including those dealing with public information and administration and finance, as well as with the appropriate senior officers of the agencies. After the creation of a Technical Assistance Board, under an Executive Chairman, and the merger of the Departments of Economic and Social Affairs, there was much to be said for combining the post dealing with inter-agency coordination and relations with that of deputy head of ESA. Such a reorganization was carried out by Hammarskjöld in 1955, the functions of the first kind to be performed as heretofore under the Secretary-General's direct authority and not as part of the functions of ESA, but in close consultation with the head of that department.

This arrangement gave the Secretary-General's Personal Representative to the specialized agencies not only the necessary authority vis-à-vis the agencies but also a wide measure of control over the relevant activities of the department as well as influence on the coordination activities carried out under ACC. There were always some on the United Nations side who resented the obligation – and the time needed – to consult with the agencies on the discharge of their responsibilities, and some in the agencies who felt that the United Nations Department of Economic and Social Affairs wielded an excessive influence. By and large, however, the system worked smoothly for almost 15 years. It was helpful to the United Nations Secretariat, since it made it easy to consult the agencies and seek their support if necessary in the carrying out of United Nations responsibilities of concern to them and United Nations-sponsored initiatives. Examples run literally into the scores: to confine oneself to institution-building and a period of four or five years, they would include the establishment of the World Food Programme in 1962, UNITAR in 1963, the merger of EPTA and the Special Fund in 1965, and the creation of the Joint Inspection Unit and the Centre for Economic and Social Information (CESI) in 1966. The arrangement also presented advantages for the agencies, facilitating, as it did, adjustment that might be necessary to secure general, but in particular United Nations, understanding and support for their positions and initiatives. It may be noted that, in a special unpublished study on possible improvements in the functioning of ACC made at ACC's request in 1958, the late Director-General of UNESCO, Mr René Maheu, then UNESCO representative at United Nations Headquarters, proposed that the Preparatory Committee should be abolished and that its task of preparing, through consultation with organizations concerned, the background material and draft reports and decisions of ACC should be transferred to an Under-Secretary working directly with the Secretary-General as Chairman of ACC and supported by an adequate staff. The heads of agencies were, however, not anxious to give up the Preparatory Committee – which, while reflecting the character of the ACC itself and capable of acting as a watchdog in the case of any United Nations initiative that might tend to be at the agencies' expense, had been functioning reasonably well – and the upshot was a decision that the Preparatory Committee would be maintained, with higher level membership and a request that the Secretary-General's representative, as its Chairman, should exercise a good deal of initiative.

Initiative has indeed always been a necessary element in the work of what is now called the Office for Inter-Agency Affairs and Co-ordination. For many years, the Office was a shoe-string operation, the Secretary-General's Representative to the specialized agencies having not more than one or two assistants permanently assigned to this work, though additional assistance was usually available from within the Department, when needed, and there were one or two senior professionals at the Geneva Office who maintained liaison with European-based agencies and followed their activities and problems under his general direction. Working mainly through, or with the help of, other senior officials of the United Nations and the agencies, it was his task to organize inter-agency action to give effect to Council and General Assembly decisions, arrange for inter-agency consultations, help find solutions where problems existed, and ensure adequate reporting and follow-up. Furthermore, it has always been his duty to arrange, where appropriate, for United Nations representation at meetings of other organizations, whether of the United Nations family or not, and ensure consultation and briefing on subjects under consideration with which the United Nations is concerned. It has fallen to him also to handle subjects of system-wide interest for which the United Nations had to assume central responsibility but with which no existing unit was equipped to deal; some of these were long-term subjects such as the coordination of action on natural disasters, others were temporary such as the negations for the establishment of new organs and institutes.

Finally, and most important, it has been part of his task to ensure so far as possible that there was proper United Nations leadership in ACC, its Preparatory Committee and its other subsidiary bodies, on which, as emphasized at the beginning of this section, the functioning of the ACC system so much depends. Such leadership was a relatively easy matter to supply when the head of the Department of ESA (or he himself as its deputy head) could brief the Secretary-General (or speak) on behalf of almost the whole range of the United Nations economic and social work; it became more difficult with the creation of UNCTAD, UNDP and UNIDO; and it becomes more difficult year by year because of the growing dispersal of authority within the United Nations itself, and the growing difficulty of harmonizing the actions of key units concerned with economic and social affairs. This trend, which successive Secretaries-General have deplored,[2] affects not only the great administrative units such as those just referred to but also numerous trust funds and has had serious effects on the whole state of order, coherence and coordination in the United Nations System. As regards inter-agency cooperation and particularly ACC, it means that the United Nations cannot always speak with one voice, and that there is often no United Nations position or leadership.

There has always been support, in principle, for bringing into the ACC Secretariat, officers on temporary detachment from agencies and United Nations programmes, and such secondments have occasionally been arranged – with indifferent results – in respect of particular assignments. More controversial has been the more far-reaching idea sometimes advanced that the Secretariat of ACC should be placed on an inter-agency basis, like the staffs of CCAQ, ICSAB, and now ICSC. All agencies would share the expenses of this secretariat, which would report to the Secretary-General not as Chief Administrative Officer of the United Nations but as Chairman of ACC. In 1966, when future staffing arrangements for ACC were being considered, the latter's views on this idea were asked for by the Council.[3] The ACC commented negatively, saying that the position of the officials of CCAQ and ICSAB was different, since they were engaged exclusively on servicing those bodies, while the staff of ACC and Inter-Agency Affairs served not only ACC but also the Council, the General Assembly and the Secretary-General.[4] Successive Secretaries-General have had reservations about this idea on both constitutional and practical grounds; nor has it been widely espoused by heads of agencies, presumably because of fears that the position of the staff dealing with inter-agency affairs within the United Nations Secretariat, and consequently of the agencies vis-à-vis the United Nations, would be weakened.

As from January 1967, the posts of Secretary-General's Representative to the specialized agencies and Deputy Under-Secretary for Economic and Social Affairs were separated. The first, now on a full-time basis, carried the title of Under-Secretary (later Assistant Secretary-General) for Inter-Agency Affairs; and it remained within the framework of ESA. At the ACC session in the Spring of 1969, the Secretary-General acceded to the request of the heads of a number of agencies that the Office for Inter-Agency Affairs should be separated from ESA and made responsible exclusively to him. Later in the year, he justified this decision in the following terms:

> In addition to matters of direct concern to the Department of Economic and Social Affairs, an increasing part of ACC's work was concerned with matters relating, for example, to budget administration, public information, decolonization and human rights which were dealt with in other departments of the United Nations Secretariat. Furthermore, there were now a number of United Nations organs, including UNCTAD, UNIDO, UNICEF, UNHCR, UNITAR, and WFP, whose executive heads participated fully in ACC and in the arrangements for inter-agency coordination. At the same time, in changing the location of the Office for Inter-Agency Affairs, the Secretary-General was mindful of the continuing need for its special links with the Department of Economic and Social Affairs.[5]

The opposition of one Government has already been recorded (see Chapter 5), but the proposal was generally endorsed and put into effect. The old practice of the head of the Office attending or being represented at meetings of directors of the Department of Economic and Social Affairs has been continued and members of the Office continue to be involved in departmental discussions affecting specialized agencies or programmes. The Office thus conserved some at least of the advantages of being part of ESA, while it undoubtedly gained standing and enhanced means of action in respect of other parts of the United Nations Secretariat and the United Nations System.

Its separation from ESA does, however, raise the question whether the traditional arrangement whereby the same unit serves ACC and the Council in regard to inter-agency coordination and relationships will always be feasible. So far, the Secretary-General's positions in such matters have been reached as a result of discussions with the agencies, usually through ACC or its Preparatory Committee, and there has seldom been any serious danger of an adversary relationship developing between the Council and the agencies. But there have been signs – for example, the Council's request in 1973 for a report by the Secretary-General himself on the past and present relationship between the United Nations and the specialized agencies and IAEA – that the Council wishes on occasion to have the Secretary-

General's own, rather than agreed, views. The creation of a special unit, or the assignment of a particular official, within the Department of Economic and Social Affairs to deal with coordination matters for the Council without the constraints felt by the Office of Inter-Agency Affairs and Coordination would be, at best, uneconomical and an administrative anomaly. The solution would seem to lie rather in recognition by the agencies of the dual responsibilities of the Office and of the need for the Office to retain a degree of discretion in regard to the manner in which it carries out requests addressed to the Secretary-General. It will normally wish to consult with the agencies. Consultation is indeed an important element in the maintenance of the mutual confidence on which ACC depends. It implies that the views of those consulted will be weighed, and, if found valid, accepted, but it should not be equated with clearance, which implies that those consulted must agree on the text or position finally adopted.

Most of the factors bearing on the way inter-agency and ACC affairs can best be handled within the United Nations Secretariat are not likely to change greatly even with considerable changes in organization, such as have been proposed in 1975 by the Committee of Experts on the Structure of the United Nations System. A great deal will, of course, continue to depend on the personality, the *modus operandi* and the attitude of the Secretary-General himself, and the time he can devote to such matters. This time factor has now become critical. The key role the Secretary-General himself must play in ACC has already been emphasized, yet no Secretary-General, because of his constant and overwhelming political preoccupations, could now devote a significant part of his time to this or indeed to playing a consistently active role in the economic and social work of the United Nations System. Arrangements must be devised, and backed by the authority of the General Assembly and the Council, under which the Secretary-General could continue to take part in essential inter-agency activities while being relieved of any unnecessary burdens. This is the subject of one of the crucial proposals of the Committee of Experts (see the Postscript) and related to the problem of overcoming or mitigating the dispersal of authority in the United Nations itself.

7 Some current constraints on order and coordination in the system

The last four chapters have been concerned with the problem of coordination envisaged in the United Nations Charter, the sort of issues that have been faced, and the approaches and instrumentalities used to meet them. But coordination, at least in the rather narrow sense in which it is usually understood, is no guarantee of order and coherence, let alone of efficiency. It often represents an attempt to make the best of a structure or set of relationships between organs which defies logic and good sense. On the other hand, one must be cautious about generalizations for an arrangement militating against order and coherence in the system may sometimes be justified by the dynamism it imparts.

One factor which has recently become disturbing is related to the United Nations Development Programme, which has to make long-term (generally five-year) commitments on the basis of uncertain voluntary contributions, voted, for the most part, year by year. This fundamental weakness in the Programme (a weakness from which UNICEF and other voluntary programmes also suffer in different degrees) was for many years of little practical significance, since total contributions were rising rapidly and steadily. It has, however, lately become a major cause of concern, the growth in contributions in 1975–1976 failing to match the growth in costs. Much has already been said about the effect of the proliferation of intergovernmental and expert organs, many with overlapping competences, which complicates the task of coordination and impedes progress because Governments are not equipped to deal properly with so much at the same time. The Council is reviewing the terms of reference of its own subsidiary organs, on the basis of an assessment and reorientation of their role. The pity is that this review cannot be extended to the whole corpus of United Nations subsidiary bodies in the economic and social field.

Two factors that have so far received little attention in United Nations organs but have a major bearing on coherence in the United Nations System and more especially the role of the Council, are the impact of UNDP and IBRD on the United Nations as a whole. (See Chapter 2.) Chapters 12 and 13 discuss some ideas for strengthening the relations between UNDP on the one hand, and the Council and the United Nations Secretariat on the other. The question of relations with the World Bank is underlined without any action being recommended at this stage apart from the sort of regular consultations between the top officials concerned that were foreseen when the relationship agreement between the United Nations and the International Development Association was concluded in 1961.

Other phenomena pervasively disturbing to order and coherence in the United Nations System are: firstly, the dispersal of authority among, and the difficulty of harmonizing the actions of, key units of the United Nations itself concerned with economic and social action, and, secondly, the shortcomings of the staff structure within the United Nations itself. Chapter 2 has cited some of the main instances and causes of the dispersal, or fragmentation, of authority, noting the effect on the system as a whole of the separation from the Council and ESA of UNCTAD, UNIDO and later UNEP. A geographical dispersal, which always compounds coordination problems, was added to the administrative and political. Judging, however, from the small advantage taken of propinquity in the case of UNDP and ESA, the influence of the geographical dispersal, however important, has probably been secondary.

Mention was also made of other cases of fragmentation of authority in recent years, including the growth in the number and size of trust and other voluntary funds. There is a natural desire to accept money for worthy and approved purposes, to meet if possible the wishes of generous donors in disbursing the money, and to enlist the services of prestigious persons of the right qualifications and nationalities to help ensure the success of the enterprise. Year by year, units and posts are set up for special tasks, mostly no doubt with the best of motives but with little regard for the effect on existing work in the same related fields. An example is provided by the arrangements made to deal with population questions. As already mentioned, a UN Fund for Population Activities, quite independent of the Population Division of ESA, was set up in 1967 as a Trust Fund under the Secretary-General. It was officially placed under the supervision of the Governing Council of UNDP in 1969 and in 1972 became a fund 'established under the authority of the General Assembly'. While the Governing Council acts as its governing body, the UNFPA has its own funds and is engaged in an active and independent programme throughout the world with its own coordinators in different countries in which projects are being undertaken. It was given main responsibility for preparations for World Population Year, 1974, of which the World Population Conference was the highlight. The process of fragmentation was compounded when an independent Secretary-General and staff for the Conference were appointed, with only quite tenuous relationships with either the Fund or the Population Division.

Another example relates to narcotic drug control, where divided authority at more than one level had been a source of friction in League of Nations days.[1] A voluntary fund to assist Governments in carrying out drug control policies was established in 1971 under a personal representative of the Secretary-General who was to have 'over-all responsibility for the Fund'. This senior official was to be independent of, but 'expected to work in close harmony with other senior Secretariat officials having responsibilities for the administration and operation of the Fund'. Such an uncompromising arrangement usually has great powers of survival, but this one was at least temporarily revised in 1973 when the then Director of the United Nations Division of Narcotic Drugs was appointed Acting Executive Director of the Fund.

Not only are important programmes launched on the basis of hopes rather than commitments that adequate voluntary funds will be forthcoming, but where budgetary provision has been made this is often quite inadequate; furthermore, there has been an incurable over-optimism as to what can be done practically without staff and funds by merely waving the United Nations flag. An example of such mistakes can be found in the recent history of United Nations arrangements for disaster relief and preparedness. For many years, the question has been how best to ensure a necessary minimum of coordination within the United Nations family, so many members of which have an essential contribution to make, and to provide a focal point under the Secretary-General, for the purpose of assisting disaster-prone and disaster-stricken countries as well as private organizations like the Red Cross which are working in the same field. In 1971, the Council approved the broad lines of a plan submitted by the Secretary-General to meet this problem and the General Assembly proceeded to create the Office of United Nations Disaster Relief Coordinator, with Headquarters in Geneva. (Resolution 2816 (xxvi).) The Coordinator was given a tiny staff of three professionals, and little more than a token budget. The idea was that he would need only a minimum of support of this kind since the UNDP resident representatives would act as his local agents in disaster-prone countries and that apart from coordinating the work of others, he could confine himself to intervening with Governments on matters which could not well be handled by the Red Cross or one of the United Nations agencies or programmes, such as obtaining over-flight authorization for relief supplies and the utilization of national military facilities and relief teams. Good and devoted work was done by officials of this and other offices in the face of an almost unprecedented incidence of major disasters in the years immediately following. But the United Nations having set up a Disaster Relief Office, it was expected to be everywhere, active and effective. Needless to say, it was not in a position fully to meet these expectations; other organs had to be given charge in particular cases and the distribution of responsibility continued to present a picture only little less confused than before. It should be added that a big effort was made to correct this situation. The staff and budget was increased, and after some voluntary contributions to the office had been made, a Disaster Relief Fund was established by the General Assembly.

Intergovernmental bodies, which have no means of cooperating with one another except through their staffs, are traditionally loath to interfere with one another, and those with a smaller membership seem to feel inhibited vis-à-vis larger ones with a more 'representative' membership; the Council's silence on broad matters of concern to it discussed in the UNDP Governing Council, the Industrial Development Board or the Trade and Development Board has been no doubt partly due to these factors – the second of which, regarding character and size of membership, has, however, now been overcome. At the Secretariat level, apart from a routine exchange of documents, routine clearance of information papers covering more than one of these units, an occasional document which must be prepared 'in consultation' and of course the normal contacts between UNDP and any executing agency, the units tend to work in water-tight compartments. It was in recognition of this fact that, as indicated in Chapter 5, the Council welcomed and endorsed the ACC's decision in 1969 that the chief executives of the major United Nations programmes should henceforth be considered as full participants in ACC. While some benefits may have resulted, not much progress can yet be claimed towards an integrated United Nations position on many important questions of programme and policy.

The degree of cooperation among administrative units always depends a great deal on the relations between the top officials concerned, and these relations are inevitably influenced not only by personal factors but also by status in the administrative hierarchy.

Here we encounter one of the fundamental weaknesses in the United Nations structure, which often escape the outside observer. The executive heads of UNCTAD and UNIDO were given the same status (that of Under-Secretary-General) as the head of the Department of Economic and Social Affairs – the Secretary-General's representative on the Economic and Social Council, the official expected to have the most comprehensive view, and the logical policy coordinator at the secretariat level. As a consequence, each naturally has tried to avoid interfering with the others, the task of policy coordination going by default.

The Executive Director of UNEP and three top officials of UNDP (one being the head of UNFPA) have since also been given Under-Secretary-General rank. The Administrator of UNDP has still higher status and it was to the then Administrator that U Thant, as Secretary-General, entrusted the chairmanship of the first United Nations Secretariat Economic Policy Board, of which more in a moment. The absence of any special status for the head of ESA is reflected in the status of ESA as a whole – not, it is true, vis-à-vis UNCTAD or UNIDO, whose staff, being paid from the regular budget, suffer the same constraints, but vis-à-vis the major specialized agencies[2] and UNDP. Given not only ESA's need for a top staff of great ability and prestige but also the unwritten convention that the chairman of an inter-agency committee or task force should be at a level not lower than that of his colleagues, the present position regarding the top staff of ESA – the result partly of budgetary parsimony and partly of prolonged bureaucratic efforts to treat ESA as just one United Nations department among the rest – has become little short of disastrous. It definitely hampers the Department in playing the central role it alone can play in the International Development Strategy, the promotion of a new international economic order and other broad programmes under the aegis of the Council.

Efforts are, of course, made to bring the top United Nations officials together from time to time for purposes of coordination. A United Nations Secretariat Economic Policy Board was set up in the early 1960s which included, for reasons of geographical and ideological distribution, a number of high officials unconnected with economic policy or programmes; in the few meetings it held, it never discussed economic policy at all and indeed never 'got off the ground'. Nor has the successor arrangement, the so-called Top Echelon meetings, started in 1968, which take place twice a year under the Secretary-General, added much of substance to the meetings, with which they are synchronized, of the executive secretaries of the regional economic commissions under the chairmanship of the Under-Secretary-General for ESA. The latter meetings have been organized and run by a chairman who is the hierarchical superior of the executive secretaries and acquainted with the policy and other issues to be discussed; they are usually attended also by the executive heads or other high officials of UNCTAD, UNIDO, UNICEF, UNEP and UNDP. They have proved to be a useful supplement to the regular contacts between ESA and the regional commission staffs – not least because they bring in the other organizations without raising questions of hierarchy or formal relationship. The scope of these meetings is, of course, rather limited.

The absence of anything approaching a UN programme, let alone a programme budget, was for many years a prime source of weakness in the system, and the arrangements recently made for the establishment of a programme budget and medium-term plan represent important steps in the right direction.[3] A Senior Budget and Policy Review Group, composed of the heads of all departments and offices of the United Nations Secretariat, meets from time to time under the chairmanship of the Under-Secretary-General for Administration and Management, one of its functions being 'to formulate a balanced and well-coordinated programme of activities expressed in terms of specific objectives' capable of being funded within the expected level of United Nations resources. Periodic meetings between the United Nations and specialized agency planning officials have also begun in the hope of improving, and achieving greater comparability among, planning and programming techniques in the whole system.

The results of this and the other coordinating devices just referred to have not so far been impressive, nor in any case are they anything like adequate for purposes of high-level consultations among the various United Nations units concerned with economic and social affairs. As a result of the dispersal of authority among these units and the fact that no top official is entrusted with organizing such consultations, there exists no means of harmonizing the thinking of executive heads and the senior staff or organs concerned with central policy issues such as ESA, UNCTAD, UNIDO, UNDP and UNEP, and directing it towards problems facing the international community and towards possible initiatives that the United Nations might usefully take. This represents a serious weakness in the whole United Nations System.

An important cause of disarray has still to be mentioned, namely, UNCTAD's growing challenge to the central position of the Economic and Social Council (ECOSOC), based both on the argument that trade, development finance and the international monetary system are interdependent and should be dealt with together and on the desire of many of the '77' to entrust the central role in respect of general economic policy to the organ and the staff that have been the spearhead of the movement towards the 'new international economic order'. This challenge also reflects the absence of coherent policy positions within the United Nations Secretariat and a lack of co-ordination within the Governments, there being frequent differences between the positions of some delegations in New York and Geneva. The Secretary-General of UNCTAD, in a paper submitted to the Trade and Development Board in August 1975[4] and referred by that body to the Seventh Special Session of the General Assembly, called attention to the duality of responsibility which 'exists at present, as between UNCTAD and the central structure of the United Nations, which makes for duplication of effort in this field, enhances the pos-sibility of conflict in advice, and weakens the effectiveness of the United Nations as a whole'. The paper went on to observe that the central organ which is now required could, in principle, be con-ceived as a new body, created as part of the central structure of the United Nations. However, 'an alternative option which deserves serious consideration would be to extend the present competence of UNCTAD – the Conference, the Trade and Development Board, and the Secretariat – so that it could become the central body of the United Nations in the field of international economic relations, thus directly supporting the General Assembly in its efforts to move towards a new international economic order'. UNCTAD's role both in the sectoral fields relating to international trade and development financing and in contributing to the formulation of economic policy is bound to increase as a result of the decisions taken at the General Assembly's Seventh Special Session; but, quite apart from its serious constitutional implications, a transfer to UNCTAD of the central Charter functions of ECOSOC would negate the positions taken not only by the Committee of Experts on the United Nations Structure, but also the General Assembly's declared policy.

Part II

SOME CONCLUSIONS
AND SUGGESTIONS

8 The context and the perspective

How far are the new orientations set forth in the decisions of the Sixth and Seventh Special Sessions of the General Assembly and the Declaration on the Economic Rights and Duties of States likely to affect the relevance of United Nations experience hitherto? Perhaps the first point to be made is that the great bulk of the total work of the system – that of the specialized areas and much of that under the Council and the General Assembly – is not directly affected by those decisions. What may be affected in some degree (though the old procedures will still have their large and essential place) is the relatively small, though all-important, part concerned with central issues of policy: the régime of international trade; the transfer of real resources for financing the development of developing countries; international monetary reform; the transfer of technology and more generally the application of science and technology for development; industrialization, food and agriculture.

These are clearly the areas most prominently in mind when it is claimed that there is need for far-reaching *structural* reforms if the purposes of the new international economic order are to be advanced. The sort of reforms that can be envisaged are more extensive than appear at first sight. On the one hand, the structure and the processes for international decision making, the functioning of the General Assembly, ECOSOC and other UN organs, and the relations among those organs and between them and the specialized agencies, are inevitably involved. On the other hand, the list must include such specific innovations as new international funds for particular purposes – among others, agricultural development in the food-deficit developing countries, and to the developing countries most seriously affected by the economic crisis. It would include new arrangements within IMF and the Bank Group whereby the transfer of financial resources from the developed to the developing countries will not only be greatly increased, but placed on a more automatic basis. There are many who would like the UN's financing organs (the Bank and the Fund, as well as UNDP and UNICEF) to be more under Third-World control; many, no doubt, would like to see the GATT machinery for trade negotiation linked to UNCTAD and brought squarely under the General Assembly. A considerable expansion of the UN's monitoring functions in different fields seems likely. Some would like to see the UN intergovernmental organs for study, exchange of views and consultation transformed into executive organs able to impose decisions by majority vote; there may also be some who would like to substitute for an objective, impartial Secretariat one that actively promotes majority views, even if these clash with those of an important segment of the Membership.

Measures have already been taken or are under active consideration in some of these directions. But, by and large, the industrialized countries have been slow to respond to the more far-reaching structural proposals that have been advanced; and it is doubtful that the developing world, which is naturally most interested in results, will wish to press such proposals against Western opposition, except possibly those affecting UNCTAD. The danger is too great of the UN being by-passed and rendered ineffective. No one can ignore the significance of the rapidly growing importance of OECD, the tendency of the EEC to take independent action (e.g. the Lomé Convention), and the fact that consultations and negotiations on how to implement some of the most important agreements reached at the General Assembly's Seventh Special Session are being pursued, not through the UN, where a majority vote still has some moral weight, but through an *ad hoc* mechanism organized by the Government of France.

The developments of the past few years bearing on our subject, and particularly the implications of the drive for a new international economic order, will be discussed further in the Postscript. Meanwhile, on the basis of the preliminary reflections set out in the last few paragraphs, one may hazard the guess that with the possible important exceptions above, far-reaching or decisive changes in the *modus operandi* of the UN, if they come at all, are unlikely to come quickly, and the conclusion that the lessons of the past thirty years have not lost their validity. In surveying the experience of those thirty years, it is well to remember that we are dealing with a working mechanism that has shown a considerable capacity both for 'harmonizing the actions of nations' and for adaptation to changing circumstances and needs, has to its credit a body of accomplishment of which the Member States and everyone who has taken part in producing it may be proud, and is envisaged by the General Assembly as becoming the centre-piece of a world-wide programme of cooperation for economic and social development more far-reaching than anything hitherto attempted. It is a mechanism that has grown up rapidly, to a considerable extent haphazardly, and in contexts that have been constantly changing both in nature and dimension. Inevitably, it contains anomalies and flaws, and will need frequent further adaptation to meet the changing demands that are being made of it. Inevitably too, if only because of the differing national interests that may be or appear to be served, its structures and organization will never be tidy or altogether free from confusion and controversy. Nor will one ever be able to reconcile completely (though one constantly seeks accommodations) the fundamental contradictions (a) between the autonomy of each intergovernmental organization and the desire for a unified United Nations policy or programme; and, (b) as regards operational activities, between decisions taken and priorities established by the central inter-governmental organs and those of individual countries under their 'country programmes'.

An element in the perspective not to be overlooked is the steady improvement in day-by-day coordination and working relationships at the staff level between the UN and the agencies, and among the agencies themselves, that have undoubtedly taken place despite the growing fragmentation of authority and finance and the other adverse factors that have been discussed. The importance of this element accounts for the emphasis placed on the ACC and restructuring within the UN Secretariat in later chapters of Part II. Other central issues to be discussed in those chapters include: the Economic and Social Council's role of leadership and coordination; how further to develop unity of purpose and concerted action within the system; and the need to curb the trend towards fragmentation, proliferation and dispersal of authority. No comprehensive discussion of the broad problems of structure, coordination and cooperation will be attempted. More will be said about organization within the United Nations itself than about the relations of the United Nations with the specialized agencies, or inter-agency problems of substantive and administrative coordination which, by and large, are dependent at least in part on the solution of more fundamental issues such as those just mentioned. The problems of individual agencies will not be referred to, nor will the handling of political issues; and the arrangements for development assistance will be discussed only briefly in Chapter 13. The Postscript will have something more to say about the new perspectives opened by the Sixth and Seventh Special Sessions of the General Assembly and their possible implications for structure and coordination; at this point it would be premature to go further.

In the organization of the UN itself, there is a crying need for simplification and concentration at the intergovernmental level. The proliferation and complexity of the present intergovernmental structure is responsible not only for much of the difficulty encountered by individual Member States in following the UN's economic and social work, let alone in controlling it or playing an active role in it, but also for much of the incoherence and lack of coordination encountered in the system as a whole. One reason for the proliferation of intergovernmental bodies in the past, namely the unrepresentative character of ECOSOC, has now been overcome, and another, the uncertain position of ECOSOC vis-à-vis the General Assembly seems to be on the way to being corrected. The serious problem of UNCTAD's competence in relation to that of the Council remains, but should that make it impossible to begin, in a modest way, a process of 'streamlining'? No sweeping centralization or 'rationalization' is suggested because a considerable degree of 'pluralism' and decentralization of support and interest in the system as a whole are as desirable as ever. But things have gone too far in that direction and unless the trend can be arrested and to some degree reversed, the prospects for the future of the system are less than encouraging. Surely, the continued separate existence of certain decision-making organs, with their individual orientations and separate staffs, and composed mainly of diplomats, can no longer easily be justified. Should it not be feasible, to begin with, for the 54-Member ECOSOC itself to take on the work of the 54-Member Committee on Review and Appraisal of the Development Strategy, which reports to it? Or even the work, which seems inadequately meshed into that of the other parts of the system, of the 58-Member Governing Council of the UN Environment Programme? Bodies responsible for the allocation of voluntary funds – for example, the Governing Councils of UNDP, the Special Fund, the Capital Development Fund – are normally constituted somewhat differently in order to maintain an appropriate balance between donors and recipients. Too, some mergers might be considered. Towards a solution of this whole problem of proliferating intergovernmental organs, the 1975 *Report of the Group of Experts on the Structure of the United Nations System* has now made a significant and helpful contribution.

That report also has valuable comments on various inter-agency matters. Furthermore, in regard to such matters, three comprehensive documents bearing on aspects of the general problem with which we are concerned, are still very relevant, namely, the Capacity Study, the second report of the *Ad hoc* Committee of Experts to Examine the Finances of the United Nations and the Specialized Agencies,[1] issued in 1966, and the final report of the Enlarged Committee for Programme and Coordination (E/4748), issued in 1969, and several of the suggestions contained in the present paper can be found, explicitly or implicitly, in one or more of them. The report of the ECPC, which was welcomed and followed up in some detail by the General Assembly in Resolution 2579 (XXIV), called attention at an early stage to

the extent of the legal, constitutional and administrative obstacles to altering the framework of relationships in the United Nations system towards central control under the General Assembly, e.g. by way of a unified programme and budget, and short of a unified budget, it is difficult to envisage how central control (in the sense of central allocation of resources) could be effectively exercised in practice. In general, therefore, there appears no practical choice but, for purposes of the present exercise, to work within the present distribution of responsibility among the governing bodies and conferences of the various agencies in respect of their own programmes and budget. This does not, however, preclude a continued effort to achieve a greater uniformity of principles, practices and standards in the programmes of the United Nations system.[2]

In the present paper, the functionally decentralized pattern of international organization is accepted as a basis not only because of the legal, constitutional and administrative obstacles to altering it but also for three further reasons: firstly, because a fundamental change to a centralized system might well place in jeopardy what everyone wants to protect and develop, namely, the effective and active cooperation of national ministries, professional groups, as well as international agencies in different fields, which has been developed under the arrangements and understandings built up among the United Nations organizations; secondly, because there is little prospect that activities so infinitely complex and so wide-ranging as those of the United Nations System could be centrally directed or controlled, except in a general way and in certain specific areas; thirdly, because there are reasonable prospects within the existing pattern, not merely for achieving a greater uniformity of principles, practices and standards and of achieving closer programme coordination through concordant work of the UN and the agencies on programme budgeting and medium-term plans, but also for strengthening the leadership of the United Nations and the coherence of the United Nations System. If some structural changes are required in the

UN–specialized agency relations, they are neither drastic nor dramatic.

An assumption must also be stated at this stage, namely, that, despite the reorientation of its priorities, the Council will continue to act not only as the coordinator of the system, under the authority of the General Assembly, but, at least for the time being, also as the governing organ for a number of sectoral activities, in some cases in the context of its general coordinating role. It has often been argued that there is a basic incompatibility between these two roles played not only by the Council itself but by the Secretariat, and to some extent by the Council's commissions and committees on its behalf. One reason, mentioned in an earlier chapter, why central inter-agency coordinating functions in the Secretariat have always been exercised under the Secretary-General himself has been the fact that coordination covers many activities – public information, adminis-tration and finance, legal and political questions – in addition to those in the economic and social fields. But another reason, no less important, has been the belief of the agencies and the Council itself that ESA, so many of whose activities impinge on or compete with those of other bodies, could not always be an impartial and objective coordinator. On the other hand, there has always been a minority view that ESA, as the secretariat of the Council, ought to be respon-sible for all the latter's staff work, including coordination undertaken on its behalf. If the Council and ESA were to find it desirable and possible to transfer a substantial proportion of their sectoral activities to agencies, regional commissions or programmes and concentrate on broad leadership and coordination, this point of view would naturally be strengthened, with important implications for the organizational arrangements for inter-agency coordination in the United Nations Secretariat, discussed in Chapter 13 below.

9 The role of the Economic and Social Council

Leadership and coordination

The Charter assigns to the Economic and Social Council, under the authority of the General Assembly, the central promotional and coordinating role in respect of the whole United Nations System: that is to say, the United Nations *per se*, including UNCTAD, UNIDO, UNDP, UNEP, UNICEF and other United Nations organs, as well as the specialized agencies and IAEA. The coordinating responsibilities of certain programmes and organs in specific sectors are subject to the proviso, usually explicit, that they do not impair those of the Council. How these responsibilities are differentiated was discussed in Chapter 3; here it will suffice to emphasize that only the Council and the General Assembly can provide *policy* coordination for the entire United Nations System – a framework within which each part of the system can play its due role; and, secondly, that the Council is in the best position to assist the General Assembly in developing the political will and taking the political decisions necessary to launch and maintain broad international actions in which the cooperation of many parts of the system is required.

If, over a long period, the Council has not fully asserted its authority under the Charter, the question arises whether it is capable of doing so. One could be defeatist in the light of the record and the increasingly difficult circumstances in which its authority has now to be exercised. But such defeatism would surely be unjustified as well as disastrous. It would be disastrous because the Council, named in the Charter a principal organ of the United Nations, provides the only constitutional basis on which to build orderly and coherent relationships within the United Nations System, and unjustified because many Governments have become convinced that the Council must be revived and many possibilities for improving its performance have yet to be explored. The answer to the question posed above must therefore be affirmative, subject, however, to a number of important conditions being fulfilled.

Some conclusions and suggestions

The support of the General Assembly itself will be crucial. This is the first condition, the second being that a strong and balanced group of Governments wants the Council to assert its leadership and is prepared to work steadfastly for this – and against the inertia and even vested interest in the *status quo* they may encounter in other organs of the United Nations and in the specialized agencies. A third condition, equally indispensable, is that the level and competence of the delegations to the Council, and the Governments' arrangements for supporting them, are such as to enable the Council's responsibilities to be exercised effectively. This condition is not likely to be fulfilled as a result merely of exhortation or for the sake of the United Nations' well-being alone. Its fulfillment will inevitably depend largely on the importance attached to the Council, in their own national interest, by individual Governments, and the use they find they can make of it for working out solutions and agreements (or even for defending their interests) in respect of major policy issues.

Another condition is that the Council's central role must be essentially catalytic and exercised through intellectual persuasion. Only the product and synthesis of many authoritative views can be persuasive. The International Development Strategy – the synthesized product of much thinking by many expert bodies, and above all UNCTAD and the Council's Committee on Development Planning – provides a model of such concerted action; several other initiatives taken in recent years, in which agencies have played a part, would also qualify. Coordination, likewise, cannot be imposed. It does not mean giving orders or even general directives; it does mean seeking consensuses through international action and initiating such action; it means providing a global perspective and encouraging inter-agency cooperation within that perspective, as well as sectoral adjustments needed to conform to it; it means a commitment on the part of the major organizations not just to offer nominal cooperation in programmes that have been jointly considered but to adjusting their own programmes and priorities in the light of such consideration and to avoid initiatives not so considered that might have important implications for the United Nations as a whole. Leadership and coordination are closely linked; both are inoperative without agency acceptance. Together they imply special concern on the part of the Council for planning, programming and evaluating the work of the system as a whole and ensuring by all practical means – and mainly by devolving responsibilities upon the Secretary-General and the Council's own subordinate bodies as well as the specialized agencies and programmes – that constraints on effective action are overcome.[1]

These considerations apply no less to the Council's role of leadership and coordination within the United Nations itself. Its role should not be considered as competitive with those of the Governing Councils of UNDP and UNEP, the Trade and Development Board and the Industrial Development Board, but as special and distinct. The Council has specific Charter duties vis-à-vis these and other organs and it should, in its coordinating role, address itself forcefully but exclusively to issues that affect the broad thrust of the work of the United Nations System or the relationships among the various programmes and organs of the United Nations, or relationships with non-United Nations organizations.[2]

If the initiative in the Council itself and in other organs on its behalf must be taken by Governments (and personally by their representatives) that are really concerned that the system should work, an outstanding President of the Council or Secretary can, during his year in office, make a real contribution, and much will always depend on the influence and active support of the Secretary-General and his representatives, despite the fact that he does not have a statutory power of initiative with regard to programmes comparable to that of the heads of several agencies vis-à-vis their governing organs.

Another condition which merits a high place on the list is that the objective of order and coherence is pursued and leadership exercised in such a way as to be broadly acceptable to all groups of Member States, developed as well as developing. While 'confrontation' may occasionally be of tactical value, it cannot be overemphasized that the success of international action in terms of human welfare depends on cooperation and the 'harmonization of policies' envisaged in the Charter.

Governments will also have to recognize that the persuasion which leadership implies requires much consultation, especially with the secretariats, and that a main and certainly an indispensable instrument for effecting such fruitful consultation in the United Nations System is ACC. The establishment of real cooperation between the Council and ACC, though often publicly urged and an objective of the annual joint meetings between the Committee for Programme and Co-ordination (CPC), the officers of the Council and ACC, has, as shown in Chapters 4 and 5 proved very elusive, partly because of the 'we and they' attitude toward the agencies which still exists rather widely in UN organs, and partly because of the restrictive view regarding ACC's proper role held by a number of Governments. One factor which should favourably affect such attitudes and views would, of course, be the demonstrated willingness of the agencies to play their part in system-wide programmes led and coordinated by the Council in the manner which has been indicated. The Secretary-General and his principal aides for economic and social affairs, as well as the executive heads of the various agencies and programmes, must identify themselves personally and actively with the task and make sure that the officials working with them are likewise dedicated to it.

The cardinal importance of support for the Council by the General Assembly has been emphasized. The Council may act on its own if generally assured of such support, or it may assist and advise the General Assembly in taking action, whichever seems most appropriate in the circumstances. The old problem of the Council's relations with the General Assembly,[3] which has often proved frustrating and embarrassing in the past, should lose its importance as the Council grows in prestige and membership. While experience has shown the difficulty of getting formal General Assembly acceptance of any code limiting its discretion, a sensible distribution of tasks between the Council and the Assembly has developed over the past few years, more especially in connexion with work arising from the Sixth Special Session. The recommendation of the Group of Experts on the Structure of the UN System that the Agenda of the General Assembly on Economic and Social Questions should be prepared by the Council is of great importance in this connexion.

How to improve the functioning of the Council

One cannot but underline the importance, for the purposes under consideration, of the recent efforts to improve and rationalize the functioning of the Council. Among the numerous authoritative documents on the subject the two most important are the reports of the Council's Working Group on Coordination (E/5259 of 1973) and of the Group of Experts on the Structure of the UN System (E/AC.62/9 of 1975). Five ideas put forward there and elsewhere seem to deserve special attention: firstly, the Council should conserve the very limited time at its disposal by refraining from the discussion and consideration of reports coming before it which are intended essentially as background information, and by confining any discussion that may be needed to aspects relating to policy planning and policy coordination. As regards the regular reports of specialized agencies and IAEA, the Council's recent practice of considering two or three each year in depth has at least been more satisfactory than the old procedure of attempting to review them all. It is possible that even this procedure might be further streamlined, (a) if the heads of the agencies are brought more fully into the 'policy-determining' discussions of the Council and its subsidiary bodies and (b) if a procedure suggested by the Secretariat is adopted, namely that when the Council examines, in alternate years, 'problems and areas of present or potential significance for development and international co-operation', 'it could select a subject which conforms to such characteristics and then decide to consider under the same item the relevant reports of its subsidiary bodies and of related agencies, organizations and programmes'.[4]

Secondly, it would be helpful if the practice were to be developed of the Council asking the Secretary-General – in consultation, where appropriate, with ACC or individual agency heads – to study, advise on and, if necessary, recast, proposals which involve or affect other parts of the United Nations System. This would not exclude the use of outside experts or intergovernmental committees for such purposes, but ensure that they had the knowledge and experience of the Secretariat availabe to them.

Thirdly, the Council's decision[5] and subsequent efforts to concentrate on major issues and initiatives and to devote less time to secondary items, as well as items that may be intrinsically important but can be dealt with at a lower level, have been encouraging. It may be hoped that such efforts will be pursued in spite of inevitable requests by delegations that pet items be fully aired or reviewed in the Council itself. Such efforts could usefully be supplemented by informal understandings and unwritten conventions, which a skilful president or committee chairman could apply without causing rancour, to limit the time spent on questions of procedure and on unnecessary oratory. The acceptance of such disciplines, including frequent recourse to informal consultations, is a matter of considerable importance, in view especially of the Council's enlargement and additional responsibilities.

Fourthly, the Council, if only in the interest of its own leadership, will surely wish to develop more active cooperation with non-United Nations global organizations and, in conjunction with the regional commissions, to extend consultative relations, and perhaps (especially if duplication exists) consider programme adjustments with major non-United Nations organizations, including the Organization for Economic Cooperation and Development (OECD), the Council of Europe, the Council for Mutual Economic Assistance (CMEA), the Organization of American States (OAS) and the Organization of African Unity (OAU). While the wide and vital questions of relations between the United Nations System and non-United Nations organizations has had to be excluded from this study, the point must at least be made that the Council's effectiveness will always be directly related to the degree of influence it brings to bear on national policies and international economic and social cooperation as a whole.

Fifth and lastly, the Group of Experts has attached especial importance to its recommendation of which more will be said in the Concluding Remarks, that small negotiating groups be set up by the Council and allowed a reasonable time, say one year or even more, 'to deal with key economic issues identified by it as requiring further negotiations with a view to bringing about agreed solutions'. The aim of this innovation, which would not involve any change on voting procedures, would be 'to enhance the authority of the Assembly and the Council by making it more likely that their decisions bring concrete results through appropriate changes in the policy of member countries'.

Needless to say, the Council's effectiveness is influenced by the degree to which it is responsive to, and has the support of, public opinion. It has never enjoyed much publicity and is indeed, like most of the United Nations' economic and social work, largely ignored by the news media. The establishment a few years ago of a United Nations Centre for Economic and Social Information, closely linked to the public information services of all United Nations organizations, has contributed to improving the situation, and some attempt has been made to involve non-governmental organizations in major recent enterprises such as the International Development Strategy and the World Population and World Food Conferences. The non-governmental organizations in consultative status with the Council under Article 71 of the Charter represent, however, a still largely untapped source of information and support to the Council, and there is no doubt that further efforts of the kind just referred to would be rewarding. The public hearings before the 'Study Group of Eminent Persons', set up under the Council's Resolution 1721 (LIII), on the role of transnational corporations and their impact on the process of development have marked a successful procedural innovation that might be used in connexion with the United Nations' consideration of other world economic problems.

The Council's schedule and the agenda for its meetings

How far would the Council's revitalized role affect its schedule? Might it even be desirable, as has sometimes been suggested,[6] for it to be, like the Security Council, in permanent session, that is to say, meeting frequently throughout the year and subject to call at any time? To the broader question, the answer must, of course, depend largely on what the Council is to do and how it organizes its subsidiary mechanisms. Some proponents of a Council in permanent session envisage it as itself exploring and attempting to deal with any existing or emerging economic and social problems of importance which seem to call for international action, and closely supervizing the steps that might lead to their solution; others want it to delegate as much as possible, and have the time to carry out more thoroughly a limited number of priority tasks, notably in the area of programming, evaluation, and coordination. On the basis of the present scope of its work, one wonders whether a Council in permanent session could avoid impinging on the narrower and more technical functions of other governmental organs, as well as on those of the Secretariat. Furthermore, the Council's authority must always be affected by the personal standing of the representatives and their influence in their Governments; and it has often been said that the Council meets too long at a stretch, especially in summer, to permit many people of the calibre needed to serve on it. The whole situation would, however, be changed if – as seems to be happening – the Council's mandate were substantially enlarged and the importance of its work significantly increased. Even now, a case could be made for it to meet more frequently but for shorter periods, and for specific items agreed in advance, possibly holding meetings at the ministerial level when the time is ripe for publicizing policy decisions, and delegating more of its tasks to subsidiary bodies or the agencies and programmes, on the one hand and to the Secretariat on the other.

Strengthening and streamlining of the Council's infrastructure

The question of the role of CPC or some alternative body to assist the Council in its coordinating task has, like many of the others, long been under study both by the Council and by the General Assembly especially in regard to the United Nations' own programme and budget. CPC has lately been doing a commendable job, providing, among other things, a critical look at the programme, thus facilitating not only the Council's task but also ACABQ's task of recommending an appropriate level of resources.[7] That some such small body to help the Council and ACABQ is more necessary than ever cannot be questioned, but there is ground for the widespread feeling, in the light of the introduction of medium-term planning and programme budgeting, that CPC, as constituted hitherto, is no longer adequate; that a body is needed whose members have had experience of the UN and budgeting techniques, would devote at least several months a year to their task and be elected for a period of years in their personal capacities – presumably on the nomination of their respective Governments, as in the case of ACABQ. It has also been felt that on coordination matters there has been a good deal of unnecessary duplication of work as between CPC and the Council's sessional Committee on Policy and Programme Coordination, as well as other bodies.

The idea, adumbrated in the report of the Council's Working Group on Rationalization some years ago, of constituting a new Advisory Committee on Programme and Coordination, to be the counterpart of ACABQ and working in close cooperation with it, was an attractive one. So *prima facie* was the idea of an eventual merger of the two bodies to constitute in effect a United Nations programme and budget committee comparable to those of some of the agencies. One practical consideration in this connexion relates to the sheer time and work involved. While the present schedule of the already burdened ACABQ covers about six months in the year, the merged committee would need to be in permanent or almost permanent session. Another problem – not necessarily a serious one – is constitutional. Would the new committee be a subsidiary of the General Assembly or of the Council, or of both and reporting to both? Would some of its members be appointed by the first and others by the second of these organs, as happened in the case of the Enlarged Committee for Programme Coordination? Yet other problems relate to size and composition. The CPC has at present 21 members and ACABQ, 13, a number considered about the maximum for effective review of budget, finance and administration. Would the new body be kept to approximately that size? This would seem doubtful, not only because of the trend towards large and politically balanced committees in the United Nations but also because of the many different kinds of expertise members of CPC and ACABQ need to provide. The issue now seems to be on the way to solution. A working group on United Nations Programme and Budget Machinery set up by the General Assembly put forward a series of recommendations (Document A/10117) under which CPC would be responsible to both the Council and the General Assembly, and would consist of 21 States Members of the UN elected by the General Assembly upon the Council's recommendation. It would review the United Nations' medium-term plan in the off-budget year and the programme budget in budget years and recommend an order of priorities among UN programmes, as defined in the medium-term plan. It would further endeavour to coordinate, on the request of the Council, activities within the UN System and in particular respond to any recommendation of the Council or the Assembly that it look into the implementation system-wide of important legislative decisions. The procedures for joint CPC–ACC consultations would be strengthened.

The General Assembly asked the Council (Resolution A/C5/1227/ Rev. 2) to put the Working Group's recommendations regarding CPC into effect on an experimental basis in 1976; by the same resolution, it requested the *Ad hoc* Committee on Restructuring of the Economic and Social Sectors of the UN 'to examine the role of ACABQ within the context of possible modifications in the structure and functioning of the UN, including *inter alia* the mandate and composition of the ACABQ'.

One may ask on the one hand, whether the Council's commissions and committees could give the Council more help in its leadership and coordinating tasks, and, on the other, whether its subsidiary machinery – which now actually includes 167 separate bodies (see E/5753, Annex, para 11) – has not become too large and complex. The answer to both questions would seem to be affirmative. Some of these bodies, including the Committee on Development Planning, the Statistical Commission and the Committee on Natural Resources, have contributed to coping with coordination difficulties with determination and success. Others have tended to avoid such difficulties. There is a legalistic – and strictly correct – view that the agencies are not subject to coordination by bodies subsidiary to the Council; but this position reflects the old conception of coordination as something imposed by a superior. Under the new and surely correct conception, these commissions and committees should, by and large, act not just as technical advisers but as instruments of the Council in a continuing consultation aimed at bringing about greater unity of purpose and coordination. There is much to be said for making greater use of the United Nations regional economic commissions in the United Nations development system; in streamlining and improving the bases of work with and among the regional structures of the United Nations System; and in establishing a stronger role for the executive secretaries of the regional commissions in regional coordination, at the staff level, regarding matters of system-wide concern.

The need for considerable streamlining is no less obvious, both among the technical bodies but also as discussed in the last chapter among the 'political' bodies that have much the same kind and size

Some conclusions and suggestions

of Membership as the Council itself, to which they report. As regards the Council's technical bodies, there are some whose membership includes an undue proportion of junior diplomats and whose performance suggests that they could be dispensed with; in other cases, the question is how far they must be permanent, with, so to speak, a jurisdiction of their own, rather than *ad hoc*, called as needed by the Council. This whole question forms an important element in the Council's current agenda.

A drastic dismantling of the Council's existing subsidiary machinery, and assumption by the Council itself of much of the work now performed by subsidiary bodies, is recommended by the Group of Experts on the Structure of the United Nations. More will be said on these subjects at a later stage. (See the Postscript.)

Attitudes, practices and policies of intergovernmental organs and Governments

No additional standing machinery for coordination, at the inter-governmental level seems to be needed: on the contrary, every pos-sibility of simplifying the existing machinery should be welcomed and emphasis laid on the development of consultations, and the opening up of channels of direct communication, among 'opposite numbers', as well as on the discipline that should be observed by all officials to ensure that their work is well-coordinated with related work in other agencies and programmes. The enforcement of this discipline, which has been repeatedly commended by the Council and the General Assembly but is far from being universally observed or even encouraged in practice, deserves constant attention by the Secretary-General and the heads of agencies and programmes, as well as by ACC.

This suggestion is linked to a change required in the attitude of the Council itself in the interest of its own effectiveness and authority, namely, to devote less time and effort to 'coordination' as such and to concentrate under that heading largely on planning and pro-gramming and on organization between the United Nations and the agencies as well as within the United Nations itself. The silence about the many critical issues of organization and structure which affect coordination, and have been discussed in Part 1, must be broken: these issues should also be aired and considered in prepara-tion, if need be, for General Assembly action. Questions of coordina-tion and cooperation of the traditional kind arising within the estab-lished institutional framework – and especially questions regarding the coordination of activities – should normally be referred by the Council to the Secretary-General, in consultation with ACC, not just for advice and report, but for action, and for immediate and decisive action, if this is required. He should be held responsible and accountable to the Council for good coordination and cooperation

at the staff level and he should report to the Council, on any difficulties he encounters either from intergovernmental organs or from
agencies.

Such a change in the Council's attitude and practice should represent not only a substantial increase in efficiency but a financial saving
for Governments and for the United Nations if only because of the
fewer meetings required. It might involve some minor increase in
respect of Secretariat time and travel for the purpose of discussions
with the agencies and programmes, and it would call for more time,
attention and personal involvement on the part of the top officials of
the United Nations and the heads of the agencies and programmes.
If the Secretary-General is to be, as suggested earlier, formally and
regularly consulted by the Council and the General Assembly on
any institutional or organizational proposals (as the executive heads
of all major agencies are by their governing bodies) he should be
ready to respond frankly and without delay and to take the initiative
in pointing out, as early as possible, any dangers that such proposals
might represent, or in suggesting preferable alternatives. He is the
primary spokesman for the system as a whole, and bears a special
responsibility both to warn against proposals that might be poten-
tially damaging from a system-wide organizational or administrative point of view, and to ensure that the fullest use is made of the
capacities of the system. The General Assembly has been singularly
slow in seeking his views on such matters.

A change is also needed in the Council's attitude towards the
specialized agencies as well as towards ACC – which although it has
sometimes been positive, has too often been defensive, especially in
recent years, as Chapters 4 and 5 have brought out. Not only the
Council, but also the General Assembly must recognize fully that the
agencies are integral parts of the United Nations System and that,
by bringing forward their different points of view and expertise, they
have a major and often decisive contribution to make to the deliberations and work of United Nations organs. This is a condition of
achieving good coordination as well as sound policy formulation.
One helpful gesture in this connexion would be reconsideration by
the General Assembly of its oft-repeated refusal formally to accept
the obligation – long since accepted by the Council[1] – to consult the
specialized agencies and IAEA, through the Secretary-General,
before taking decisions that might affect them. Furthermore, before
deciding on any new project involving the cooperation of specialized
agencies, the Assembly (and the Council) should surely have before
it an estimate of financial implications not only, as at present, for the

United Nations itself, but also for the United Nations System as a whole, even if this means delay. Most important, however, for the purposes in view would be a change in the current practice, due to the enlarged membership and the development of group action, of working up all major decisions in the General Assembly committees and the Council, through group meetings, informal consultations, and closed sessions, thus largely excluding agency representatives from the processes of consultation.

In addition to such changes, a new effort is needed on the part of Governments (which, as indicated below, the Secretariat should be ready to assist, if so desired) to assimilate the positions they take in different international bodies, at least on matters of consequence (including matters relating to programme coordination, structure and organizations). While this may, in some cases, require a considerable strengthening of national coordinating arrangements, it should be made easier by every improvement in coordination among international organs. More weight than in the past will have to be given to administrative as against purely political considerations in deciding on international organizational arrangements. The high priority of streamlining the structure of intergovernmental bodies has been emphasized; at the same time, efforts must be made to avoid, except where really indispensable, the creation of new organs, with all that that implies in terms, on the one hand, of staff, administration, representation and other trappings of independent existence, and, on the other, of new coordination problems, particularly where the tasks to be assigned to the new organ would conflict or overlap with those of organs that exist. If some new organ is indispensable, it is important to ensure that its terms of reference are carefully defined in relation to other organs and that it is brought under the coordinating authority of the Council.

The Secretary-General and the United Nations Secretariat can do much to influence the United Nations' intergovernmental organs in the desired directions. They can also influence governmental attitudes toward ACC, which has often been regarded – and not without occasional justification – as the mouthpiece of the specialized agencies. Strong support of ACC by the Secretary-General, and leadership by him or his representative – not only in ACC itself but also in the Preparatory Committee and its other subsidiary bodies – are indeed essential if ACC is to operate successfully, if the Council's innate suspicion of it is to be kept at bay and a partnership between the two organs is to become a reality. This aim is likely to be furthered if and when there is closer integration and policy alignment at the higher echelons of the Secretariat, a subject which is discussed in Chapter 13.

The new approach to coordination questions and the role of the secretariats implies a change also in the attitudes and practices of the heads of agencies and programmes as well as of the Secretary-General and his staff. Some of the implications for the organization of ACC's work will be discussed separately. Here it will suffice to make a few quick points: firstly, that because of the number and importance of the many broad and multisectoral tasks that have to be dealt with, membership in ACC, meetings of ACC and the standing relationships maintained between the Secretary-General and the heads of agencies have acquired additional importance. Much thought, discussion and acceptance of responsibility is required on the part of the members themselves in regard to not just their own organizations' performance but to the concerted contribution the United Nations System can make. Secondly, the agencies should be careful to avoid giving the impression, at any time, of 'ganging up' against the United Nations especially in ACC; conversely, the United Nations Secretariat should be careful to consult, and seek accommodation with, the specialized agencies and refrain from exploiting its position as the arm of the Council and the General Assembly to the agencies' disadvantage. Thirdly, ACC ought to pursue an active programme of review and reform on its own. Part of this programme should concern its own functioning, but part must relate to the tasks it decides to undertake. In this respect, the first thrust of its efforts in the area of general policy, where its somewhat imprudent claims to competence were rebuffed by CPC and the Council in 1969,[2] will no doubt be guided by the Council's request, 'when it submits suggestions and studies, to state options and alternative courses of action in order to facilitate the decision-making role of the appropriate legislative organs'.[3] It will also have to address itself to the difficult task of coordinating the actions of the different organizations under the decisions of the Sixth and Seventh Special Sessions of the General Assembly, and at the same time to correcting miscellaneous situations that have been causing trouble. These could include programme difficulties such as those already mentioned, but also administrative situations that have been under criticism, such as what many Governments consider to be inadequate interorganizational cooperation on electronic data-processing systems. They must also include difficulties even of a minor nature which have tended to be neglected or 'swept under the carpet'. It would, for example, be inexcusable if an end were not quickly put to unedifying disputes on such petty matters as precedence and the use of the United Nations flag in field posts. It is no less essential that progress be made in regard to the pooling of services in the field (including official cars as well as offices). The ground could be prepared for a gradual simplification of the regional structures of the United Nations System, and the possibilities carefully explored of cutting down time and money spent on agency (and United Nations) representation at less essential intergovernmental and non-governmental meetings as well as on certain inter-agency discussions.

Some ideas for developing and adapting the ACC machinery for such purposes as well as for strengthening it generally are discussed later. What is essential, above all, is a determination by the Secretary-General and the heads of agencies and programmes to ensure, so far as this lies within their power, more coherence and better coordination within their organizations and among members of the system.

Improvement of internal organization should be sought not only at Headquarters and in respect of global activities but also at the regional level and in the field, where the possibilities of cutting down on personnel and of streamlining activities seem at least as great in the case of some agencies as in that of the United Nations and its programmes. Obstacles will no doubt be encountered, not least in the field, where centrifugal tendencies are particularly marked, and compromises will be necessary on some matters on which rigid positions may have been taken in the past.

Possibilities of system-wide programme and budget review

One type of reform, *prima facie* attractive, would be to have the major programme agencies submit their programme and budget *for comments* to the Council (through CPC or its successor) and the General Assembly (through ACABQ) before being finally adopted by their respective legislative bodies. This procedure would require an adjustment of the timing of the budgetary process in the agencies, as well as in the United Nations; in order to provide a solid basis for findings by the General Assembly and ECOSOC affecting coordination, it would also presuppose a far greater degree of comparability between the United Nations' and the agencies' budgetary classifications and practices than has so far been reached; it would presuppose an active and competent CPC meeting for long periods, and a considerable strengthening of its staff and that of ACABQ. It would avoid direct infringement of the agencies' constitutions; unless, however, rather tight restrictions were placed on the character of the comments that might be made by the General Assembly or ECOSOC, there is little doubt that serious difficulty would arise. The first relates to competence and work-load if the whole programme and budget were reopened for examination. Would the Governments agree to the work of the agencies' experienced intergovernmental organs being thus reviewed by an outside body, however distinguished? Would they tolerate an aggravation of what is already so much complained of, namely, duplication of discussions, negotiations and time? Another difficulty concerns the sensitivity of Governments and intergovernmental majorities to criticism, especially by experts and staff. Every agency draft programme and budget, even if not finally adopted, will nevertheless embody the wishes of Governments. It would be a rash central organ of the United Nations, even if of a political rather than an expert complexion, which would challenge such wishes. One of the sources of strength of the ACABQ, and one which it would discard at its peril, is that it challenges no intergovernmental decisions – even decisions of commissions – but the Secretary-General's financial and administrative proposals for giving effect to those decisions. Not that its comments on the administrative budgets of the agencies should remain almost entirely descriptive, the exceptions consisting of unprovocative references to such general matters as the rate of budgetary increase, or of the proliferation of documentation, or the control of travel expenditure. But the possibilities of change are limited, and, however well the new arrangements for CPC may work, it would not be realistic to expect any central UN organ to exercise any real control over the programmes and budgets of the UN System as a whole.

This does not mean that no approach to closer central review should be attempted, but rather that the approach itself should be gradual, cautious and tentative. Two elements seem to be vital. Firstly, efforts might be made to give fuller effect to the provision in the agreements with the major agencies (apart from IMF and the Bank Group) that the agencies will consult the United Nations in the preparation of their budgets. So far, consultations, when they have been held, have been concerned with form, terminology and presentation. How far would it be possible to extend their scope to content? At the staff level, emphasis is being laid on the need to make the programming systems of different organizations more comparable with one another. As indicated earlier, this will inevitably be a long process, involving additional work and possible difficulties for individual organizations without necessarily offering them much immediate and tangible advantage. But in so far as those efforts succeed, medium-term planning and plan harmonization would open up new possibilities for a clearer definition of objectives, a stricter ordering of priorities and more systematic thinking about the future.

Secondly, one might envisage ACABQ and CPC, or its successor, commenting more fully than at present on agency programmes and budgets not in lieu, or duplicating the work of the agencies' own competent organs, but to ensure that those organs are aware of the priorities as well as the standards and criteria applied in the United Nations, and the implications of agencies' plans for the broader objectives of the system as a whole.

Review of the UN–agency agreements

The sort of measures so far proposed would not require revision of the United Nations–agency relationship agreements but would represent, at least in part, a fuller and more active implementation of them. The agreements are, in many respects, out-of-date, especially because so many new and additional elements have been introduced over the years as a result of requests by the Council and the General Assembly and the spontaneous development of cooperation, particularly through the secretariats. They will continue to serve a purpose and no harm, if little good, would be done by adding uncontentious provisions to meet new situations – such as those dealing with decolonization and technical assistance which are to be found in the UN–WIPO Agreement of 1974. If substantial changes in existing practices or relationships are considered indispensable, it would probably be better to avoid the formal revision procedure which would be likely to produce a maximum of resistance and a minimum of agreement. At any rate, before embarking on it, it would seem wise to try an alternative, namely to get the necessary understandings and interpretations formulated by the Council and/or the General Assembly with the help of bodies like ACABQ and CPC and after due consultation with the agencies through ACC and the governing organs concerned. The understandings would finally be submitted to the General Assembly for approval, in a form which, depending on their scope and effect on the agencies, could be endorsed or simply noted by the agencies' governing organs. Some measures might be taken spontaneously without intervention of the General Assembly or the Council, but, in any case, given the desire of so many Governments to 'strengthen the coherence of the system' and judging from the record of agency compliance with requests of the General Assembly and the Council over many years, it should require no more than such a request in order to secure wide concurrence in any reasonable innovations. Every effort would no doubt be made to avoid modifications in the agreements incompatible with the agencies' constitutions – as would be, for example, an attempt to remove from the agencies' intergovernmental organs the formal control of their programme and budget. As brought out long ago in successive discussions of the possibility of the General Assembly approving the budget of the specialized agencies or of incorporating agency budgets in a consolidated budget of the United Nations,[4] any attempt to effect such a major revision of agency constitutions would inevitably be a lengthy and divisive undertaking, and probably an unnecessary one because so much could be done and more easily, by simple decisions supported and pressed for by Governments in the General Assembly and the Council and in the organs of the agencies themselves. Some fairly far-reaching measures in the direction not only of budgetary assimilation but of building up system-wide institutions have already been accepted by agencies on the basis of General Assembly action. Examples include the creation of the Joint Inspection Unit recommended by the Committee of 14, and the establishment of the International Civil Service Commission.

Apart from action that the United Nations might wish the agencies to undertake, there are certain powers under the Charter and the agreements that the United Nations itself might wish to utilize more fully. The decisions of the General Assembly in respect to the recent Special Session of the General Assembly suggest that the Assembly may be prepared to do more than it has hitherto done by way of 'making recommendations to the agencies concerned'. Would the Council likewise wish to make greater use of its power to make specific recommendations, after consultation, to specialized agencies and the International Atomic Energy Agency (IAEA)? Another group of powers, so far little utilized by the United Nations, concerns 'reciprocal representation' and 'liaison'. The Coordination Unit at Geneva and the Office for Inter-Agency Affairs and Coordination in New York (which holds regular meetings with agency and programme representatives there) fulfill some liaison functions with the agencies, but the United Nations has no liaison offices at the seats of the major agencies such as the latter have at United Nations Headquarters. An exception existed in the case of IAEA, which was intended to have a closer relationship to the United Nations than the specialized agencies, and for many years a Permanent Representative of the Secretary-

General to IAEA was stationed at Vienna. That post has, however, been eliminated. Budgetary considerations reinforced a once widely held doctrine that the agencies should maintain day-to-day contact with the United Nations, rather than *vice versa*. A related doctrine, strongly held by Hammarskjöld, was that while the agencies should be represented at, and put their views before, the United Nations organs, the main burden of ensuring that the agencies' intergovernmental organs are kept aware of United Nations views and encouraged to act accordingly should be borne by Governments and agency heads. Before his time it was the practice to send a strong United Nations delegation, led by a top official, to meetings of the major agencies' governing organs and conferences to put forward, in consultation with agency heads, United Nations views on important issues. (Hammarskjöld himself addressed a number of such conferences, though always on general UN themes.) United Nations officials still follow major meetings and a high official may briefly attend and make a formal statement, but the practice of active participation by the United Nations has, at least partially, lapsed. It is worth considering whether it should not, at least in some degree and circumstances, be revived.

One set of conclusions to which this discussion leads, is that there are many possible approaches to an updating of United Nations–agency relationships and practices, that such approaches need not involve confrontations and that it would be useful to explore, as informally as possible, the points requiring agency action on which agreement could quickly be reached. A second conclusion is that much of this possible updating depends upon decisions of the United Nations itself to give fuller effect to existing provisions and to play a more active role in furnishing guidance and in contributing from the centre of the system to the objectives and purposes of the agencies.[5] How far it will be possible to ensure that the priorities of the agencies reflect the Council's overall view of what they should be depends on the other factors that have been mentioned, including the manner in which the Council conceives and carries out its coordinating role and the support given to United Nations positions by Governments in the agencies' governing organs.

Some promising initiatives in administrative and programme coordination

Many measures which have recently been initiated in the interests of coordination are promising and need to be actively pursued. The work of the International Civil Service Commission, at last established, must now be developed in the interest of improving system-wide administrative coordination; and the work of the United Nations Administrative Management Service, which studies and advises the Secretary-General on internal organization and possible improvements in the management and distribution of tasks in the United Nations Secretariat as well as in arrangements for cooperation among its different parts, deserves fuller support than it has so far received. Nor must one underestimate the possibilities of improving management and coordination in the wider inter-agency field offered by the Joint Inspection Unit.

While the United Nations and many of its Members derive great advantage from the voluntary financing of particular United Nations projects and types of work, it is clearly desirable to ensure:

(a) consolidation, wherever possible, of the separate funds;
(b) fuller administrative and budgetary control over them and due integration of activities financed by them with related activities financed by the regular budget;
(c) respect tor two principles which have been cited by both the Joint Inspection Unit and the ACABQ, namely, the collective responsibility of Members, and collective decision making, in regard to the United Nations economic and social programme.

Yet another promising set of ongoing measures is aimed at bringing about accommodations between the United Nations and different agencies in particular substantive problem areas. Some of this work has been in hand for years, at the intergovernmental and inter-secretariat levels, in certain areas very successfully, in others without much positive result, and a determined effort is needed by the Council and ACC to reach solutions quickly in those areas. Current candidates for such consideration include the division and coordination of work on the application of science and technology for development and on the transfer of technology; work on natural resources, including water use and conservation; and work connected with marine science.[6] As emphasized earlier, there is still much uncertainty as to the future roles of ESA and UNCTAD and the allocation of responsibilities between them; adjustments have still to be made among different organizations in respect of work on the human environment, while the distribution of work on industrial development stands more in need of review than ever since the adoption of the Lima Declaration. Nor must one overlook the long-term potentialities for improved substantive coordination (although the results have so far not been impressive) in the current United Nations work on programme budgeting and on medium-term planning, combined with the early inter-agency consultations on such plans that are beginning to be organized. Here a laborious process lies ahead of securing general acceptance of uniform terms, concepts and methods, on which there are still wide discrepancies, quite apart from that of reorienting the traditional United Nations approach to budget making, and no sensational results in the short run should be expected. As brought out in Chapter 2, much is likely to depend on whether the United Nations itself develops an effective form of central decision making in internal programme matters. This would imply that the present embryonic central programming machinery would be reinforced under a high official who would be responsible for ensuring, in due consultation with the intergovernmental organs as well as other officials, implementation in the various United Nations organs concerned of decisions reached. As mentioned earlier, the establishment of the Senior Budget and Policy Review Group under the Under-Secretary-General for Administrative and Management represents a step in the direction indicated.

Finally, this chapter must include a reference to the undramatic work of the Office for Inter-Agency Affairs and Coordination at United Nations Headquarters and the Coordination Unit at Geneva, as the parts of the Secretariat responsible for keeping in regular contact with agency representatives, and, so far as feasible, briefing them on government attitudes, draft resolutions or other initiatives under consideration in United Nations organs, and assisting them in making their agencies' points of view known and taken into account. This function means much to the agencies – especially the smaller ones which have no regular representation at United Nations Headquarters or at Geneva – and should be fostered.

Chapter 5 has attempted to describe ACC's central role in inter-organizational coordination; it has hinted at some of ACC's unfulfilled potentialities and suggested that the Council might call on ACC directly or through the Secretary-General more than in the past for advice on the best means of modifying the resources of the system; it has also made clear some of ACC's inherent limitations. There is reason to think that the need for ACC and its importance will continue to increase; indeed the actions of the two special sessions of the General Assembly imply an extensive further enlargement of its responsibilities. Resolution 3362 of the General Assembly's Seventh Special Session sets in motion a series of measures 'as the basis and framework for the work of competent bodies and organizations of the UN system'; and to the considerable degree to which these measures (which include not just studies and reports, but international conferences and meetings of experts, intergovernmental negotiations and in some cases institutional changes) involve joint or collective action by several organizations, a clear responsibility falls upon ACC. How is it to be strengthened and restructured to meet its enhanced responsibilities in the new context that has been moulded by the General Assembly, which aspects of its structure and functioning should be preserved and which modified? The ACC has been wrestling with these questions and much of what follows reflects ideas and decisions that have emerged from this exercise.

The first point to be made is that the ACC's biggest achievement, one of vital importance, has been to develop mutual confidence, a sense of common purpose, an *esprit de corps*, a desire to cooperate, among the executive heads of the organizations of the United Nations System, and through them – if only partially and imperfectly – among their staffs. Here is a source of strength, unforeseen and unsought in 1945, without which it is difficult to imagine that the United Nations System could now function; and it must be preserved. This implies the preservation of ACC's fundamental characteristics – especially the personal participation of the Secretary-

General and heads of agencies, and its essentially consultative character. As noted earlier, its consultative character has, however, not prevented it, and should not prevent it in future, from acting also as, in a sense, an executive organ, each member voluntarily implementing or sponsoring within his own governing organs the measures or policies generally agreed upon.

In order better to meet its growing commitments, the ACC has already added one full day to its Spring Session. This probably represents a limit to the time the Secretary-General and some of the agency heads can normally give to the meetings. Solutions will have to be sought largely in other aspects of the functioning of the ACC machinery, including the organization of work at the meetings themselves, the assignment of work to small groups from especially interested organizations, finding means to relieve the Secretary-General of part of his present burden, delegating more to the Preparatory Committee and other subsidiary bodies, and enhancing the contribution of the Secretariat. In much of this terrain, which has been gone over many times in the past fifteen or twenty years, no very dramatic results are likely to occur. On certain aspects, however, significant changes do seem feasible and these must be considered with care.

It has been noted earlier that the ACC has long suffered, especially when dealing with economic and social policy matters of central importance, from the excessive numbers of participants and the extreme disparity between the interests and potential contributions of its members. Arrangements are, of course, made to schedule items in such a way that the executive heads not concerned need not attend all meetings, or even all sessions. At a lower level, satisfactory arrangements on an open-ended basis have been found in some cases through the established machinery of subcommittees and working groups. Other models have been provided by *ad hoc* panels for specific subjects, including the so-called Functional Groups of ACC itself by temporary task forces on numerous specific questions, as well as by the Environmental Coordination Board (ECB), all having considerable latitude in working as they think best. In general, there seems to be wide agreement that ACC should work increasingly through groups consisting only of members closely concerned with the subject under consideration or their immediate assistants. Such arrangements, normally at a level just below that of the executive heads, might be envisaged to prepare the ground on general organization and policy questions and be helpful in solving intractable problems affecting a group of agencies in particular fields. They would not necessarily provide an alternative to the Preparatory Committee – which must continue to bear the main burden – or existing consultative arrangements bringing together the heads of the responsible divisions in different agencies, but they might constitute a useful complement. The ECB pattern which provides maximum autonomy within the ACC framework, would seem well-suited for regular high-level consultations on the Development Programme under the Chairmanship of the Administrator of UNDP – an arrangement which would replace the Inter-Agency Consultative Board of the United Nations Development Programme (IACB).

The original version of the present study contained the above suggestions; in the meantime, the Group of Experts on the Structure of the United Nations System has made a number of recommendations directly affecting the issue, of which two are of especial importance: firstly, the establishment of a post in the United Nations Secretariat of Director-General for Development and International Economic Cooperation, who would serve as a *primus inter pares* among the heads of the United Nations organizations and agencies dealing with economic and social affairs and would be in charge of directing all activities at present being carried out by the Department of Economic and Social Affairs and the various UN offices and programmes with respect to research, policy-making support, inter-agency coordination and operational activities; secondly, the creation of an Advisory Committee on Economic Cooperation and Development to be chaired by the new Director-General and consisting of the executive heads only of the major international organizations and unions dealing with development issues. The main task of this Committee would be '. . . to review the world economic and social situation and bring to the attention of high-level meetings of the Economic and Social Council, together with its own assessment and recommendations, all issues which, in its view, require international decisions and actions. . .'[1]

The Group of Experts thought that the proposed Committee should be independent of ACC, but should keep it regularly informed in order to avoid possible duplication. It seems right that it should not be just a subgroup of ACC, since the latter, being so heterogeneous does not have the standing which some of its individual members enjoy in major matters of policy. On the other hand, to deprive the ACC and its Chairman, the Secretary-General, of all say in such matters, would tend to weaken their authority in other matters. It would seem advisable, therefore, that the new Committee, while being independent and issuing its own reports, should be formally 'within the framework of ACC', in which its work and its finances would from time to time be discussed.[2]

The recommendation for the creation of a Director-Generalship for Development and International Economic Cooperation, naturally has a close bearing on another long-standing problem, which is steadily becoming more acute, namely that of relieving the Secretary-General of part of the burden involved in his Chairmanship of ACC in respect of inter-agency affairs generally. The recommendation of the Group of Experts should provide an easy and satisfactory solution: the new Director-General would deputize for the Secretary-General, as needed, as Chairman of ACC, and assume general responsibility for most of the appropriate work and follow-up for ACC within the UN Secretariat. Pending adoption of that recommendation, or should it not be accepted, the options are rather narrow. No UN official has the standing to replace the Secretary-General in ACC and, except as a temporary replacement at a particular meeting, the head of a specialized agency cannot appropriately act as the Secretary-General's alternate, if only because of ACC's basic terms of reference and the nature of most of the work carried out under it. One would probably have to make do with arrangements for chairing ACC, in the Secretary-General's absence, based on the nature of the discussions, the Secretary-General himself continuing to preside at the regular private meetings of ACC and when decisions are taken on general policy or important administrative issues.

In so far as he acts as Chairman of ACC, the Secretary-General is not in a good position to advance actively on his own aims and interests or those of the United Nations itself. Nor is the head of the Office of Inter-Agency Affairs and Coordination (OIAAC) in ACC and in the Preparatory Committee. That task must fall upon the UN heads of departments or the executive heads of one of the United Nations economic and social programmes. But these officials are inferior in rank, as in status in ACC, to the heads of the big agencies. This anomaly, which tends to weaken the leadership of the United Nations in ACC, is compounded by another, namely, that, as between the Secretary-General and the senior Headquarters officials, on the one hand, and the executive heads of UN bodies such as UNCTAD, UNIDO, UNDP, UNICEF and UNEP, on the other, there are no arrangements for prior consultation regarding United Nations positions or possible United Nations initiatives in ACC. It is only too understandable that without such consultations, the Secretary-General himself and the top UN officials are often hesitant to take positions. The institution of regular consultations among the United

Nations departments and programmes in preparation for ACC meetings – a step which would be facilitated by, but is not dependent upon the structural reform recommended by the Group of Experts – could not but help. Furthermore, it would be quite indispensable if another weakness is to be overcome, namely that ACC, whose members are inevitably concerned primarily with the affairs of their respective organizations, has not been noteworthy in proposing new approaches or better means of utilizing the resources of the system. If the Council and the General Assembly have made insufficient use of it, the ACC itself has initiated little, although such initiatives have frequently been invited, at least implicitly and are indeed inseparable from the role that has been outlined by the Council for it. The ACC might, for example, usefully look beyond the current range of work of the system and take up significant issues overlooked by inter-governmental organs, such as relations with non-United Nations international organizations like the Red Cross.

Any such development would, of course, depend not only on much more high-level consultation within the UN Secretariat, but even more on the preparatory work, that can be undertaken by ACC's subsidiary bodies and by the ACC Secretariat.

As regards the inter-agency machinery that might be brought into play, recourse might be had to such temporary devices as task forces and the designation of 'lead' agencies in particular fields. In this and in almost all other aspects of ACC work, including follow-up, the Preparatory Committee will inevitably continue to play the decisive role and its further functions as an executive committee, taking decisions and action on matters that do not need ACC's special attention, have recently been explicity confirmed. If, in some questions, it were once thought to be an expendable body, the Preparatory Committee is clearly indispensable now and the respected – but never implemented – decisions of ACC that the level of representation of all organizations on the Preparatory Committee should be that of Deputy or Assistant Director-General, have lost much of their force in view of the need for members not only well versed in the attitudes and thinking of their principals (which deputy executive heads not always are) but able to deal authoritatively with a far more formidable range of issues (many relating to different aspects of programme coordination, including experimental exercises in joint planning in numerous fields) and in greater depth, than in the past – in greater depth, because the failure so far to achieve the hoped for improvements in programme coordination from the widespread introduction of programme planning has meant that the onus must be borne by the existing mechanisms. The members of the Preparatory Committee also need to give more time to meetings and preparations for them than deputy executive (especially in the case of 'lead' agencies) heads, whose calendar is often as full as that of their superiors, are usually able to do.

The subsidiary inter-secretariat bodies, permanent and temporary, dealing with particular programme areas are constantly being adjusted and 'streamlined' and, because of the rapid growth in the number and interdependence of such bodies – and especially of *ad hoc* consultative groups – this process will need to be rather vigorously pursued. There will also need to be more decentralization, if ACC and the Preparatory Committee are not to be overwhelmed with technical reports and detailed coordination problems, and a closer relationship between such bodies and the corresponding intergovernmental organs.

The ACC has always wanted the Preparatory Committee to 'vet' the reports and recommendations of all subsidiary groups or inter-secretariat meetings. This has never caused any difficulty in the case of bodies dealing with economic and social matters or most other matters such as public information, legal questions, or publications, but this has not been altogether true in the case of CCAQ, which brings together most of the heads of administration and finance. Because of the central importance of these subjects, occasional differences of view between the two committees was not surprising, and differences tended to be compounded because of the geographical or administrative factors set forth in Chapter 2. It is certainly an anomaly that CCAQ should have its autonomous inter-agency Staff Office at Geneva, jointly financed, like the Inspection Unit and certain other institutions, by the United Nations and the agencies, and it has often been suggested that the Staff Office should be fully incorporated in the UN Secretariat. But the old differences have become less acute and, in view of the general need now for more decentralization and delegation of authority, and the close working relationship that is being developed between the CCAQ and the ICSC, it would seem wiser not to press for any change.

The key to the success or failure of inter-secretariat activities is normally to be found in the character and quality of the staff responsible for organizing them. This is certainly true of ACC and its Preparatory Committee, for almost all of whose work, other than the strictly administrative and financial, the Office for Inter-Agency Affairs and Coordination provides the essential basis of thinking and documentation. This contribution has been growing steadily in quality and volume. Since its separation from ESA, the Office has gained some additional staff, but it is still very small (at the professional level and above) and must be further strengthened if it is to carry the load now facing it. As mentioned earlier, it has sometimes been suggested that the Office should have more of an inter-agency, and less of a purely UN, character and include seconded staff from some of the agencies. If officials highly qualified in the matters dealt with by the Office are offered a position on a trial basis, this offer would no doubt be accepted, although past experience has not been over-encouraging.

The most important question affecting the staffing of ACC is, however, of a quite different character, namely, whether it is desirable to maintain the present status of the Office, which is independent of ESA and the Secretariat of the Economic and Social Council. Some advantages of the reorganization that took place in 1970 have been indicated (Chapter 5), but it is not certain that the present arrangement is most conducive to the full cooperation between the Council and ACC. as well as the individual agencies, that is so necessary. It should be noted that the restructuring of the UN Secretariat recommended by the Group of Experts would bring inter-agency coordination within the responsibility of the new Director-General for Development and International Economic Cooperation.

Three final points may be made before closing this chapter: one has been made before but bears repeating, namely, that a large proportion of the total work of the United Nations System is self-contained and does not need to be coordinated with that of the other organizations. This is particularly true of WHO and highly technical organizations such as ITU and UPU; it applies least to the United Nations itself. The second point is that the mechanisms of ACC, however convenient, flexible and generally acceptable, should enjoy no monopoly, and that, for questions of overwhelming concern to say two or three organizations only, it is often preferable, and entirely legitimate, to make *ad hoc* arrangements for coordination and cooperation. Nor, thirdly, does the ACC provide a substitute for the Secretary-General's own direct consultation and cooperation, on behalf of the UN, with individual agencies. Such direct contacts will indeed always be at least as essential and extensive as the broader consultations for which the ACC is uniquely fitted.

12 Some structural and organizational issues[1]

Suggestions involving change in United Nations administrative and organizational arrangements must always be subject to the imponderable factor of the personalities, capacities and nationalities of the officials concerned. How many excellent paper schemes have had to be rejected because of this factor or have come to grief because of the appointment of the wrong person to administer them! The converse – poorly conceived schemes being made to work well by the right people – is less common, though not unknown. These considerations are relevant to Part II of this study as a whole, but more particularly to the suggestions made in the present chapter.

The position of the United Nations Development Programme (UNDP)

One may begin by considering the position of UNDP, which continues to pose a number of questions of structure, relationship and organization within the United Nations System. Among such questions are those arising from the fundamental difficulties of making commitments to Governments and agencies for a period of years on the basis of fluctuating contributions pledged usually on an annual basis, of reconciling fully the objective of an integrated programme for the UN System with the autonomy and independent programmes of the participating agencies, those relating to the coordination of field activities financed from regular budgets and from voluntary contributions, and questions affecting UNDP's relations to the Council and the regional commissions. Such issues, and many others, have been analyzed, and solutions have been proposed, in the Capacity Study. The present study must confine itself to one broad question which can reasonably claim a certain priority, namely, how to ensure the fuller integration of UNDP in the central Secretariat of the UN itself, maximum mutual support as between it and the regular UN services, and avoidance of further fragmentation and unjustified administrative disparities. These goals should be pursued with the aim of strengthening UNDP's contribution to development always in view.

The question has been squarely faced by the Group of Experts on the Structure of the UN System, a summary of whose recommendations appears in Appendix 6. Here a few comments must suffice. One change that experience suggests relates merely to attitudes – the fostering of the idea among the staff of UNDP that it is an integral part of the United Nations, under the Secretary-General, whatever the special needs and circumstances that call for special administrative arrangements. It is a change that should not be difficult to induce – indeed it has clearly started; it implies a break with the one-time tenet that, for UNDP, the United Nations organization is – in respect of development work – just one participating and executing agency similar to the specialized agencies. This view not only lacks perspective, but also overlooks the special need and potentialities for collaboration between UNDP and ESA. The fact that UNDP has not used ESA's extensive know-how and network of experts in development planning and programming, indeed the virtual absence of any intellectual contacts between it and CDPPP, has become increasingly indefensible, as the emphasis in UNDP assistance has shifted from development projects to assistance in the preparation, support and implementation of country development programmes. At the same time, there is surely room and need for UNDP's very close association, firstly, with the International Development Strategy and, more particularly through the network of resident representatives, with the processes of review and appraisal, in which so much emphasis is laid on country appraisals, and secondly, and more generally, with the aims of the new international economic order and the broad measures that have been agreed on to implement it, especially the measures to be taken by or directly affecting the developing countries. In order better to meet the second of these desiderata a shift in UNDP priorities and assistance and greater flexibility in its functions have been proposed by the Administrator and approved by the General Assembly.[2]

With regard to the more specific first desideratum, it is clear that the resident representatives, who play a key role in coordination at the country level, should have more direct contact both with the UN's central organs and with the system-wide coordinating arrangements under the Council and ACC. This is all the more important because, as noted in Chapter 2, quite apart from their role in the strategy, one looks to the resident representatives to help the Governments to which they are accredited in reconciling country programmes with global programmes and priorities worked out in the intergovernmental organs of the United Nations and the agencies. There is no easy way and – pending a possible move in the direction of administrative integration of UNDP and the regular UN services, as contemplated later in this chapter and by the Group of Experts – one must rely mainly on a variety of partial measures, such as discussions with Headquarters officials during the periodic meetings of UNDP resident representatives and keeping the latter regularly informed from Headquarters about developments and problems affecting policy and coordination.

In order to meet hardship cases in the field and make it possible to recruit top-quality experts, one cannot but accept the need for exceptional arrangements regarding emoluments and even such factors as housing and home leave, provided they do not threaten the 'common system', at the same time, it is clearly important to reduce the striking discrepancies between the top structure of UNDP and those of UNICEF, UNHCR, UNRWA, UNCTAD, UNIDO and the Department of Economic and Social Affairs. The fact that such discrepancies have arisen calls attention to the differences that exist in the nature and degree of administrative and financial control exercised by the General Assembly through ACABQ in regard to activities financed from the regular budget and those financed from funds voluntarily contributed. It seems important to pursue the efforts now being made to rectify this situation[3] which affects, of course, many aspects of United Nations and agency activity and remains a serious obstacle to coherence and coordination in the system.

Policy coordination within the UN Secretariat

The urgent need to devise some means to avoid placing an impossible additional burden on the Secretary-General has already been stressed, as has the unfortunate effect of the absence of any top-level official who is specifically instructed on behalf of the Secretary-General to bring together, for purposes of policy harmonization, planning and coherence of action, and to be in regular contact with, the executive heads of the various UN organs and programmes. The filling of this gap is certainly one of the most pressing structural reforms required in the interest of coordination and coherence in the United Nations' own machinery. It should be undertaken in such a way as to reinforce the Council's role in overall planning and co-ordination and to facilitate the policy review of operational activities throughout the system which the Council has decided to undertake in alternate years.

It should be possible to achieve this objective as well as the aim discussed earlier in this chapter of relating UNDP more closely with the thinking and activities of the central organs of the United Nations without affecting the constitutions of UNDP and other UN organs and programmes concerned or the basic conditions necessary for their effective functioning; and a good deal could be done by administrative decisions and arrangements without even requiring action by the intergovernmental bodies. However, the possibilities of adjustment within a given organizational framework (in this case, more especially the existence of entirely separate commands) are limited and one may ask whether some broad organizational change likely to further the purposes in view, should not be considered. Might not the need for leadership and coordination in economic and social affairs, as well as the strengthening of mutual support, unity of philosophy and general policy, between UNDP and ESA, be served if UNDP and ESA were placed under a single top official who would be in charge both of UNDP and the Department of Economic and Social Affairs? The post could carry some such title as Director-General for Economic and Social Affairs and a rank comparable to that of the Director-General of a major specialized agency[4] – a rank already held by the Administrator of UNDP.

Such an official's position in the United Nations itself and vis-à-vis the agencies would be second only to that of the Secretary-General and his task would be no less many-sided, exacting and important. A full merger such as occurred in 1966 between EPTA and the Special Fund would not necessarily be involved and UNDP and ESA could even – at least during an experimental period – retain their separate identities, under the supervision of the Administrator-Director-General. The constitutional position of other United Nations organs, such as UNCTAD, UNIDO and UNEP, need not be affected, while they should derive benefit from the regular consultations on general economic and social policy and programmes which it would be one of the tasks of the Administrator-Director-General to organize among the heads of all the United Nations programmes and organs concerned. It would, moreover, naturally fall to him to chair and lead what has so long been needed – an ACC subgroup on development policy and major issues of international economic and social cooperation, consisting of the heads of the agencies and programmes principally concerned. Such a group would presumably absorb the existing IACB.

Any suggestions for a major structural reform of this kind naturally raise a number of questions. Some of these – for example where it might affect adversely UNDP's capacity to raise funds, or undermine the degree of administrative independence which UNDP finds essential, or tend to subordinate the UNDP management to the political constraints to which the Secretary-General is subject – would, it is believed, not be difficult to answer satisfactorily. Then there might be the objections of some specialized agencies and their corresponding ministries in national administrations that such an arrangement would involve an unacceptable further concentration of authority at the centre of the UN development system. The strength of such objections would depend, at least in part, on the future range and character of ESA's work, a matter discussed in the next section. Finally, one must ask how much weight, if any, should be attached to maintaining the separation between operations, on the one hand, and research and general policy, on the other, which underlies the relationship between UNDP and its executing and participating agencies? In this case, the separation has been due to the functional pattern of international organization rather than to administrative principle. While the separation works to the advantage of the parts rather than the whole, the essential problem now is precisely to reinforce the system as a whole and bring together thinking and action. It should be noted, too, that as an administrative principle, the separation of policy and operations is of questionable validity. It had to be abandoned in the 1950s when the United Nations sought to make its maximum contribution to technical assistance. The administration of the United Nations Fund for Drug Abuse Control was first (1971) kept separate from the Division of Narcotic Drugs, but after two years' experience, it was vested, temporarily at least, in the Director of the Division. Still more significant, perhaps, the Executive Director of UNEP has been made responsible for the administration of the Environment Fund as well as for much of the intellectual leadership and general coordination of the programme.

Factors such as those indicated would naturally have to be carefully weighed and the major organizational change envisaged should certainly not be attempted without a strong consensus, as well as circumstances, in its favour. In the meantime, it would be all to the good to proceed with less far-reaching measures, which, even if likely individually to contribute only modestly towards a solution of the major issues, should offer definite advantages. A few suggestions and comments additional to those mentioned earlier are offered below.

Some conclusions and suggestions

Functions, structure and level of the Department of Economic and Social Affairs (ESA)

Apart from the questions of coordination among United Nations units and UNDP–ESA relationships, there are several aspects of organization within the United Nations itself which bear with considerable force on coherence and coordination in the system. The first concerns the functions, structure and level of ESA, or whatever unit may take over its central functions. It has been suggested in several contexts, including the Capacity Study, that the primary and overriding responsibility of ESA is to be a 'brain' as regards general economic and social policy at the disposal of the UN development system as well as the General Assembly and Council. The idea is that ESA should strengthen its capacity to fulfill these central functions and, in order to avoid dissipating its energies, gradually divest itself of its operational and even its substantive responsibilities in such fields as housing, transport and perhaps natural resources[5] as and when they could be taken over by other components of the system, including the regional commissions. ESA would, however, have to retain such responsibilities in regard to economic and social planning, public administration and statistics which have a general non-sectoral bearing on development.[6] It should probably also retain a central role in regard to the application of science and technology to development and in regard to population, a role which no individual agency is in a position to play.

Some shifts in the direction indicated seem to be desirable; certain functions in the area of housing are indeed in the process of being transferred. But (a) the feasibility of making effective alternative arrangements for carrying out central Secretariat functions in other areas seems to be rather limited; and (b) any move that would disrupt the integral relationship between the operational and substantive work, particularly on central issues of economic and social development, should be viewed with caution. In the absence of an overall 'boss' for UN economic and social work, the position in ESA is quite different from that prevailing in the specialized agencies, where the Director-General or Secretary-General, and – in the case of the larger agencies – the Deputy Director-General, direct, control and consult with the various technical units day-by-day and where, consequently, a special operational unit, such as exists in FAO, is neither isolated from, nor unable to contribute to, the thinking and knowledge of the substantive divisions. A completely separate unit for UN technical assistance operations such as existed prior to 1959 (see Chapter 2) could scarcely fail to result not only in increased staffing but also – at a time when it is more than ever important to make optimum use of the resources available – in divided counsels as well as an impoverishment of thinking and experience on both sides of the Department's work.

There are other aspects of the structure of ESA, as well as the question of its 'level' in the UN Secretariat, on which action is long overdue. The Department has at present a range of responsibilities in the economic and social field comparable to that of the staff of a major specialized agency and should surely be provided with a senior structure at least approaching that of the substantive services of such agencies. The need for a modest 'upgrading' of ESA is *sui generis*, and the argument that it would set a precedent for other departments of the United Nations Secretariat, which are in no way comparable with it in size or professional scope, would be difficult to sustain. Nor could one accept objections on the grounds of finance, since the costs involved would be extremely small.[7]

Location in the United Nations Secretariat of central responsibility for ACC affairs and coordination

The tasks performed by the Office for Inter-Agency Affairs and Coordination, which assists the Secretary-General in such matters and in providing the Secretariat for ACC as well as the Chairmanship of the ACC's Preparatory Committee, are often not easy to reconcile. The Office must serve the ACC, speak for that body and assist the agencies vis-à-vis the Council and the General Assembly and their subbodies, serve these organs on matters affecting the agencies and the UN System as a whole, further the interests of the Secretary-General and the UN Secretariat, and promote coordination in economic and social programmes without impinging on the role that ESA, constituting the substantive staff of the Council, alone can play. Changes in emphasis on these different roles are reflected in the changes that have several times been made in the location and status of the unit, the last major change, decided upon in 1969 – namely the full separation of the Office for Inter-Agency Affairs from the Department of ESA – having been at the demand of the heads of some of the major programme agencies.

The question must be faced whether the arrangements that have since been in force are still the best, or whether some further structural shift is desirable. Several new factors bearing on this question have asserted themselves. Firstly, the emphasis on – and need for –

unity of purpose and action throughout the UN system has immensely increased. Secondly, programming – both short-term, for the purpose of the programme budget, and medium-term – has been given ever-greater emphasis as an instrument for the achievement of greater coherence and better coordination throughout the system. Such programming in the economic and social field is carried out within ESA, working directly with the Department of Administration and Management. Thirdly, Governments have shown an increasing interest, not only in institutional matters affecting the system, but also in supervizing the functioning of the coordination processes. They have, moreover seemed inclined to prefer that questions of structure and such aspects of coordination, joint or concerted as the follow-up by different organizations (and more especially by the programmes) of the decisions of the General Assembly's recent special sessions, should be handled primarily by the staff directly servicing the General Assembly and the Council. Finally, for reasons given in earlier chapters, the need to strengthen internal coordination within the United Nations itself has become increasingly urgent.

The 1970 terms of reference of the Office for Inter-Agency Affairs, confirming a long-term practice, required that, among its various tasks, the Office should 'maintain contacts, for purposes of coordination, with the programmes and organizations established by the General Assembly (including UNDP, UNICEF, WFP, UNHCR, UNRWA, UNCTAD, UNIDO and UNITAR)'[8]. The addition in 1973 of the words 'and Coordination' to the title of the Office was generally understood to imply that the Office would henceforth be expected to play a more direct and active part in promoting coordination, internal as well as inter-agency, than in the past; and efforts have been made to fulfill this expectation through the machinery of the ACC. These efforts have not been without a good deal of success, but they have inevitably been limited by the second and third factors referred to above, and have been subject to the usual constraints felt by small coordinating authorities which lack adequate substantive support.

Should the recommendation of the Committee of Experts for the creation of a post of Director-General for Development and International Economic Cooperation be adopted, there is no doubt that that official should have overall responsibility for coordination, as the experts propose. The same could be said in the event of a less far-reaching concentration of authority in the UN Secretariat being decided upon, such as that suggested earlier in the present chapter.

And what if the present structure is maintained without significant change? Some of the factors that prevailed in 1969, including the fear of ESA felt by some of the major agencies, would seem to have lost much of their importance and it is difficult to escape the conclusion that, despite certain advantages still offered by the present arrangements, the balance of advantage would now lie in some form of reintegration of the Office for Inter-Agency Affairs and Coordination in the Department dealing with economic and social programmes and policies.

Travel for coordination purposes

The desirability of strengthening United Nations participation in important agency meetings was mentioned in the review of United Nations–agency relationships in Chapter 10. While programme budgeting should ease the problem of providing the necessary finances, a special earmarking of funds to finance travel for coordination would continue to be required so far as travel funds are allocated to individual departments and divisions for use at their discretion. The same consideration applies in the case of travel from Headquarters to the regions and vice-versa. For the travel credits of ESA and the regional commissions, there are always pressing claims, in respect of representation and the prosecution of substantive work, which tend to be given priority, and the executive secretaries, who tend to travel extensively, must come to the summer sessions of the Council and the winter staff meetings at United Nations Headquarters. Small wonder that there is often no money available for the regional programme staff to meet their colleagues from United Nations Headquarters and from the agencies and programmes at consultations arranged by ACC, or for the appropriate Headquarters staff (including the Regional Commissions Section) to visit regional headquarters for purposes of ensuring coordination. An effective and inexpensive means of checking centrifugal tendencies in the regional commissions themselves is often missed when there is no official present from Headquarters at regular high-level meetings of a regional economic commission to tell the delegates and the staff about the positions taken by the General Assembly, the Council and individual Governments on organizational matters and about the bearing the commission's decisions will have on the United Nations System as a whole. It may be added that there is not enough in the exiguous budget of OIAAC to cover more than a single trip to Bangkok, Santiago, Addis Ababa or Beirut in any one year.

Some conclusions and suggestions

Overlapping jurisdiction and proliferation of coordinating machinery

With the enormous increase in the scope and range of international activity, continued efforts are needed to meet the cases, or dangers, of overlap or disputed 'jurisdiction', between some of the programmes created by the General Assembly and the Council as well as certain agencies. Meetings of Governments or of experts on closely related groups of subjects, such as resources, energy, technology, manpower, environment, are moreover often convened under slightly differing titles by one (or perhaps jointly by two) of the numerous interested units, sometimes indeed with little or no consultation with, or even unbeknownst to, the others; confusion as to responsibilities and failure to achieve satisfactory follow-up naturally follow. At the moment, one is keenly aware of problems of overlap in connexion with the expanding scope of the interests of UNCTAD and the United Nations Environment Programme. The relations of UNCTAD and the United Nations Industrial Development Organization (UNIDO) with the Council and some of the agencies are not yet firmly based or fully satisfactory;[9] furthermore they are, as noted in Chapter 2, complicated by ideological factors. No one would wish to press for immediate decisions in areas where opinions and loyalties have been sharply divided and efforts to find pragmatic solutions conscientiously sought. But now that the attention of the world is concentrated on the means of increasing the effectiveness of the United Nations System in promoting international economic co-operation *for development*, it is clearly timely to reflect, and, if possible, to reach decisions, on the best structural arrangements for achieving that objective.

A system of 'regular consultations' or the creation of joint bodies for coordination may often be necessary, but is time-consuming and expensive and has contributed to much of the proliferation of bodies so generally complained of. Indeed in some cases, the cure is worse than the disease. The explanation that different expertises need to be brought to bear on a problem – as in the case of the parallel responsibilities of WIPO and UNESCO under the Paris Convention on Copyright and the Universal Copyright Convention respectively – is not always convincing. An allocation of overall responsibilities to one agency or a clear division of responsibilities among several of them offers great advantages, where it is feasible.

In general, such problems would without doubt be reduced in scope if there were a move towards bringing close together and reducing the number of semi-independent United Nations intergovernmental organs, as contemplated in Chapter 2. But uncertainty as to competence is also to be found in areas little affected by that factor or by overlapping conventions or controversy over the purposes and methods of the organs concerned. In an earlier chapter, the area of disaster relief has been mentioned in this connexion; one could also mention the potential overlap between UNITAR and the newly established United Nations University (UNU), both being concerned with the study of the problems of peace, human welfare and human survival, both having suffered from the beginning from not a little vagueness and difference of opinion as to their purposes and functioning, and both being dependent on voluntary financing, so far entirely inadequate. It has been assumed that UNITAR will take its place as part of the decentralized University structure, but the modalities of such an arrangement raise difficulties and will need attention as the University becomes a going concern.

13   Expansion, adaptation, concentration and the responsibilities of the General Assembly

Year-by-year the areas in which the United Nations System is active expands and the work takes on new forms. Already there is scarcely any aspect of human life and environment which is the concern of Governments that is not within the programmes of the system: the subject of study, of exchanges of experts and expertise, of standard setting, of assistance programmes. And a host of new problems await international action, from the control of the disposal of nuclear waste to water utilization and resources, from the Law of the Sea and the Ocean Floor, to the attack on the vicious circle of ignorance, poverty and disease affecting two-thirds of mankind. While it reflects the innate strength of the United Nations System, the fact that far too much is being attempted at the same time, that there are far too many committees than can be properly manned by national delegates and supported by national administrations, and far too much pressure to find quick 'solutions' is an inevitable source of administrative weakness. In most instances, there is little enthusiasm on the part of the Membership as a whole to accept the financial obligations involved in new programmes. The line of least resistance is to create a new fund to which interested States may contribute and through which a special staff can be recruited and financed. Hence, as we have seen, the proliferation of semi-autonomous units and funds, the consolidation or rationalization of which it has become a priority task to bring about. The greater concentration of authority and administration required implies a considerable degree of flexibility and adaptation at the intergovernmental as well as the staff level. The rigidities of bureaucracy, which are often an obstacle to reform in national administrations, are probably still more difficult to overcome in international organizations because of the factor of geographical dispersal, the absence of a central international authority and of coordination within most Governments, together with Governments' reactions to anything that might seem directly to affect their own interests or those of their citizens. The recommendation in the Capacity Study that there should be a single focal point – the Council – for intergovernmental control of all activities in the UN develop-ment system, and the analogous recommendation of the Group of Experts for an integration of policy-making and management organs, as well as an integration at the Secretariat level, are ever more clearly valid. While recognizing the strength of the resistances that would have to be overcome, one cannot but conclude that without some moves in this direction, the United Nations System is headed for chaos.

The old controversy regarding the coordinating authorities of the General Assembly and the Council, respectively, has been blunted in recent years. When the General Assembly has taken an initiative it now tends to assign responsibility for ensuring due and coordinated follow-up action to the Council. The Council's responsibility, under the General Assembly's authority, to ensure coordination throughout the system, is scarcely in dispute as a general proposition, subject to the general qualification, noted in Chapter 7 above, regarding the substantial coordinating role necessarily exercised by organizations like UNCTAD, UNIDO and UNEP within certain sectors. But it would be too much to claim that there is unanimity as to the precise scope of the Council's coordinating functions. Unless it is to be purely mechanical and administrative, limited to the scheduling of meetings and so on, the Council's authority cannot be separated from its role as the central organ under the General Assembly dealing with general economic policy. As indicated in the discussion at the end of Chapter 7, this position is widely supported and corresponds to the logic of the Charter,but it is not altogether acceptable to some supporters of a greatly expanded role for UNCTAD. The most serious danger, because it is so largely political, comes from this quarter. Less intract-able are the questions of competence involved between UNEP, whose sectoral functions are promotion and coordination, and ECOSOC, in the latter's capacity of general coordinator of the United Nations System and as governing organ for UN activities in many fields which affect the environment, including housing, urbani-zation, natural resources (including water resources and energy), transportation, and population, and other aspects of social policy. Such issues also arise between UNEP and UNIDO, as well as several of the specialized agencies, one of the major UN programmes (UNIDO) and the regional economic commissions. Any serious con-troversy has so far been avoided, partly no doubt because the essential lesson about coordination has begun to be learned, namely that the exercise of coordinating authority does not imply active intervention or even necessarily the setting up of coordinating machinery in the organ or organs concerned, but rather bringing influence to bear by indirect means, particularly through the Governments, through standing arrangements for referring UNEP's recommendations and comments to other agencies for consideration, and through the established mechanisms for coordination under the Council and ACC.

The fact that the UN has learned somehow to survive so far with a multiplicity of policy-making organs, in no way detracts from the importance of streamlining policy-making, management and secretariat activities and seeking a greater concentration of authority in the Council. Both the Capacity Study and the Group of Experts centered their attention on the sector within the UN organization itself. Action within the UN is the essential first step, but the end in view must be broader; it must include an attempt to introduce a greater measure of coherence and rationality into the UN System as a whole. This task has many aspects. First, it requires review of the structure of the whole system, terms of reference and the functioning of the individual agencies, the possible desirability of mergers. Among the more urgent practical issues to be considered is no doubt that of the overlapping – and to some extent, conflict – between UNCTAD and GATT, and the possibility contemplated in recent UNCTAD documents of replacing both by a comprehensive International Trade Organization. Many other issues that seem in need of such review have been identified in earlier chapters, but the process will not be an easy one, since it must take into account such imponderables as future need for action. What, for example, is to be the extent of IAEA's responsibility a decade or two from now? Or the responsibility of ITU and WMO, and for that matter, of ILO? Or the respective roles of the World Bank Group, with its close mutual support relationship with FAO, UNESCO, WHO and UNIDO, and the UN organization itself, with its regional commissions, and UNDP and other funding authorities? In part recurrent problems of coordination here are of a practical character and it should be possible to deal with them case by case. This applies, for example, to difficulties in carrying out the understandings that exist between the Bank and UNDP and between the Bank and ESA, regarding economic development planning and the relationship between the UNDATS and the Bank's country missions. A coordinating procedure, endorsed by the Council and the General Assembly, already exists in the form of a liaison committee established under the relationship agreement of 1961 between the UN and IDA. This committee, which consists of the President of the Bank Group, the Secretary-General and the Administrator of UNDP, has seldom met in recent years, but perhaps could be usefully revitalized, subject to some adjustment. It might be desirable, for example, to provide for the Secretary-General to be represented by the executive heads of UNCTAD as well as ESA, and to bring in IMF and, as required, the major programme agencies and units of the United Nations. In part, however, the areas referred to go deeper. They involve the relationship between the World Bank and the UN General Assembly in respect of development policy and development programmes and they point towards a possible evolution of a more far-reaching character in development assistance, such as has been hinted at in the Capacity Study as well as by UNCTAD and the recent General Assembly Special Sessions.

The most important immediate question is, however, how to work best within the present structure. Several years ago as indicated earlier, an unsuccessful attempt was made to integrate the agricultural work of FAO and the UN regional economic commissions. One may ask whether a real integration of the work of the UN family is ever to be possible in that or other fields? Is consultation and 'cooperation' among separate autonomous entities, global or regional, the most one can hope for? Can there never – except in the cases of real emergency – be genuine unified UN action? As in the case cited, a good measure of integration without affecting constitutions might have been achieved by simple decisions by the intergovernmental organs of two or more institutions involved to assign full responsibility to one (subject to its obligation to consult when necessary, and to help being provided by the other(s), if needed) rather than to create cumbersome coordination arrangements under which each institution remains in the act.

The task of bringing about a greater measure of coherence and rationality in the UN System as a whole, must, of course, address itself to innumerable underlying issues, such as the distribution of resources among existing UN agencies and organs, ensuring that all sectors in which international cooperation is needed are adequately covered and effectively dealt with. What answer would be given whether, for example, energy as a whole, or transportation as a whole, or the development and utilizations of water resources, are being tackled to the best advantage? Are the present arrangements for determining priorities the best that, in all the circumstances, can be devized? Should more authority be given to the UN General Assembly by the agencies and international organs? Are relations and cooperation adequate between the UN and the great non-UN intergovernmental organs, world-wide and regional, dealing with economic and social policy? The same questions might be posed in regard to UN relations with intergovernmental and non-governmental organs in particular professional fields. Are the lines between the organizations which are Members of the UN System and these non-UN bodies too sharply drawn?

This study must leave such questions largely unanswered, concentrating on the more pedestrian issues of structure and coordination, with due emphasis also on cooperation, in the system as it stands.

Despite their limited scope, the preceding chapters have set out, in effect, an extensive notional agenda for Governments and the central organs of the UN, as well as for the specialized agencies.[1] A beginning might be made almost immediately on carrying out certain parts of it, especially items within the competence of individual Governments, ACC and the secretariats; other parts, calling for intergovernmental decisions and more far-reaching adjustments, might need a period of gestation; others again represent ideas for longer-term study and reflection. It is believed that the United Nations System, basically sound, needs the care of the physician rather than the knife of the surgeon; and the structural changes envisaged are modest. Most of the prescriptions concern adjustments in attitudes and practices that have been accepted in principle, not a few of them being implicit in ideas already put forward by the General Assembly and the Council. The results would depend, above all, on the degree to which the Governments wished to see such a programme as a whole carried out, stage by stage.

If few items have been directly imputed to the General Assembly, this is mainly because so many are likely to go first through a process of study and preliminary consideration by one or more of the other organs, the General Assembly coming in at the end of the process. Nevertheless, the omission might be misleading and should be rectified, since the General Assembly has recently taken such a noteworthy lead in the demand for structural reform and greater efficiency in the system, and in any case has an essential part to play from the outset. The whole movement for reform requires the General Assembly's broad endorsement and steadfast support if it is to generate and maintain the momentum essential to its success. More than that, it is to the General Assembly, drawing on the Council, the United Nations programmes, the specialized agencies and IAEA, as well as the Governments direct and the United Nations Secretariat, that one must mainly look for the flow of ideas and initiatives that is the life-blood of the United Nations System; it is also the forum for review and consideration by the Governments of the world of the performance of the United Nations System, as well as of the nature and shape of desirable change in its institutional arrangements for economic and social cooperation. It is only the General Assembly, as the highest international forum, advised by the Council, or the Council acting under its authority, that can formulate guidelines as to programmes and priorities and as to possible structural changes in the United Nations System as a whole; and it is only through the General Assembly that one can hope to achieve both a full integration of the budgets of United Nations organs, whatever the source of their financing, and a reasonable degree of coherence and complementarity among the United Nations budgets and those of the specialized agencies.

At the same time, on many of the specific issues which have been mentioned, the General Assembly's contribution at some stage would be vital. It has already in hand important immediate work bearing on the functioning of the United Nations System, ranging from the machinery and methods for formulating, reviewing and approving programmes and budgets to consideration of the very bases of international economic relations; it must bear the responsibility for resisting a further fragmentation of the system and any further undercutting of the Council; it will also be responsible for ensuring an appropriate division of functions between itself and the Council, and generally for supporting the assumption by the Council of an active coordinating role. It will be directly concerned with reviewing the mechanisms for administrative and budgetary coordination within the system, including the possibilities of an enlarged role for ACABQ, closer control over voluntary funds and other specific financial and administrative issues; and the Assembly alone can decide on the crucial problem of UNDP's place in the system. While much of what emerges from the deliberations of other United Nations bodies concerning items on the notional agenda can be implemented under their own authority, a considerable part of it will come one day to the General Assembly for endorsement and action.

Reference has been made to the general tendency to expand existing international activity and undertake major initiatives, without due budgetary provision or even the assurance of extra-budgetary funds, and the whole problem of financing has assumed very serious proportions as the work of the UN System has been rapidly enlarged. Without relieving this problem, the improvement in budget presentations would be one modest way of encouraging increased financial support, especially among the larger contributors whose government services and general public are naturally concerned to know precisely how funds are being spent. Despite the improvements in budgetary comparability and presentation that have occurred (and some of the budgets, for example that of FAO, are admirably full and informative), there remain big discrepancies and some agencies still confine themselves to objects-of-expenditure budgets, without a word of text to explain the work that is to be financed.

In dealing with the UN budget, and in reviewing the budgets of the agencies, the Fifth Committee of the General Assembly will no doubt continue to rely on ACABQ and the Under-Secretary-General for Administration and Management, as well as CCAQ and the inspectors; and there is no doubt that the establishment of much closer relations between budgetary and 'programme' planning and administration at the intergovernmental, the 'expert' and the secretariat levels, is a matter of real importance. The attendance of the Chairman of ACABQ at an ACC or CPC meeting once or twice a year has not proved in any way adequate; nor has the brief appearance of a JIU delegation at the ACC spring session. Such arrangements and close contacts at the staff level can usefully be developed; but hope of attaining the end in view would seem to lie mainly in a combination of measures now in train or under consideration, especially the improvement and greater comparability of programme budgets and medium-term plans, and the creation of suitable machinery to assist the Council and ACABQ on programme and coordination matters. On this last point, the decision reached at the General Assembly's Thirtieth Session (see Chapter 9) has been encouraging.

Even without the organization measures mentioned in Chapter 11 above, the difficulties in the way of carrying through to success a programme such as has been outlined should not be underestimated. To seek drastic solutions and root and branch reforms, to abolish constitutions and impose compliance with decisions taken at the centre would serve no good purpose, but it would be, in some ways, an easier course to pursue than merely to encourage and cultivate new approaches and attitudes, in the hope of obtaining gradual improvements. And in this case, however successful the programme, some of the features would remain which have been a source of complaint by Governments and individuals who seek the orderliness of a centralized system. There would still be separate agencies located in a number of different capitals each with its own programme, budget and staff and – in some cases – its own network of regional and sub-regional offices. But one may hope that there would be a difference, and a major one: that the Council's role of coordination and leadership, under the authority of the General Assembly, would be further consolidated and its work and that of the United Nations programmes rendered more coherent; that the United Nations regular Charter responsibilities and its operational activities would have begun, at least, to be more closely integrated and a first step would have been taken towards structural simplification; that the United Nations and the agencies, each providing its expertise and the special points of view of its constituents, and mobilizing the technical support of national administrations, would be working in fuller mutual understanding; that the General Assembly and the Council, in carrying out more purposefully their coordinating and promotional functions, would be aided and advised by a more highly developed and active inter-Secretariat mechanism, under the leadership of the Secretary-General. Such a vision may appear naïve to those who have been exposed to the recent tensions and conflicts within the UN and especially in the General Assembly, and it is, at best, overoptimistic, for no one with experience in international organization can ignore the fact that even the best intentioned Governments are primarily interested in their countries' economic and political ends, rather than in administrative and procedural means. But this does not make it any less important to strive for attainable improvements in the functioning of the system that should help the UN to be of maximum benefit to humanity.

Postscript*
New objectives, prospects and problems

The remarkable Sixth and Seventh Special Sessions of the General Assembly, the developments within the United Nations and the welter of events which have followed have, by and large, confirmed the trends and reinforced the conclusions reached in this study. But new issues and new complexities have been introduced, and the final impact of the whole exercise on structure and coordination of the UN System, and, indeed, on the effectiveness of that system, is still too early to assess. Some description of the economic objectives and policies which have been the real issue, to which structure and organization are only means, cannot be avoided; nor can one altogether overlook the possible effect of the tactics of confrontation, through use of the voting power of the Third World, on the future potentialities for the use of UN machinery for negotiation or even for the objective consideration of world economic problems.

The Declaration on the Establishment of a New International Economic Order, which was adopted at the Sixth Special Session (Resolution 3201 (S–VI)) opens with the portentous words:

We, the Members of the United Nations solemnly proclaim our united determination to work urgently for THE ESTABLISHMENT OF A NEW INTERNATIONAL ECONOMIC ORDER based on equity, sovereign equality, interdependence, common interest and co-operation among all States, irrespective of their economic and social systems which shall correct inequalities and redress existing injustices, make it possible to eliminate the widening gap between the developed and the developing countries and ensure steadily accelerating economic and social development and peace and justice for present and future generations...

It goes on to state that the New International Economic Order should be founded in full respect for a number of principles, some of a primarily political character – including non-interference in the internal affairs of other States, full permanent sovereignty of every

---

* This section is a first draft by Mr Hill. He was unable to put the final touch to it. It has been only slightly revised after the author's demise by a group of his closest former colleagues.

Postscript

State over its natural resources, with the right to nationalization –
others concerned directly with economic policy.

The most important of the economic policy provisions call for the
establishment of a just relationship between the prices of raw materials,
primary commodities, manufactures and semi-manufactured goods
exported by developing countries and the prices of raw materials,
primary commodities, manufactures, capital goods and equipment
imported by them; the extension of active assistance to developing
countries by the whole international community, free of any political
or military conditions; ensuring that the development of developing
countries and the adequate flow of real resources to them shall be a
main aim of the reformed international monetary system; preferential and non-reciprocal treatment for developing countries, whenever
feasible, in all fields of international economic cooperation; securing
favourable conditions for the transfer of financial resources to
developing countries; providing the developing countries access to
the achievements of modern science and technology and promoting
the transfer of technology; the strengthening of mutual economic
trade, financial and technical cooperation among the developing
countries, mainly on a preferential basis; facilitating the role of pro-
ducers' associations within the framework of international cooperation. Emphasis was laid on the role that the Charter of the Economic
Rights and Duties of States, which was then being adopted would
have in the establishment of a new international economic order.

Some of these provisions are of special interest to this study:

...all Member States pledge to make full use of the United Nations
system in the implementation of the present Programme of Action,
jointly adopted by them, in working for the establishment of a new international economic order and thereby strengthening the role of the
United Nations in the field of world-wide cooperation for economic and
social development...

All organizations, institutions, subsidiary bodies and conferences of
the United Nations System are entrusted with the implementation of
the Programme of Action, and the Economic and Social Council
shall define their policy framework and coordinate their activities in
order to enable it to carry out its tasks effectively:

(a) All organizations, institutions and subsidiary bodies concerned within
the United Nations system shall submit to the Economic and Social
Council progress reports on the implementation of the Programme of
Action within their respective fields of competence as often as necessary, but not less than once a year;

154

(b) The Economic and Social Council shall examine the progress reports as a matter of urgency, to which end it may be convened, as necessary, in special session or, if need be, may function continuously. It shall draw the attention of the General Assembly to the problems and difficulties arising in connection with the implementation of the Programme of Action...

It is also stated that: 'Urgent and effective measures should be taken to review the lending policies of international financial institutions, taking into account the special situation of each developing country – *inter alia* – and to ensure more effective participation by developing countries, whether recipients or contributors, in the decision-making process through appropriate revision of the pattern of voting rights...' The last point is made in more detail in the section on International Monetary Reform, which specifically called for a '...review of the methods of operation of the International Monetary Fund, in particular the terms for both credit repayments and "stand-by" arrangements, the system of compensatory financing, and the terms of the financing of commodity buffer stocks, so as to enable the developing countries to make more effective use of them ...'.

Finally, the General Assembly decided to establish a Special Programme to mitigate the difficulties of the developing countries most seriously affected by the economic crises and bearing in mind the particular problems of the least developed and land-locked countries. As a first step, the Secretary-General was requested to launch an emergency operation for the purpose of ensuring essential imports over the subsequent twelve months for the most seriously affected countries and invited the financial support of 'industralized countries and other potential contributors'. He appointed Dr Raul Prebisch, former Secretary-General of UNCTAD, to be his representative for the emergency operation and negotiate for contributions to the Special Account. By the middle of 1975, about $276 million had been contributed direct to the Special Account and allocations provided to more than 40 countries. The Secretary-General's main preoccupation was, however, not to channel funds through that Account, but to encourage maximum contributions through bilateral or other means. Total commitment of emergency assistance during this period, as reported by the donor countries, was approximately $5 billion.[1] The *modus operandi* and the financing of the Special Fund are under study, the hope having been to begin operations with large scale assistance from oil-rich as well as industrialized countries in the course of 1975. This hope has not yet been realized.

Postscript

The Sixth Special Session also made a series of requests to the financial agencies and UNDP, one notable request being to the IMF 'to expedite decisions on the establishment of an extended special facility with a view to assisting the most seriously affected developing countries; the creation of a link between the allocation of special drawing rights (SDRs) and development financing; and the establishment of a new special facility to extend credits and subsidize interest charges on commercial funds borrowed by Member States. Action since taken by the IMF is referred to below.

The two sessions of the Economic and Social Council that followed the Sixth Special Session of the General Assembly again deferred discussion of a number of pending matters, including the future and terms of reference of subsidiary bodies – an item that included institutional arrangements for science and technology and for natural resources. It also deferred action on its own machinery for Programme Coordination in the face of opposing positions, some favouring a relatively small expert body, meeting for relatively long periods, others a larger intergovernmental group which might carry more direct political authority. It, however, adopted a number of organizational measures concerning the implementation of a programme of action on the establishment of a new international economic order and created a Preparatory Committee for the Seventh Special Session of the General Assembly, open to the whole UN Membership.[2] It also set up a new Commission on Transnational Corporations, a substantive achievement of importance. No discussion took place on UN–specialized agency relationships, but the Council had before it a descriptive and analytical report[3] on the subject which the Secretary-General had been requested to prepare, together with the views of the executive heads of those agencies.[4] In addition, the Council had before it the original version of the present study, which was made available by UNITAR. The positions taken in the Secretary-General's report and the UNITAR paper were very similar on all key issues, such as the need to enhance the coordinating authority of the Council and to arrest the proliferation of decision-making organs, the importance of mobilizing political will to bear on issues of economic development, and the importance of inter-secretariat cooperation.

The only point of minor divergence between the Secretary-General's report and the UNITAR paper concerned the question of the review of the UN–agency agreements. The Secretary-General's report suggested that the Council might wish either to: (a) 'negotiate supplementary agreements with the agencies, which would include the necessary modifications to the present agreements as well as additional provisions in respect of questions which have arisen since the conclusion of such agreements. . .' or '(b) defer revision until the General Assembly has decided upon the structural changes that it considers necessary. . .' The item was, in the event, deferred until 1975 and then until 1976.

The reports of the executive heads of the specialized agencies and IAEA referred to above contained a number of views and suggestions of interest. Among them was the recognition most explicitly by the then Directors-General of ILO (Mr Jenks) and FAO (Mr Boerma) of the overriding importance of policy coordination which the Council and the General Assembly alone can ensure, and a strong plea for more leadership on broad policy by the Council, as well as more reliance by the Council on the agencies' expertise and advice. A passage from the report of the President of the World Bank, Mr Robert McNamara, was likewise significant, especially because of the Bank's traditionally independent attitude. Referring to the steps which the Bank Group is taking to tackle the problem of poverty in the developing world, he wrote: 'These plans and programs are an implicit response to the guidance which ECOSOC has provided in identifying the areas in which the interests of all parts of the international community converge and on which a broad measure of consensus can be achieved. This is a unique and an essential function. . .' Most of the reports emphasized the essential role of ACC in the coordination of programmes. The then Director-General of UNESCO, the late Mr Maheu, went more deeply into the changes needed in the UN System in his report to the 1974 UNESCO General Conference on 'Ways and Means whereby UNESCO could contribute to the Establishment of a New International Economic Order' (18 C/103). He noted the powerful influence exercised by some organizations, first and foremost the International Bank and the UNDP, on the programmes of the specialized agencies, and noted 'that the secretariats of these two banks . . . quite often make decisions concerning Member States' requests in UNESCO's sphere of competence which do not take UNESCO's views into account or may even set them aside'. Secondly, Mr Maheu felt that the development of true concerted planning for the economic and social activities of the system as a whole must be a primary objective and that this calls for new arrangements to strengthen the central organs at the intergovernmental and secretariat levels. Among possible innovations to meet this need, he suggested the establishment at the secretariat level 'of a joint planning body, associated with ACC, which would directly serve the Economic and Social Council'.

Postscript

The third main issue raised by Mr Maheu was that of the increased resources he felt would be required if the UN System was to carry out its tasks effectively, and of the importance of using such increases, in the first place, to bolster the regular budgets of the UN and the specialized agencies which provide the foundation for the operational activities generally financed from extra-budgetary resources.

Actions taken within the United Nations

The Sixth Special Session asked that '...All the activities of the United Nations System to be undertaken under the Programme of Action as well as those already planned, such as the World Population Conference, the World Food Conference, the Second General Conference of the United Nations Industrial Development Organization and the mid-term review and appraisal of the International Development Strategy for the Second United Nations Development Decade should be so directed as to enable the special session of the General Assembly on development, called for under Assembly Resolution 3172 (xxviii) of 17 December 1973, to make its full contribution to the establishment of the new international economic order...'

We may take a brief look at the way the request of the Sixth Special Session was taken into account in two of these activities; firstly, the World Food Conference and secondly, UNIDO.

The idea of a World Food Conference at the ministerial level, to meet the alarming food shortages confronting vast areas of the world, came from the Algiers meeting of the Heads of State of the Non-Aligned Nations in September 1973. Their suggestion that it be organized by FAO and UNCTAD encountered difficulties, especially because the USSR was not a member of FAO, and the USA, the world's principal supplier of grain, preferred the responsibility to be borne by the UN as a whole, rather than by one of its subsidiary organs. So the proposal which was put before the General Assembly by the USA in October, and eventually adopted, was for a conference to be held in Rome, under UN auspices, ECOSOC to have overall coordinating authority.

The Rome Conference, held in November 1974, recommended an ambitious long-term international approach to the problem, which was, in part, the fulfillment of a plan for a World Food Bank, that had been advanced by Sir John (later Lord) Boyd Orr, when he was Director-General of FAO in the late 1940s, but this approach went

158

much further. The Conference placed primary emphasis on increasing food production in the developing countries, and especially those with a chronic food deficit, and on ensuring the availability of food aid of at least 10 million tons of cereal grains for each of the coming three years, as well as the establishment of adequate reserves. It recommended the establishment of a large International Fund for Agricultural Development to finance development projects primarily for food production in developing countries; and the establishment of a World Food Council at the ministerial or plenipotentiary level, to be serviced within the framework of FAO with Headquarters in Rome, to function as an organ of the UN, reporting to the General Assembly through ECOSOC, its members to be nominated by ECOSOC for election by the General Assembly. The Council should, *inter alia* 'review periodically major problems and policy issues affecting the world food situation, and the steps being proposed or taken to resolve them by Governments, by the United Nations system and its regional organizations, and should further recommend remedial action as appropriate'. The Conference recommended further the establishment of a Committee on World Food Security as a standing committee of the FAO Council to keep under review and evaluate the current and prospective demand, supply and stock position for basic food-stuffs, and that the Intergovernmental Committee of the UN–FAO World Food Programme be reconstituted so as to enable it to help evolve and coordinate short- and longer-term food aid policies recommended by the Conference, in addition to discharging its existing functions. The reconstituted committee should be called, and function as, the Committee on Food Aid Policies and Programmes.

Both the Committees – on World Food Security and on Food Aid Policies and Programmes – should submit periodical and special reports to the World Food Council, as should the Governing Board of the proposed International Fund for Agricultural Development and the FAO Commission on Fertilizers. Periodic reports to the World Food Council from UNCTAD, through ECOSOC, on the world food trade situation and relevant information from GATT were also called for. FAO was requested to examine any new arrangements which might be necessary in regard to the development of a Global Information System and Early Warning System, and ECOSOC was asked to examine whether organizational rearrangements in the UN System in respect of nutrition might be justified; IBRD, FAO and UNDP were asked to organize a Consultative Group on Production and Investment in Developing Countries and to keep the WFC informed of its activities to increase, coordinate and improve the efficiency of financial and technical assistance to agricultural production in developing countries; and the Development Committee of IBRD and IMF were asked to keep under review the adequacy of external resources available for these purposes.

The General Assembly duly approved the resolutions of the Conference the following month, established the World Food Council, and requested the Secretary-General, in consultation with the Director-General of FAO, to set up the secretariat and report to the General Assembly's Thirtieth Session on the implementation of the Conference's resolutions. Apart from the expansion of international action all this represented, the change in organizations' relationships involved within the UN System was not without interest. Although the organs of FAO will have to bear the brunt of the work envisaged, it was clearly intended that the world food problem as a whole was one which required policy decisions, and should be kept under constant scrutiny, at the highest level of government and by the central political organs of the United Nations. The relevant provisions may be contrasted with those adopted in 1962, when the World Food Programme was created as a joint enterprise of the UN and FAO, reporting to both organizations equally. The UN has since taken little part in WFP's affairs, including the choice of its successive Executive Directors. How far this practice will change in the case of the WFC and how far the Council will be able to fulfill the role envisaged for it, are difficult to foresee. One wonders how a Council dependent for its expertise and servicing on the FAO staff in Rome, while reporting to ECOSOC, can exercise the independent authority envisaged: certainly, the first session of the Council was unimpressive as regards accomplishment and level of government representation. Be that as it may, one notes that the Conference has already to its credit many important follow-up actions. Prominent among these are the preparations already well advanced for the establishment of the International Fund for Agricultural Development. That Fund will no doubt provide valuable and much-needed resources; at the same time, being organically separate, not only from the UN and the FAO, but also from UNDP and WFP, there is no little risk that it will constitute a fresh source of duplication and confusion.

In the other instance, at the Second General Conference of UNIDO, held in Lima in March 1975, the keynote was the assertion of intent by almost all Governments that by the year AD 2000 the share of the developing countries in the world's industrial production would, so far as possible, be raised from the present 6 % to approximately 25 % – a higher goal than that set by the International Development Strategy. Among the many means to this end were to be the creation of a major Industrial Development Fund under UNIDO's control; the transformation of UNIDO into a specialized agency; measures to be taken by industrialized countries to relocate and promote industries in the developing world and to facilitate the transfer of technology, and the creation at the Secretariat level, of a Coordinating Committee of all interested UN bodies, under the Chairmanship of UNIDO's Executive Director.

The Declaration and Plan of Action adopted at Lima represents in large measure aspiration and hope, for UNIDO has so far been suffering less from a deficiency of means or from constraints resulting from its status as an organ of the General Assembly than from an insufficiency of requests for its service in national development programmes and its relative isolation from the principal sources of finance. One cannot but note also that certain of the actions proposed represent a further fragmentation of the UN System and that the new draft constitution of UNIDO, since prepared under the decisions of the Industrial Development Board, would give it the full autonomy that, in the case of the existing specialized agencies, has been so widely criticized over the years. The Lima proposals and the declaration were adopted by huge majorities of the Third-World countries in spite of certain reservations by some industrialized countries and have now been approved at the Thirtieth Session of the General Assembly. The slightly incongruous intergovernmental exercise of first separating a UN organization from its parent body and then establishing formal agreement between them was to be worked out.

In the general policy area, the Second Committee of the previous regular session (the Twenty-ninth) of the General Assembly was largely occupied with the implementation and underpinning of the decisions of the Sixth Special Session, pride of place being taken on the one hand by the adoption of the Charter of the Economic Rights and Duties of States and on the other by certain decisions made in direct preparation for the Seventh Special Session. These decisions referred first to the timetable of the Preparatory Committee for the Special Session, which had been set up by ECOSOC, and went on to request the Secretary-General (i) in cooperation with the heads of organizations directly concerned, to prepare and submit to the Preparatory Committee 'a comprehensive report on the state of international economic activities, focusing on constraints of a general policy nature which face the implementation of a programme of action on the establishment of a New International Economic Order...'; and (ii) 'in close consultation with Member States, to appoint immediately a small group of high-level experts to submit a study containing proposals on structural changes within the UN System so as to make it fully capable of dealing with problems of international cooperation in a comprehensive manner....'.

These requests gave rise to two important documents. The first – of more ephemeral interest – generally known as the Report on 'Constraints' (E/AC.62/8 of May 1975) constituted a statement of the international economic situation at mid-decade. The report reviewed general economic conditions and also touched upon other special issues such as trade, financing, international monetary reform, agriculture and industrialization. These aspects were presented in the context of the progress in implementing the programme of action and the international development strategy, and indicated possibilities for corrective action. It represented the sort of contribution that the international secretariat can and must be able and willing to make if the intergovernmental machinery of the United Nations is to function in a responsible manner. It is no reflection on its value that it evoked practically no comment from the Preparatory Committee or other intergovernmental organs.

The second document followed from the appointment of a highly distinguished and geographically well-balanced Group of 25 Experts. The Chairman of the Group was Al Noor Kassym of Tanzania, a former Secretary of the Economic and Social Council, and its Rapporteur, Professor Richard Gardner of Columbia University, former United States Assistant Secretary of State for International Organization Affairs; its members included such people as Dr Manuel Perez Guerrero, former Secretary-General of UNCTAD. Having met from time to time during March to May 1975, it produced a report entitled 'A New United Nations Structure for Global Economic Cooperation' (Document E/AC.62/9). This report, on which certain comments will be offered in the next section of this chapter, together with the Secretary-General's Report on Constraints referred to above, were available as planned to the June meeting of the Preparatory Committee, together with a number of key position papers which represented a considerable *rapprochement* on certain policy matters and avoided some of the more contentious issues. The papers from the 77 and the European Economic Community may be mentioned in particular. The first covered international trade (the regulation of the raw material and commodity market and access to markets of developed countries for raw materials and manufactures of developing countries), the transfer of real resources for financing the development of developing countries and international monetary reform, science and technology, industrialization, food and agriculture and restructuring of the economic and social sectors of the UN System. The submission from the European Economic Committee concentrated on industrialization, committing itself to strong measures pursuant to the Lima Declaration and Plan of Action, with particular reference first to the establishment of a consultation system within UNIDO, and other UN agencies where appropriate, with a view to coordinating the policies of the developed and developing countries, secondly to incentives for the establishment of industrial concerns in developing countries, and third to the working out of joint industrial cooperation agreements.

Signs of such *rapprochement* had appeared earlier in the conclusion at Lomé in February 1975 of a comprehensive agreement between the 9 members of the European Economic Community and 46 developing countries of Africa, the Caribbean and the Pacific. This agreement embodied many of the undertakings on the part of the 9 that had been requested by the 77 in regard to trade arrangements, the stabilization of commodity export earnings, industrial cooperation, financial and technical cooperation and the establishment of appropriate machinery to ensure that the agreed arrangements are carried out. Another landmark in the harmonization of policies was provided by the Declaration on Relations with Developing Countries adopted by the OECD in May, making clear the determination of the OECD's members 'to pursue the dialogue with the developing countries ... in order to make real progress towards a more balanced and equitable structure of international economic relations'; yet another was the statement by the British Prime Minister, Mr Harold Wilson, at the Kingston Meeting of Commonwealth Heads of Government in April on the need to find ways to correct the relationship between the rich and the poor countries, with special emphasis on the needs of the poorest. Such developments were paralleled by the constructive attitude and restraining influence exercised by a number of statesmen from developing countries. How effective and successful such actions, buttressed by the ceaseless efforts of the Secretariat, proved to be is in part reflected in the documents that came before the Preparatory Committee, but became fully apparent only when the Seventh Special Session opened on September 1st.

So far as the UN organs and agencies are concerned, the Rome and Lima meetings dealt essentially with the longer term, even though – and this was strikingly true in the case of food supplies – they

163

stimulated emergency bilateral action. Also of a long-term character were the all-important efforts, at the centre of which stands the IMF, to work out a new international monetary system and (likewise), the current GATT negotiations. The general objectives of these negotiations are the expansion and further liberalization of world trade and the securing of additional benefits for developing countries. Under the Tokyo Declaration of 102 participating Governments of September 1973, the interests of the developing countries are specifically to be kept in view, one of the subsequent aims being to achieve full application of generalized preferences for the manufactures of such countries.

In so far as the immediate financial and balance of payments difficulties – difficulties threatening the lives of people as well as of local industries and development plans – of so many of the poorer countries could be dealt with through UN organs, it was mainly by the International Monetary Fund and the World Bank.

In the Spring of 1974, IMF created an oil facility, financed largely by oil-producing countries, to help members meet the balance of payments impact of the increased cost of petroleum products. Assistance was given to some forty members for a total amount of almost 2·5 billion SDRs. A joint Ministerial Committee of the Governments of the Fund and the World Bank, known as the Development Committee, was set up in September 1974, to deal with the various aspects of the transfer of real resources to developing countries. At its behest, the Fund enlarged its facilities for compensatory financing to meet the export fluctuations of developing countries and to assist members in connexion with the financing of commodity buffer stocks. It also created a special Trust Fund to provide largely concessional resources to meet the balance of payments needs of low-income developing countries for the next few years. The World Bank unanimously supported the establishment of a 'third window' lending facility – a subsidized facility providing loans at rates intermediate between the regular bank rates and those of IDA for the benefit of poorer countries.

In 1975 the Fund's oil facility was extended, with the help of finance from both oil-exporting and industrial countries, to an amount close to 4 billion SDRs and steps were taken to create a subsidy account for the purpose of reducing the interest payable by the poorest countries under the oil subsidy. As a result of the Kingston Agreement in 1976, measures have also been taken to increase the total size of the Fund itself, and part of the profits the IMF will realize on the sale of a portion of its gold holdings and the total additional resources these and other measures should make available for the developing countries is expected to exceed $3 billion a year. The Bank has created an interest-subsidizing Fund for the purpose of subsidizing the so-called 'third window', through which it hopes to be able to provide concessional loans to a total of as much as $1 billion. At the same time, it is planning to raise the level of its regular lending programme to some $40 billion over the years 1975–1980, a 58% increase in real terms from the previous five-year period. Furthermore, it is preparing to seek a further replenishment of IDA.

Certain decisions of the Twenty-ninth Regular Session of the General Assembly were in the direction of bringing greater cohesion to the system. These include the resolution stressing the need for further reorganization of ECOSOC in order to enable it to fulfill its expanded role; and some far-reaching changes proposed by the Secretariat were, in fact, adopted by the Economic and Social Council shortly after. Another such action was the final establishment of the International Civil Service Commission (see Chapter 3) and the adoption of the Agreement bringing WIPO – an existing intergovernmental organization, closely concerned, *inter alia*, with the transfer of technology – into relationship with the United Nations as a specialized agency. The Agreement followed the pattern of the earlier agreements but included some additional provisions, on cooperation in providing technical assistance in the field of intellectual creation, in promoting the transfer of technology to developing countries and – within the field of its competence – in giving effect to the General Assembly Resolution on Decolonization. The clause concerning the coordinating authority of the General Assembly and the Council was also made more explicit.

On certain other matters, however, the General Assembly moved in the opposite direction. As already noted, it invited the forthcoming UNIDO Conference to consider a shift in its status to that of an autonomous specialized agency; furthermore, it envisaged the creation of an unprecedented number of new semi-autonomous voluntary funds. These included the United Nations Special Fund for Emergency Relief and Development Assistance to the most seriously affected countries, which has been proposed by the Sixth Special Session; an International Fund for Agricultural Development recommended by the World Food Conference; an International Habitat and Human Settlements Foundation, to be funded by voluntary contributions; a revolving Fund for the Exploration and Utilization of Natural Resources; and the United Nations University. It also asked for additional resources for the Capital Development Fund, for

Postscript

UNICEF and for UNITAR. The proliferation of such funds, as we shall see, was one of the subjects on which the expert group on structural changes within the UN System was to have some important proposals to make.

The proposed new United Nations structure for global economic cooperation

The Report of the Group of Experts entitled 'A New United Nations Structure for Global Economic Cooperation' has been called by Secretary-General Waldheim 'the first real endeavour since the adoption of the UN Charter to review in a comprehensive way the institutions of the UN System as an instrument for achieving the goals of the international community'.[5] It is so central to the subject of the present study that a full summary of it must be included. Such a summary, which was made by the UN Secretariat and appeared as an annex to the Group's Report, is reproduced in Appendix 6 below.

The first version of the present study was before the Group of Experts and the broad lines of the conclusions reached as regards major weaknesses in the present arrangements and the essential roles and functioning of the General Assembly, ECOSOC and the Secretariat, are very similar in the two documents. Similar too is the emphasis on the need for much consultation and adjustment and a step-by-step approach if the broad thrust of the recommended reforms is to be achieved. However, the findings of the UNITAR paper were much more limited in scope – as are those in the present study – and more concerned with attitudes and practices than with structure; where they deal with structure, moreover, they are tentative and general, while many of the Experts' proposals are precise and specific; they devote more attention than those of the Experts to relations and cooperation between the UN and the specialized agencies, and concentrate on a few areas of importance only, notably, the role of ECOSOC and the General Assembly in regard to co-ordination, the problem of proliferation of organs and the fragmentation and dispersal of authority, and the contribution that can be made by the staff and by ACC. Little is said of the operational side of the UN's work. While references are made to coordination in sectoral fields, such as trade, monetary reform, development financing, food and agriculture and industrial development, little is said about the possible structural implications. Above all, the Experts responded to a far broader mandate than the search for greater cohesion and coordination in the system. Their proposals are designed, in the words of paragraph 14 of their Report, to:

(a) Deal with international economic and social problems in a more effective and comprehensive manner, with better coordination throughout the United Nations system as a whole; (b) Harmonize, as far as possible, the views and approaches of Member countries towards these problems; (c) Contribute to a significant improvement in the transfer of real resources and technology to developing countries; (d) Promote economic cooperation between States, including those with different social systems; (e) Increase the capacity of the United Nations system to provide essential services for all its Members; (f) Improve the management of United Nations resources available for assistance to the developing countries so as to maximize the benefit to these countries; (g) Respond effectively to new opportunities, problems and challenges arising from changing requirements of world economic cooperation; (h) Foster better utilization of the capabilities of developing countries for economic and technical cooperation among themselves; (i) Make the United Nations a more effective instrument for the establishment of a new, more rational and just international order . . .

Some of the Experts' proposals seem to have been widely approved, including the central proposal regarding the rationalization of the Council's Sessions. Others have been well-received in many quarters though not always without certain questions and reservations. One may mention a number of areas where such reservations have been most apparent.

The Experts' Report was referred to by several speakers at the Summer (Fifty-ninth) Council, and was the principal subject of discussion at the Joint Meeting of the Policy and Programme Coordination Committee that preceded it. At that joint meeting (E/5709), the Secretary-General made clear the general support of the executive heads for the Experts' proposals, emphasizing that they supported all measures that would 'serve to strengthen the effectiveness of the General Assembly and the Council in carrying out their Charter responsibilities for global policy-making'. A number of special points were made, the Secretary-General for example stating that the UN should maintain a substantial role in the field of social policy and again that the relationship between the proposed Advisory Committee on Economic Cooperation and Development should be such as to enable all Members of the ACC to make their full contribution to the Committee's tasks. The Chairman of the PPCC, Ambassador Smid of Czechoslovakia, observed that the structural changes should not be considered as an end in themselves, but as a necessary means for the implementation of the Declaration and Programme of Action for the Establishment of the New International Order and also for the implementation of the Charter of Economic Rights and Duties of States.

Postscript

Both executive heads and government representatives appeared to support the expanded facilities offered for interdisciplinary analysis and research as a basis for more effective global policy making by the central organs, the creation within the central secretariat of joint research and planning staff drawn from different agencies, as well as the more effective integration of planning and operations and the consolidation of the various funds. The Administrator of UNDP backed the recommendations on the organization of operational activities which were in line with the consensus reached at the Governing Council's Twentieth Session.

The first, and perhaps more important recommendation of the Expert Group's Report, relates to the future arrangements in the field of international trade, on which there was some division in the Group which the Report leaves deliberately vague. The experts from the developing economies tended to favour equipping UNCTAD with the elements necessary to transform it gradually into a World Trade Organization, while those from the developed countries tended to support a strengthening of GATT and bringing the latter into closer association with the UN. There were also differences of view as to how far any new international trade organizations should deal not only with matters directly concerned with trade, but also other issues such as restrictive business practices, transfer of technology, private investment and transnational enterprises.

Secondly, there was the proposal that the Council should establish on the pattern laid down for UNCTAD in 1964, but never put into operation, small negotiating groups to deal with key economic issues requiring further negotiations, with a view to improving the chances of achieving agreed solutions. Great importance is attached by several industrialized countries to procedures of this kind – for which a reasonable time, perhaps a year or even on occasion two years must be allowed – in order to avoid the 'confrontations' that have occurred at ECOSOC, the General Assembly and in other bodies. Any mandatory procedures of this kind tend to be opposed by developing countries on the ground that they limit the authority of the majority, but in practice there is often considerable leeway and possibility of friendly arrangements for the purpose in view. Another such proposal refers to the dismantling of much of ECOSOC's subsidiary machinery, direct responsibility for whose work would be taken over by the Council itself, using the devices of specially oriented sessions and/or by the appointment of *Ad Hoc* groups. Excluded would be the regional commissions, expert bodies performing highly technical work that cannot be performed by the Council, and certain bodies like the Commissions on Human Rights and on Transnational Corporations. There has been some criticism that this proposal may go too far on the grounds firstly that if ECOSOC is to perform its central task of policy formulation and harmonization, it will not have time to cope with the numerous subjects now being handled by its commissions and committees (reference being frequently made to questions of science and technology) and secondly, that many Governments now participating in the Council's work through its subsidiary organs would lose the opportunity of doing so. The recommendation that ECOSOC assume responsibility for the policy functions of the Governing Council of UNEP, with the management of the UNEP Fund being taken over by the proposed Development Operations Board, has also encountered opposition.

There has naturally been much question as to the desirability and feasibility of the Experts' radical proposal of consolidating operational activities and funds for the purpose of more effective policy making, administration and management, into a new United Nations Development Authority. The proposal would maintain the separate identity of different funds while bringing them under a single authority; a related proposal aiming at integrating the inter-governmental policy-making organs with the establishment of a single Operations Board responsible for the general conduct of the UN Development Authority has also been criticized as unrealistic and going too far in the direction of centralization.

This list of proposals must include that for the establishment within the UN Secretariat of a new post of Director-General for Development and International Economic Cooperation, who would be directly responsible to the Secretary-General and *primus inter pares* among the executive heads of UN organizations and the agencies dealing with economic and social affairs. It should also include proposals for (a) reorienting the work of the new Director-General's staff to assist the sectoral organs of the UN in the development of global priorities, the formulation of system-wide decisions and priorities and the overview of the implementation of such decisions by the various components of the system; and (b) the more disputed proposal for divesting ESA gradually of most of its sectoral technical functions and especially its sectoral operational responsibility. There has also been resistance to the idea that the activities of individual agencies should be directed more towards planning standard-setting and back-stopping than to actual execution of projects.

Finally, there is the question of the relation of ACC to the proposed Advisory Committee on Economic Cooperation and Development, under the Chairmanship of the new Director-General for Development and Economic Cooperation. This Advisory Committee would have the executive heads of the IMF and IBRD, ILO, FAO, UNESCO and WHO, the Executive Secretaries of the Regional Economic Commissions, the proposed Deputy Director-General for Research and Policy and the Administrator of the new UN Development Authority, as *ex officio* members. The Director-General of GATT and heads of other agencies would be invited to participate as necessary. The proposal for this committee is not altogether to the liking of the agencies and programmes excluded from participation in it. This recommendation addressed itself to a problem which has been raised earlier in this study and is in line with the thinking of this writer, provided the committee is placed within the framework of ACC.

Recent developments within the United Nations

At the Seventh Special Session, the burning priorities were the broad issues of international economic policy and cooperation, together with the immediate needs especially of the most seriously affected developing countries, which, despite some international and much bilateral aid, remained at least as acute as a year before. Neither the Experts' Report, nor the ideas that had come up or were in the air on restructuring were discussed by the Special Session which recommended (Resolution 3362 (S–VII)) that the regular Session immediately following should establish an *Ad Hoc* Committee of the whole of the General Assembly, open to the participation of all States, 'to prepare detailed action proposals with a view to initiating the process of restructuring the UN system so as to make it more fully capable of dealing with problems of international economic cooperation and development in a comprehensive and effective manner'. A further objective was included, namely that the restructuring 'should make the system more responsive' to the requirements of the two basic policy documents approved by the General Assembly in 1974 – the Declaration and Programme of Action on the Establishment of a New International Economic Order and the Charter of the Economic Rights and Duties of States'.

The *Ad Hoc* Committee was to take into account in its work the proposals and documentation submitted in preparation for the Seventh Special Session and other decisions, including the May 1975 report of the Group of Experts on the Structure of the UN System, the records of the Economic and Social Council, the Trade and

Development Board, the Governing Council of the United Nations Development Programme and the Seventh Special Session of the General Assembly, as well as the results of the forthcoming deliberations on institutional arrangements at the Fourth Session of the United Nations Conference on Trade and Development (UNCTAD) (Nairobi, 5–28 May) and of the Governing Council of the United Nations Environment Programme (Nairobi, 3 March–14 April).

The *Ad Hoc* Committee was duly set up and requested to report to the Thirty-first regular session of the Assembly (1976) through the Economic and Social Council. In addition the tasks set out in the resolution just cited, was asked 'to examine the role of the ACABQ within the context of possible modifications in the structure and functioning of the UN, including the ACABQ mandate and composition' (Resolution 3392 (xxx)). The Committee held an organizing session in November and elected as its Chairman, Kenneth K. S. Dadzie, Ambassador of Ghana in Geneva, who had long served with distinction in the Secretariat, having held among other posts that of Deputy Head of the Office of Inter-Agency Affairs and Coordination. Arrangements were made for further sessions in February–March and for the setting up of an informal working group under the Chairman of the Committee to meet between the second and third sessions. The executive heads of all specialized agencies, United Nations programmes and regional economic commissions were invited to participate personally in the second session.

To revert to the Seventh Special Session, a remarkable degree of agreement was reached on the broad measures that should form 'the basis and framework for the work of the competent bodies and organizations of the UN system'. Intensive consultation and negotiation has indeed been under way on many aspects of international trade, the transfer of real resources to developing countries, monetary reform, industrial cooperation, the transfer of technology, food and agriculture – consultations and negotiation, the results of which surface from time to time as in the case of the momentous Kingston Agreement of the IMF, and the establishment of the International Fund for Agricultural Development.

Action has by no means been confined to UN bodies. An *ad hoc* international conference at the ministerial level was called in Paris in December on the initiative of the French Government to deal directly with a number of issues including raw materials and energy. While various forms of relationship and cooperations have been arranged between this conference and the UN System, there is no organic relationship between them; the conference has its own secretariat and indications were not lacking that the four main commissions into which it was divided, each composed of representatives of 8 developed and 19 underdeveloped countries would function in considerable independence. It is already apparent that in certain agencies (IMF, IBRD, FAO, UNIDO) main structural changes are required to meet the new tasks laid upon them; changes no less significant will no doubt be canvassed in others – GATT and UNCTAD, first and foremost. The centre of balance and distribution of authority in the UN Development System may be shifted; new relationships will inevitably be required between IBRD and the UN.

Certain broad trends of the utmost, and not altogether reassuring, significance for our study have also been emerging. One is the *accelerated* creation of independent entities, defying the timeless principles of Occam's razor. This is happening – as in the case of the Agricultural Development Fund – not because of any administrative advantage it presents, but essentially because use of any existing organ would raise political difficulties for one of the States or groups whose cooperation is vital. Another trend is to make coordination rather than action the main function of the new organ, to the detriment of the work to be performed and with the danger of making confusion worse confounded. The World Food Council is a case in point. A third is exemplified in the Paris Conference, namely, the setting up of alternative and unrelated procedures for the achievement of particular ends – another process that, however worthy its object may be and occasionally valuable for political reasons, is inevitably fraught with the danger of frustration and wire-crossing.

A Resolution was adopted by the General Assembly (A/RES/32/197) on 20 December 1977 giving effect to many of the proposals referred to in this book – notably a new post of Director-General 'to ensure leadership and coherence' in the whole UN System of agencies. Many of the details of the Resolution remain to be worked out by the Secretary-General.

Appendix 1
Abbreviations and glossary of institutions

ACABQ	Advisory Committee on Administrative and Budgetary Questions – An organ of the General Assembly. (See Appendix 2.)
ACC	Administrative Committee on Coordination – Standing Committee set up in virtue of ECOSOC Resolution 13 III, consisting of the executive heads of all specialized agencies, with the executive heads of all UN Programmes participating fully, under the Chairmanship of the Secretary-General.
CCAQ	Consultative Committee on Administrative Questions – Subsidiary organ of ACC, with panels on Personnel and Financial and Budgetary subjects, composed of senior administrative officers of the UN, the specialized agencies and UN Programmes.
CCPI	Consultative Committee on Public Information – (See CESI below.)
CDF	Capital Development Fund – Was established under General Assembly Resolution 2186 XXI, to assist developing countries by supplementing existing resources of capital assistance through grants and loans, particularly long-term loans, free of interest or at low interest rates. Sufficient funds have not been forthcoming to enable the CDF to become operational and the Administrator of UNDP was requested in virtue of General Assembly Resolution 2321 XXII to perform the functions of the Managing Director of the CDC.
CDPPP	Centre for Development Planning, Projections and Policies – A major unit of the UN Department of Economic and Social Affairs, responsible for research on world economic conditions, trends and prospects and on policies relating to economic development and stability; acts as substantive secretariat for the Committee for Development Planning and the Committee for Review and Reappraisal of the Intergovernmental Development Strategy.
CESI	Centre for Economic and Social Information – Part of the UN Office of Public Information with special responsibility for providing informational support for the development activities of the UN and for coordinating economic and social

information activities of the UN System. Its inter-agency Programme Committee was merged with the UN's Consultative Committee on Public Information (CCPI) in 1974 to form the Joint United Nations Information Committee.

CPC   Committee for Programme and Coordination – (See Appendix 2.)

ECA   Economic Commission for Africa – Set up by ECOSOC, with its seat at Addis Ababa, in 1958. (See Appendix 2.)

ECAFE   Economic Commission for Asia and the Far East – (See ESCAP and Appendix 2.)

ECB   Environmental Coordination Board – (See UNEP and Appendix 2.)

ECE   Economic Commission for Europe – (See Appendix 2.)

ECLA   Economic Commission for Latin America – (See Appendix 2.)

ECOSOC   The Economic and Social Council – A principal organ of the UN, consisting of 54 member states. Its functions and powers are defined in Chapter 10 of the United Nations Charter. (See Appendix 2.)

ECPC   Enlarged Committee for Programme and Coordination – 1966–1969. (See CPC and Appendix 2.)

ECWA   Economic Commission for Western Asia – Created in 1973 replacing the United Nations Economic and Social Office in Beirut which had been set up in 1963. (See Appendix 2.)

EPTA   Expanded Programme of Technical Assistance – Established by the General Assembly in 1950 (Resolution 304 IV,) on the basis of a recommendation by ECOSOC (Resolution 222 IV) for the purpose of strengthening the means available to the United Nations and Specialised Agencies to assist developing countries in their economic development effort. The Programme was run by the Technical Assistance Board established by ACC, consisting of the heads of the participating organizations or their representatives, and an Executive Chairman. The Board reported through ACC to the Technical Assistance Committee of the Council. EPTA was merged with the Special Fund (q.v.) in 1965 to form the United Nations Development Programme (UNDP).

ESA   Department of Economic and Social Affairs of the United Nations Secretariat – (See Appendix 2.)

ESCAP   Economic Commission for Asia and the Pacific (formerly ECAFE) – (See Appendix 2.)

FAO   Food and Agriculture Organization of the United Nations –. Specialized agency with Headquarters in Rome. (See Appendix 3.)

G.A.	General Assembly of the United Nations – (See Appendix 2.)
GATT	General Agreement on Tariffs and Trade – (See Appendix 3.)
IACB	Inter-Agency Consultative Board of the United Nations Development Programme – Consisting of the executive heads of agencies participating in UNDP, it is advisory to and chaired by the Administrator. (See Appendix 2.)
IAEA	International Atomic Energy Agency – (See Appendix 3.)
IBRD	International Bank for Reconstruction and Development – (See Appendix 3.)
ICAO	International Civil Aviation Organization – (See Appendix 3.)
ICSAB	International Civil Service Advisory Board – Predecessor of ICSC (q.v.)
ICSC	International Civil Service Commission – (See Appendix 2.)
IDA	International Development Association – (See Appendix 3.)
IDB	Industrial Development Board – (See UNIDO, Appendix 2.)
IFC	International Finance Corporation – (See Appendix 3.)
ILO	International Labour Organization – (See Appendix 3.)
IMCO	Inter-Governmental Maritime Consultative Organization – (See Appendix 3.)
IMF	International Monetary Fund – (See Appendix 3.)
IOB	Inter-organizational Board for Information Systems and related activities – Set up in Geneva by ACC with a view especially to developing and rendering more comparable computerized data to support the development activities of Member States and the United Nations System.
IRO	International Relief Organization – Established and recognized as a UN specialized agency in 1946, wound up in 1952.
ITU	International Telecommunication Union – (See Appendix 3.)
IUOTO	International Union of Official Travel Organizations – (See WTO.)
JIU	Joint Inspection Unit of the United Nations – (See Appendix 2.)
OAS	Organization of American States.
OAU	Organization of African Unity.
OECD	Organization for Economic Co-operation and Development, Paris – Came into operation in 1961 as successor to the Organization for European Economic Cooperation. Membership: 18 Western European states plus Canada, USA and Japan.
OIAAC (IAA and IAAC)	Office for Inter-Agency Affairs and Coordination – A unit of the UN Secretariat, working directly under the Secretary-General. (See Appendix 2.)

S.G.	Secretary-General – Used without qualification, refers to the Secretary-General of the United Nations.
Special Fund	Special Fund – (i) Created by General Assembly Resolution 124 (XIII); in 1958 as a major extension of UN assistance to the economic and social development of the less developed countries; merged with EPTA in 1965 to form UNDP. (ii) Created by the General Assembly at its Sixth Special Session 1974 as part of its Special Programme to provide emergency relief and development assistance to countries most seriously affected by economic crisis. The Fund, which depends on voluntary contributions, is placed under an *Ad Hoc* Committee of 36 Member States. (See Appendix 2.)
TAB	Technical Assistance Board – (See EPTA.)
TDB	Trade and Development Board – (See UNCTAD.)
UNCTAD	United Nations Conference on Trade and Development – (See Appendix 2.)
UNDP	United Nations Development Programme – (See Appendix 2.)
UNEP	United Nations Environment Programme – (See Appendix 2.)
UNESCO	United Nations Educational, Scientific and Cultural Organization – (See Appendix 3.)
UNESOB	United Nations Economic and Social Office in Beirut – Replaced by ECWA. (See Appendix 2.)
UNFPA	United Nations Fund for Population Activities – (See Appendix 2.)
UNHCR	Office of the United Nations High Commissioner for Refugees – (See Appendix 2.)
UNICEF	United Nations Children's Fund – (See Appendix 2.)
UNIDO	United Nations Industrial Development Organization – (See Appendix 2.)
UNITAR	United Nation Institute for Training and Research – (See Appendix 2.)
UNRRA	United Nations Refugee and Rehabilitation Administration – A war-time humanitarian organization which was terminated 1946–1947.
UNRWA	United Nations Relief and Works Agency for Palestine Refugees in the Near East – (See Appendix 2.)
UNU	United Nations University – (See Appendix 2.)
WFC	World Food Council – (See Appendix 2.)
WFP	World Food Programme – (See Appendix 2.)

Appendix 2

Principal organs of the United Nations (General Assembly, Economic and Social Council and Secretariat), with main subsidiary organs directly concerned with economic and social cooperation and coordination (Status as of Spring 1976)

GENERAL ASSEMBLY

(a) *Organs of the General Assembly directly concerned with administrative and budgetary matters and whose reports are considered by the Assembly's Fifth Committee:*

Advisory Committee on Administrative and Budgetary Questions – Consisting of 13 experts nominated by Governments and appointed by the General Assembly to assist the latter body in the discharge of its responsibility under Article 17 paragraph 1 of the Charter (consideration and approval of the budget of the organization) and paragraph 3 (consideration and approval of any financial and budgetary arrangements with the specialized agencies and examination of the agencies' administrative budgets).

Joint Inspection Unit – Consisting of 8 individuals, set up by the General Assembly Resolution 2150 (xxi) and reporting to the United Nations and the other Organizations participating in the 'common system of salaries and allowances'. The Unit, administratively attached to the Secretary-General as chief administrative officer of the United Nations and as Chairman of the Administrative Committee on Coordination, has 'the broadest powers of investigation in all matters having a bearing on the efficiency of the services and the proper use of funds'. The members are 'chosen from among members of national supervision or inspection bodies, or from among persons of similar competence, on the basis of their special experience in national or international administrative and financial matters'.

International Civil Service Commission – Created under General Assembly Resolution 3357 (xxix) and replacing the eleven-member International Civil Service Advisory Board (ICSAB) which had been set up by the ACC in 1948. The Commission, which reports to the General Assembly, has been established 'for the regulation and co-ordination of the conditions of service of the United Nations common system ...' and it 'performs its functions in respect of the United Nations and those Organizations which participate in the common system and accept the present Statute'. Its thirteen members are appointed by the General Assembly, under a procedure set out in paragraph 4(a) of the Resolution:

> After appropriate consultations with Member States, the executive heads of the other organizations, and with staff representatives, the Secretary-General, in his capacity as Chairman of the Administrative Committee on Coordination, shall compile a list of candidates

for appointment as Chairman, Vice-Chairman, and members of the Commission and shall consult with the Advisory Committee on Administrative and Budgetary Questions before consideration and decision by the General Assembly.

(b) *Main programmes and funds established by the General Assembly under the general powers given it by Article 22 of the Charter*:

Since it may be useful for the reader to have a general idea of the relative scope of the activities carried out through each of these organs, an indication is given of the appropriations for each in the United Nations Budget for the biennium 1974–1975, and, in the case of work financed by voluntary contributions, the actual expenditure incurred in the year 1974. The budgetary appropriations for these UN organs are taken from the 'Programme Budget for the Biennium 1974–1975' (A/9006 Add. 2). They are in no way comparable to the total budgets of the specialized agencies shown in Appendix 3. The 1974 expenditures are taken from 'Financial Report and Accounts for the year ended 31 December 1974' (A/9607).

UNICEF (United Nations Children's Fund) – Established by the General Assembly in 1946, Resolution 57(1), as the United Nations International Children's Emergency Fund to provide aid to children and nursing mothers, victims of the World War, thus taking over some of the functions that had been exercised by the war-time UNRRA. In 1953 the Fund was made permanent and its title, but not its initials, were changed. Its intergovernmental organ is the thirty-member Executive Board; its Executive Director is appointed by the Secretary-General after consultation with the Board. The Board reports to the General Assembly through the Economic and Social Council. 1974 income: $101 million, expenditure: $89 million.

UNHCR (Office of the United Nations High Commissioner for Refugees) – Established by the General Assembly in 1949, Resolution 319 (IV), to take over some of the major functions, especially in the matter of the protection of refugees and displaced persons, from the International Refugee Organization (IRO), which was shortly to be wound up. The Programme is supervised by an Executive Committee consisting of representatives of thirty-one States. The High Commissioner is elected by the General Assembly on the nomination of the Secretary-General. Appropriations for biennium 1974–1975: $10,904,000. 1974 income (voluntary funds): $11 million, expenditure: $11.5 million.

UNRWA (United Nations Relief and Works Agency for Palestine Refugees in the Near East) – Established by the General Assembly in 1949, Resolution 302 (IV), replacing an earlier temporary UN organization. It is financed by voluntary contributions exclusively. The Commissioner General of the agency is assisted by an Advisory Commission of representatives of principal donor countries and the host countries of the refugees in the Middle East. The Commissioner General reports directly to the General Assembly. 1974 income: $89 million, expenditure: $88 million.

World Food Programme – A Joint Programme established by the United Nations General Assembly and the FAO Conference in 1962 and located in Rome, whose purpose is to provide food aid (originally surplus foods) in support of economic and social development projects, to assist in pre-school and school feeding and to help meet emergency food needs. The Executive Director is appointed by the Secretary-General and the Director-General of FAO. Half of the membership of the Intergovernmental Committee, which provides guidance on policy, administration and operations is appointed by ECOSOC and half by the FAO Council, to both of which organs the Committee reports. Under a decision giving effect to a recommendation of the World Food Conference, 1974, the General Assembly has enlarged the mandate of the Intergovernmental Committee, modified its name to 'Committee on Food Aid, Policies and Programmes' and requested it to report to the World Food Council in addition to the Economic and Social Council and the Council of the FAO. The operations of the Programme, made possible by contributions in cash and in kind, are running at a level of more than $400 million a year.

United Nations Conference on Trade and Development – As a result of the first UNCTAD Conference in Geneva in 1964, the Conference was made a permanent organ of the General Assembly (Resolution 1995 (xxix)) with its Headquarters in Geneva; its own governing organ, the Trade and Development Board; and its Secretary-General, who is appointed by the Secretary-General of the United Nations and confirmed in office by the General Assembly. Appropriation for biennium 1974–1975: $28,135,000.

United Nations Development Programme – Established by General Assembly Resolution 1240 (xiii), as a result of the merger of the EPTA and the Special Fund, for the purpose of assisting developing countries in their efforts to accelerate their economic and social progress. The principal intergovernmental organ of the UNDP, which reports to the Council, is the Governing Council, consisting of 48 members, and its chief executive is the Administrator, who is appointed by the Secretary-General, subject to the approval of the General Assembly. The Administrator is advised by an Inter-agency Consultative Board consisting of the executive heads of the participating agencies and programmes and chaired by himself. Total 1974 income: $367 million, expenditure: $385 million.

UNIDO (United Nations Industrial Development Organization) – Established by the General Assembly under Resolution 2152 (xxi) in 1966, as 'an autonomous organization within the United Nations' to promote and accelerate the industrialization of the developing countries and coordinate the activities of the UN System in the field of industrial development. The Headquarters of UNIDO are in Vienna; its principal intergovernmental organ is the Industrial Development Board (IDB) which reports to the General Assembly through the ECOSOC and its principal Executive Officer is the Executive Director appointed by the Secretary-General subject to confirmation by the General Assembly. By Resolution 3306 (xxix) of the General Assembly, the Second General Conference of UNIDO was requested to consider the desirability of UNIDO being transformed into a specialized agency. This suggestion was endorsed by the Conference and the Statute of a new specialized agency was to be worked out. Appropriation for biennium 1974–1975: $30,798,000.

United Nations Fund for Population Activities – Created as a voluntary Trust Fund under the Secretary-General in 1967 to enable organs of the UN System to respond more fully to the needs of countries seeking assistance in the field of population policy. The General Assembly placed the Fund under the management of the Administrator of the UNDP in 1969 and, pursuant to General Assembly Resolution 3019 (xxvII), the Governing Council of UNDP now exercises surveillance over the programme. Total 1974 income: $57 million, expenditure: $61 million.

United Nations Environment Programme – Set up by the General Assembly under Resolution 2997 in 1972 to give effect to the recommendations of the United Nations Conference on the Environment held earlier that year in Stockholm. The Programme, under a governing council of 58 members and an Executive Director appointed by the General Assembly on the nomination of the Secretary-General, has its Headquarters in Nairobi, Kenya. The purpose of the programme is to promote international co-operation, recommend policies and provide guidelines for environmental programmes. General Assembly Resolution 2997 provided for the establishment of an Environmental Coordination Board (ECB) under the Chairmanship of the Executive Director and 'under the auspices and within the framework of the Administrative Committee on Coordination'. Appropriation for biennium 1974–1975: $6,090,000. Fund of the UNEP, total 1974 income: $21 million, expenditure: $8 million.

Special Programme – Created by the General Assembly at its Sixth Special Session in 1974 has two components: (a) an emergency operation to provide timely relief to the most seriously affected developing countries. The amount received by 31 May 1975 in the UN account set up under this operation was $229,471,000. (b) a Special Fund to be established under UN auspices for emergency relief and development assistance and 'to provide an alternative channel for normal development assistance after the emergency period'. An *Ad Hoc* Committee of 36 Member States was set up to make recommendations on the scope, machinery and operation of the Special Fund, which depends upon voluntary contributions. This Committee has so far been stalled because of uncertainty whether large aid contributions which had been expected, especially from OPEC countries, would in fact be channelled through the Fund.

UNITAR (United Nations Institute for Training and Research) – Established by the Secretary-General in virtue of General Assembly Resolution 1934 (xvIII), as an autonomous Institute within the framework of the United Nations, for the purpose of enhancing, by the provision of training and the undertaking of research and study, the effectiveness of the United Nations in achieving the major objectives of the Organization, in particular the maintenance of peace and security and the problems of economic and social development. A Board of Trustees lays down the principles and policies to govern the activities and operation of the Institute, approves its work programme and adopts its budget; the Executive Director of the Institute is appointed by the Secretary-General of the United Nations after consultation with the Board. Total 1974 income (General Fund plus special-purpose grants): $1·8 million, expenditure: $1·5 million.

United Nations University – On the basis of an idea launched in 1969 by the then Secretary-General, U Thant, a series of studies by the United Nations and UNESCO led to the formulation, by a jointly-sponsored panel and then a Founding Committee, of a design, highly decentralized in character, for a United Nations University, which was finally endorsed by the General Assembly and the UNESCO Conference. Responding to a generous offer of financial support by Japan amounting in total to $100 million, and an invitation by that Government to locate the central programming unit of the University in Tokyo, the General Assembly formally established the University in 1973 (Resolution 3313 (xxix)). The members of the University Council, and the Executive Director, chosen jointly by the Secretary-General and the Director General of UNESCO, were appointed in 1974.

World Food Council – Established by the General Assembly under Resolution 3348 (xxiv) (December 1974), at the ministerial and plenipotentiary level, to function as an organ of the United Nations reporting to the General Assembly through the Economic and Social Council and having purposes, functions and mode of operation set forth in Resolution (xxii) of the World Food Conference called by the United Nations in 1974. By that Resolution, the World Food Council is, *inter alia*, called upon 'to serve as a coordinating mechanism to provide overall, integrated and continuing attention for the successful coordination and follow-up of policies concerning food production, nutrition, food security, food trade and food aid, as well as other related matters, by all the agencies of the United Nations system'.

The World Food Council consists of 36 members nominated by the Economic and Social Council and elected by the General Assembly. Its Executive Director is appointed by the Secretary-General in consultation with the Director-General of FAO.

ECONOMIC AND SOCIAL COUNCIL

The Economic and Social Council (54 members) whose functions and powers are set out in Chapter x of the Charter, acts as:

(a) The governing body for the United Nations work programme in the economic, social and human rights fields;

(b) The coordinator of the activities of the United Nations system of organizations in these fields;

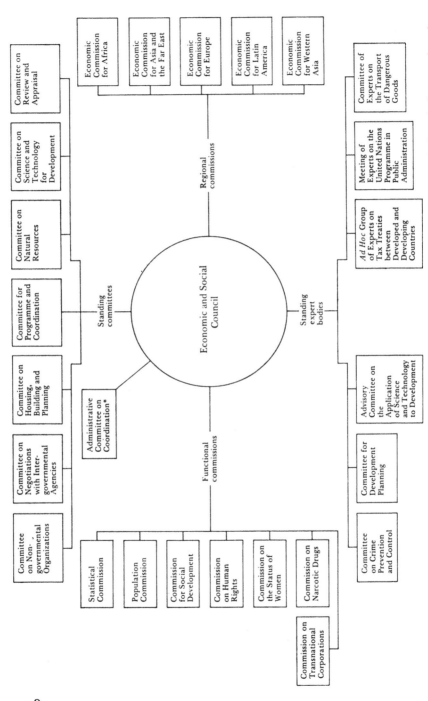

Committee on Review and Appraisal

Committee on Science and Technology for Development

Committee on Natural Resources

Committee for Programme and Coordination

Committee on Housing, Building and Planning

Committee on Negotiations with Inter-governmental Agencies

Committee on Non-governmental Organizations

Administrative Committee on Coordination*

Standing committees

Economic Commission for Africa

Economic Commission for Asia and the Far East

Economic Commission for Europe

Economic Commission for Latin America

Economic Commission for Western Asia

Regional commissions

Economic and Social Council

Functional commissions

Standing expert bodies

Committee of Experts on the Transport of Dangerous Goods

Meeting of Experts on the United Nations Programme in Public Administration

Ad Hoc Group of Experts on Tax Treaties between Developed and Developing Countries

Advisory Committee on the Application of Science and Technology to Development

Committee for Development Planning

Committee on Crime Prevention and Control

Statistical Commission

Population Commission

Commission for Social Development

Commission on Human Rights

Commission on the Status of Women

Commission on Narcotic Drugs

Commission on Transnational Corporations

*Although not a subsidiary organ of the Council, the Administrative Committee on Coordination reports to that body and plays a major role as a link between it and the specialized agencies.

(c) A forum for the discussion of issues of international economic and social policy, and for formulating recommendations for the United Nations system of organization.

The Council works through three sessional committees of the whole, namely, the Economic Committee, the Social Committee and the Policy and Programme Coordination Committee.

The subsidiary bodies of the Economic and Social Council, a chart of which appears on p. 182, are the following:[1]

(a) *Regional commissions*

 (i) Economic Commission for Africa (42 members and 4 associate members);

 (ii) Economic and Social Commission for Asia and the Pacific (31 members and 8 associate members);

 (iii) Economic Commission for Europe (34 members);

 (iv) Economic Commission for Latin America (29 members and 4 associate members);

 (v) Economic Commission for Western Asia (12 members).

All five commissions were established according to similar terms of reference to function in an analogous manner in their respective regions. Their main objective is to initiate and participate in measures for facilitating concerted action for economic and social development in order to raise the level of economic activity and advance the levels of living and to maintain and strengthen economic relations among their members and other countries of the world. The commissions may, after discussion with any specialized agency functioning in the same general field, and with the approval of the Council, establish such bodies as they deem appropriate in order to facilitiate the carrying out of their responsibilities. The appropriations for the biennium 1974–1975, exclusive of Trust Funds, for each of the commissions are as follows: ECE – \$10,113,000; ESCAP – \$11,066,000; ECLA – \$12,677,000; ECA – \$13,602,000; ECWA (preliminary appropriation) – \$2,422,000.

While the regional commissions approve their respective programmes of work, the functional commissions and standing committees of the Council, in accordance with the decision of the Economic and Social Council, on 10 January 1973,[2] 'state their programme objectives so that the Secretary-General can examine and elaborate the most effective and economic means of achieving the objectives in question and make appropriate recommendations in the biennial programme and budget and the medium-term plan'. The functional commissions and standing committees are as follows:

(b) *Functional commissions*

 (i) The Statistical Commission (24 members) promotes the development of national statistics, the coordination of statistical work, and the development of central statistical services; and advises the organs of the United Nations on general questions of statistical information;

(ii) The Population Commission (27 members) studies and advises on the size and structure of populations, the interplay of demographic factors and policies designed to influence the size and structure of populations and changes therein;

(iii) The Commission for Social Development (32 members) advises on social policies of a general character, on vital social problems and on related required measures;

(iv) The Commission on Human Rights (32 members), and its Sub-Commission on Prevention of Discrimination and Protection of Minorities (26 members), submits proposals, recommendations and reports regarding an international bill of rights, the protection of minorities and the prevention of discrimination.

(v) The Commission on the Status of Women (32 members) prepares recommendations and reports on promotion of women's rights in political, economic, civil, social and educational fields;

(vi) The Commission on Narcotic Drugs (30 members) assists in exercising powers of supervision over the application of international conventions and agreements dealing with narcotic drugs, advises the Council on all matters pertaining to the control of narcotic drugs, and prepares such draft international conventions as may be necessary;

(vii) Commission on Transnational Corporations established by Resolution 1913 (LVII) of the Council in 1974, as an advisory body to the Council. Its membership comprises 48 States, each of which appoints a high level expert as its representative.

(c) *Standing committees*

(i) The Committee on Non-governmental Organizations is a committee which recommends the status of individual Non-governmental Organizations.

(ii) The Committee on Negotiations with Inter-governmental Agencies is a committee which is called whenever it is necessary to negotiate an agreement with a newly created agency.

(iii) The Committee on Housing, Building and Planning (27 members) examines reports, makes recommendations to Governments and United Nations bodies, and promotes research in the field of housing, related community facilities and physical planning;

(iv) The Committee on Natural Resources (54 members) establishes guidelines, examines reports, analyzes existing resolutions and makes recommendations in areas related to natural resources.

(v) The Committee on Science and Technology for Development (54 members) promotes international cooperation, encourages the formulation of overall policy, and evaluates and reviews policies and new developments in the field of science and technology.

(vi) The Committee on Review and Appraisal (54 members) assists the Council and the General Assembly in the overall review and appraisal of the Second United Nations Development Decade. The Economic and Social Council, by Resolution 1768 (LIV), decided that the review and appraisal should be undertaken by each organ which has responsibility in a particular field or sector of the International Development Strategy, that each organ should examine all the relevant information and that the results of all sectoral or regional reviews should be transmitted to the Committee on Review and Appraisal. The Council further decided that the Committee on Review and Appraisal should (a) examine the obstacles and reasons for shortfalls identified in the various sectoral and regional reviews, and (b) on the basis of such reviews as well as its own conclusions, recommend measures to overcome the obstacles and shortfalls, including new or revised goals and policy measures as required.

(d) *Expert bodies*

(i) The Committee on Crime Prevention and Control (15 members) advises on devising programmes for international study and formulating policies for international action in the area of crime prevention;

(ii) The Committee for Development Planning (24 members) considers and evaluates programmes in their progress, analyzes major trends and studies individual questions in the area of economic planning, programmes and projections;

(iii) The Advisory Committee on the Application of Science and Technology to Development (24 members) reviews programmes and progress in programme application and proposes practical measures for such application and advises on desired changes in the area of science and technology;

(iv) The *Ad Hoc* Group of Experts on Tax Treaties between Developed and Developing Countries (19 members) explores ways and means for facilitating the conclusion of tax treaties between developed and developing countries;

(v) The Meeting of Experts on the United Nations Programme in Public Administration (varying membership) elaborates, in close collaboration with the specialized agencies and non-governmental organizations concerned, specific objectives and programmes in the field of public administration, and examines the Secretary-General's proposals in public administration for the Second United Nations Development Decade;

(vi) The Committee of Experts on the Transport of Dangerous Goods (9–16 members) revises and updates the list of dangerous goods, considers existing transportation practices and studies problems of packing and related matters.

The Committee for Programme and Coordination – to be responsible to the Economic and Social Council and through it to the General Assembly. It would advise and assist the Council in discharging its coordination functions under Articles 58, 63 and 64 of the Charter of the United Nations and, in particular, it would keep under review the activities of the United Nations and its related agencies and programmes, study the present procedures for coordination and cooperation and submit its conclusions to the Council on the issues and problems arising thereon.

The Committee would prepare and submit to the Council recommendations to the specialized agencies, the General Assembly and to Members of the United Nations as envisaged under Article 63, paragraph 2, of the Charter.

The Committee would receive continuing authority from the Council to review programmes and procedures in particular sectors on a system-wide basis as well as the interaction of different sectors in order to ensure that programmes in a particular sector respond to the objectives set forth in General Assembly Resolution 2188 (xxi). In particular, the Committee would be concerned with the review of programme planning, implementation of programmes, their evaluation and the effectiveness of coordination machinery.

The Committee, in accordance with paragraphs 1 and 2 of General Assembly Resolution 2370 (xxii), would develop, in consultation with the Secretary-General, its own processes for carrying out the envisaged system of long-term planning and programme formulation; and, in accordance with Economic and Social Council Resolution 1275 (xliii), section iii, paragraph 2, the Committee would keep under continuous review further steps required to implement within the United Nations the recommendations of the *Ad Hoc* Committee of Experts to Examine the Finances of the United Nations and the Specialized Agencies concerning the development of an integrated system of long-term planning, programming and budgeting.

In the light of Council Resolutions 1093 (xxxix), 1171 (xli), 1177 (xli), 1275 (xliii), 1367 (xlv) and 1378 (xlv) in relation to the work programme of the United Nations in the economic, social and human rights fields, the Committee would carry out the following programme functions:

(a) An annual general review of the totality of the Secretary-General's work programme in the economic, social and human rights fields, and in the light of its budgetary implications, covering the various units of the Department of Economic and Social Affairs including those of the regional economic commissions, the Division of Human Rights, the Division of Narcotic Drugs, the United Nations Conference on Trade and Development and the United Nations Industrial Development Organization, giving particular attention to programme changes arising out of the decisions by intergovernmental organs and conferences or suggested by the Secretary-General;

(b) A review in depth of selected sectors of the work programme phased over a period of time in accordance with the recommendations set forth in the reports of the Committee for Programme and Co-ordination on its second session and the first part of its third session, as endorsed in Council Resolutions 1367 (XLV) and 1456 (XLVII), respectively. This review would concern itself in particular with long-term plans formulated for these sectors and an assessment of results achieved from current activities, the continuing validity of legislative decisions of more than five years' standing, and the effectiveness of coordination with other units of the Secretariat and members of the United Nations family;

(c) Assist the Council and the General Assembly in the establishment of programme priorities within the United Nations and the formulation of programmes clearly responsive to such priorities as specified in paragraphs 8 to 17 of the report of the Committee for Programme and Coordination on its second session;

(d) Assist the Council in meeting its responsibilities under rule 34 of the Council's rules of procedure.
(Subject to the Council's authorization, the Committee would communicate its views directly to the specialized agencies, the International Atomic Energy Agency and to United Nations programmes with respect of any matters coming within its terms of reference.)

The same Resolution emphasized that 'the effective discharge of the duties of the reconstituted Committee is dependent upon the existence of the closest working relationship between the various units of the Secretariat dealing, respectively, with inter-agency affairs and economic and social affairs. The Committee would also have to work in close collaboration with the Administrative Committee on Coordination and the Advisory Committee on Administrative and Budgetary Questions.'

THE SECRETARIAT

The resouces of the Secretariat can be drawn upon by the Secretary-General as needed for the work of the General Assembly, the Economic and Social Council and other subsidiary organs. The Offices of Legal Affairs and of Public Information serve all United Nations organs, as do the Departments of Administration and Finance, Conference Services and General Services, while different aspects of particular issues may be assigned to a variety of different units. At the same time, for each of the main organs and programmes in the economic and social fields created by the General Assembly, whether financed from the regular budget or by extra budgetary funds, as well as for each of the Regional Economic Commissions, there is a special staff which is primarily concerned with its work. UNCTAD has its own Secretary-General and a Secretariat based in Geneva; UNIDO has its Executive Director and a Secretariat based in Vienna; UNDP under its Administrator and UNICEF under its Executive Director have their respective staffs with Headquarters in New York. The Office of the United Nations High Commissioner for Refugees is based in

Geneva and that of the United Nations Environment Programme, under its Executive Director, in Nairobi. The United Nations Relief and Works Agency for Palestine Refugees with Headquarters in Beirut, as well as UNITAR and the United Nations Fund for Population Activities in New York, all have their particular staffs, which in all important respects, except tenure, are assimilated to the regular staffs forming part of the United Nations Secretariat proper. The executive heads of all these units are administratively under the general responsibility of the Secretary-General of the United Nations. The five Regional Economic Commissions have their respective secretariats, which formally form part of the Department of Economic and Social Affairs, and their Executive Secretaries report to the Secretary-General through the Under-Secretary-General in charge of that department.

Among all these staff units dealing with economic and social affairs, the Department of Economic and Social Affairs, as the right arm of the Economic and Social Council, has a quite special role. In the words of the 1974–1975 (A/9006 p. 43) United Nations budget estimates:

> The Department of Economic and Social Affairs assists the Secretary-General in providing leadership and, from an overall perspective, providing policy guidance for the total effort of the United Nations system in economic and social development. The Department also has the responsibility for providing substantive support in the economic, social and humanitarian fields for the General Assembly, the Economic and Social Council and their subsidiary bodies. It conducts research, performs programme evaluation and assists governments in making policy and standard-setting recommendations relating to overall development objectives as well as to the sectors for which it is responsible. It provides developing countries, at their request, with direct advisory services in a number of key areas and renders technical and related assistance to them in fields within its substantive responsibility.

The Department comprises at the time of writing, in addition to the Secretariat of the Economic and Social Council, an Office for Technical Cooperation, and a small Special Projects Unit, the following Centres and Divisions dealing with substantive issues: Centre for Development Planning, Projections and Policies; Statistical Office; Centre for Social Development and Humanitarian Affairs; Population Division; Centre for Housing, Building and Planning; Division of Public Administration and Finance; Centre for Natural Resources, Energy and Transport; Office for Science and Technology. The budgetary appropriation for ESA for the biennium 1974–1975 was $32,983,000.

A key role is reserved, finally, for the Office for Inter-Agency Affairs and Coordination, which reports directly to the Secretary-General and whose functions have been defined (ST/SGB/131/Amend. 21) as follows:

> To assist the Secretary-General in promoting inter-agency coordination and cooperation at the executive level and to act as secretariat of the Administrative Committee on Coordination (ACC) and its Preparatory Committee;

To assist the General Assembly, the Economic and Social Council, and their subsidiary organs in respect of questions involving relations and coordination with or among the specialized agencies, IAEA and other intergovernmental organizations;

To maintain contacts, for purposes of coordination, with the Programmes and organizations established by the General Assembly (including UNDP, UNICEF, WFP, UNHCR, UNRWA,UNCTAD, UNIDO, UNITAR);

To assist the Secretary-General and the departments and offices of the Secretariat in regard to the United Nations' own relations with the specialized agencies, IAEA and other intergovernmental organizations, and in particular to assist the Under-Secretary-General and senior officers of the Department of Economic and Social Affairs in the discharge of their responsibilities vis-à-vis these agencies and organizations in economic and social matters;

To assist those agencies and organizations in their relations with the United Nations and to maintain contacts with their executive heads and senior officials on all matters of coordination;

As appropriate, to exercise initiative with regard to inter-agency problems and to facilitate the smooth functioning of inter-agency coordination arrangements . . .

The budgetary appropriations for the Office for the biennium 1974–1975 was $825,000.

Appendix 3
Chart of Agencies related to the United Nations[1]

The agencies are:

IAEA	International Atomic Energy Agency
ILO	International Labour Organization
FAO	Food and Agriculture Organization of the United Nations
UNESCO	United Nations Educational, Scientific and Cultural Organization
WHO	World Health Organization
IBRD	International Bank for Reconstruction and Development
IFC	International Finance Corporation
IDA	International Development Association
IMF	International Monetary Fund
ICAO	International Civil Aviation Organization
UPU	Universal Postal Union
ITU	International Telecommunication Union
WMO	World Meteorological Organization
IMCO	Inter-Governmental Martime Consultative Organization
WIPO	World Intellectual Property Organization

IAEA is an agency established 'under the aegis of the United Nations'; it reports annually to the United Nations General Assembly and, as appropriate, to the Security Council and the Economic and Social Council.

The United Nations and GATT cooperate at the secretariat and intergovernmental levels. The GATT secretariat was originally set up to serve as the secretariat for the Interim Commission for the International Trade Organization, an organization that failed to come into existence.

Intergovernmental agencies related to the United Nations

Agency and Members*	Functions	Gross budget† and Headquarters	Chief officer and number of staff	Constitution and agreement with United Nations
IAEA (104)	Promotes uses of atomic energy for peaceful purposes; assists in atomic research and applications. Arranges exchange of information and specialists, and supply of materials, equipment and facilities. Applies safeguards against diversion of materials to military use, as provided in Treaty on Non-Proliferation of Nuclear Weapons. Gives technical aid and training, sets safety standards, helps draft laws and conventions.	For 1975: $29,675,000 Karntner Ring 11–13 A-1010, Vienna Austria	Director-General: Sigvard Eklund (Sweden) Staff: about 1,000 at headquarters	IAEA Statute entered into force 29 July 1957. Relationship with United Nations approved by General Assembly 14 November 1957.
ILO (126)	Brings together Government, labour and management to solve pressing international labour problems. Provides technical cooperation. Conducts World Employment Programme, which helps countries combat unemployment. Develops world labour standards for consideration by Governments. Runs research and publications programmes centered on basic social and labour problems.	For 1975: $55,247,000 4, route des Morillans, CH-1211, Geneva 22 Switzerland	Director-General: Francis Blanchard (France) Staff: about 3,000, including about 900 experts in the field	Original Constitution came into force 11 April 1919. Revised Constitution came into force 20 April 1948. Relationship with United Nations approved by General Assembly 14 December 1946.

* Number of members, as of 1 January 1975.
† Amounts are in United States dollars, except where otherwise indicated. The figures for agency budgets are from the latest annual report of the Advisory Committee on Administrative and Budgetary Questions on administrative and budgetary coordination with the specialized agencies (Document A/9857) and are adjusted for comparability between budgets.

Agency and Members*	Functions	Gross budget† and Headquarters	Chief officer and number of staff	Constitution and agreement with United Nations
FAO (131)	Helps countries, through expert assistance, to increase production from farms, forests and fisheries, and to improve distribution, marketing and nutrition. Coordinates the Freedom-from-Hunger Campaign. In collaboration with the United Nations, administers the World Food Programme, which provides food for economic development and relief.	For 1975: $63,885,000 Viale delle Terme di Caracalla Rome Italy	Director-General: Addeke H. Boerma (Netherlands) Staff: over 5,000, including experts in the field	Constitution came into force 16 October 1945. Relationship with United Nations approved by General Assembly 14 December 1946.
UNESCO (136 plus 1 associate member)	Seeks to broaden the base of education in the world, bring benefits of science to all countries, and encourage cultural exchange and appreciation. 1975–1976 programme includes: Assistance for educational planning and development; Functional literacy projects combining literacy with economic advancement; Promoting research and cooperation in basic sciences, including hydrology and life sciences; special studies on preservation of the environment; improvement of science teaching; Peace studies; interdisciplinary studies on human rights; Protection of cultural heritage.	For 1975: $88,409,000 7, place de Fontenoy 75700 Paris France	Director-General: Amadou-Mahtar M'Bow (Senegal) Staff: 3,581, including experts in the field	Constitution came into force 4 November 1946. Relationship with United Nations approved by General Assembly 14 December 1946.

Agency and Members*	Functions	Gross budget† and Headquarters	Chief officer and number of staff	Constitution and agreement with United Nations
WHO (140 plus 3 associate members)	Serves as directing and coordinating authority on international health work. Helps Governments, at their request, in carrying out public health programmes. Sets standards for drugs and vaccines, establishes guidelines and criteria in environmental health, and provides other technical services in international health. Promotes medical research.	For 1975: $129,574,000 20 Avenue Appia 1211 Geneva 27 Switzerland	Director-General: Dr Halfdan Mahler (Denmark) Staff: over 3,800, including regional offices and field staff	Constitution came into force 7 April 1948. Succeeded Interim Commission for WHO 1 September 1948. Relationship with United Nations approved by General Assembly 15 November 1947.
IBRD (125)	Furthers economic development of members by loans for productive projects and by furnishing technical advice. All loans are made to or guaranteed by Governments. Loans totalling $21,653 million made by end of 1974.	$134,200,000 administrative budget for 1974 fiscal year for IBRD and IDA, to be met from income. 1818 H Street, N.W., Washington, D.C. 20433	President: Robert S. McNamara (United States) Staff: about 3,500	Articles of Agreement came into force 27 December 1945. Began operation 25 June 1946. Relationship with United Nations approved by General Assembly 15 November 1947.
IFC (99)	Seeks to assist less developed member countries by helping promote growth of private sector of their economies. Provides risk capital without government guarantee for productive private enterprises, assists development of local capital markets and stimulates the international flow of private capital. Gross commitments at end-1974 totalled $1,049·1 million.	$9,176,417 administrative expenses for 1974 fiscal year, met from income 1818 H Street, N.W., Washington, D.C. 20433	President: Robert S. McNamara (United States) Staff: 203 (IFC is an affiliate of IBRD.)	Charter came into force 20 July 1956. Relationship with United Nations approved by General Assembly 20 February 1957.

Agency and Members*	Functions	Gross budget† and Headquarters	Chief officer and number of staff	Constitution and agreement with United Nations
IDA (113)	Furthers economic development of members by providing finance on terms bearing less heavily on balance of payments of members than those of conventional loans. (Its credits have been for terms of 50 years, interest free.) Development credits totalled $7,414 million by end-1974.	(See IBRD.) 1818 H Street, N.W., Washington, D.C. 20433	Same officers and staff as IBRD. (IDA is an affiliate of IBRD.)	Articles of Agreement came into force 24 September 1960. Began operation 8 November 1960. Relationship with United Nations approved by General Assembly 27 March 1961.
IMF (126)	Promotes monetary cooperation and currency stabilization, facilitates trade expansion. Sells currency to help members meet temporary foreign payments difficulties. Aids Governments by consultation on financial problems. Supplements reserve assets of participants in Special Drawing Account. Members' drawings totalled 30,305·6 million Special Drawing Rights and repayments by repurchase totalled SDR 16,657 million at end of December 1974.	$56,070,594** administrative budget for 1975 fiscal year, met from earnings 700 19th St., N.W., Washington, D.C. 20431	Managing Director: H. Johannes Witteveen (Netherlands) Staff: 1,402	Articles of Agreement came into force 27 December 1945. Began operation 1 March 1947. Relationship with United Nations approved by General Assembly 15 November 1947.
ICAO (128)	Promotes safety of international civil aviation by standardizing technical equipment, services and training, and by encouraging the use of safety measures; specifies location of air navigation services. Provides economic and statistical information. Works to reduce the red tape of customs, immigration and public health formalities. Extends technical assistance. Codifies international air law. Arranges joint financing of air navigation facilities and services.	For 1975: $16,426,000 International Aviation Bldg. 1080 University St. Montreal 101, P.Q. Canada	Secretary-General: Assad Kotaite (Lebanon) President of Council: Walter Binaghi (Argentina) Staff: 889, including regional office and technical assistance personnel	Constitution came into force 4 April 1947. Relationship with United Nations approved by General Assembly 14 December 1946.

** Budget in Special Drawing Rights; converted at the rate SDR 1 = $1.19401.

Agency and Members*	Functions	Gross budget† and Headquarters	Chief officer and number of staff	Constitution and agreement with United Nations
UPU (154)	Unites countries for reciprocal exchange of correspondence. Organizes and improves postal services and promotes international collaboration in this sphere. Every member agrees to transmit, as well as to admit in transit, mail of all other members by the best means used for its own mail.	Estimate for 1975: $5,044,000‡ Case postale 3000 Berne 15 Switzerland	Director-General International Bureau of UPU: Mohamed J. Sobhi (Egypt) Staff: 120	Established 1874. Constitution came into force 1 January 1966, additional protocol on 1 July 1971 Relationship with United Nations approved by General Assembly 15 November 1947.
ITU (144)	Regulates, standardizes, plans and coordinates international telecommunications (radio, telegraph, telephone and space radio-communications). Promotes the development of technical facilities and their efficient operation. Is instrumental in allocating radio frequencies.	For 1975: $23,593,000‡ Place des Nations 1211 Geneva 20 Switzerland	Secretary-General: Mohamed Mili (Tunisia) Staff: 605	Originated as International Telegraph Union 1865. Present title adopted under Convention of 1932. Relationship with United Nations approved by General Assembly 15 November 1947.

‡ Budget in Swiss francs; converted at the rate Sw. fr. 2·55 = $US 1.

Agency and Members*	Functions	Gross budget †and Headquarters	Chief officer and number of staff	Constitution and agreement with United Nations
WMO (139)	Promotes international cooperation in meteorology and operational hydrology, especially in establishment of world-wide network of meteorological stations and rapid exchange of weather data. Promotes standardization of observations and publication of observations and statistics. Furthers the application of meteorology to the activities of mankind and encourages research and training in meteorology.	For 1975: $8,568,193 41 Avenue Giuseppe Motta 1211 Geneva 20 Switzerland	Secretary-General: David A. Davies (United Kingdom) Staff: 348, including field staff in technical assistance projects	Preceded by International Meteorological Organization, a non-governmental organization founded in 1873. Convention came into force 23 March 1950. Began operation 4 April 1951. Relationship with United Nations approved by General Assembly 20 December 1951.
IMCO (85 plus 1 associate member)	Promotes intergovernmental cooperation on technical matters affecting international shipping. Recommends and encourages adoption of highest practicable standards of maritime safety and navigation. Fosters international action, notably through technical and legal studies, to prevent marine pollution caused by ships and other craft. Drafts and concludes conventions, agreements and recommendations. Advises other international bodies on shipping matters.	For 1975: $3,031,500 101–104, Piccadilly London, W1V OAE England	Secretary-General: C. P. Srivastava (India) Staff: 151	United Nations Maritime Conference in 1948 drew up IMCO Convention which came into force 17 March 1958. Formally established 13 January 1959. Relationship with United Nations approved by General Assembly 18 November 1948.

Agency and Members*	Functions	Gross budget† and Headquarters	Chief officer and number of staff	Constitution and agreement with United Nations
WIPO (74)	Promotes protection of intellectual property; encourages conclusion of new international treaties and harmonization of national legislation. Ensures administrative cooperation among intergovernmental 'unions' by centralizing and supervizing their administration. Assembles and disseminates information, carries out technical and legal studies, and maintains services for international registration or other administrative cooperation. Extends legal and technical assistance to developing countries.	For 1975: $6,898,823‡ 32, chemin des Colombettes CH-1211 Geneva 20 Switzerland	Director-General: Arpad Bogsch (United States) Staff: 186, including experts in the field	Originated as International Bureau of Paris Union (1883) and of Berne Union (1886), and is successor to United International Bureau for the Protection of Intellectual Property (BIRPI). Convention came into force 26 April 1970. Relationship with United Nations approved by General Assembly 17 December 1974.
GATT (83 Contracting parties, 19 additional countries participating under special arrangements)	Establishes and administers code for orderly conduct of international trade. Helps Governments reduce customs tariffs and abolish other trade barriers, and provides forum for other trade negotiations. With United Nations Conference on Trade and Development, operates International Trade Centre, which provides export promotion assistance for developing countries. GATT rules govern some 80% of international trade.	For 1975: $11,085,098‡ Villa Le Bocage Palais des Nations CH-1211 Geneva 10 Switzerland	Director-General: Olivier Long (Switzerland) Staff: 198, excluding 139 in International Trade Centre	Charter of International Trade Organization drawn up at United Nations conference in Havana 1947–1949, but never ratified. GATT drawn up in 1947, came into force 1 January 1948.

‡ Budget in Swiss francs; converted at the rate Sw. fr. 2·55 = $US 1.

Appendix 4
Regional and branch offices of organizations of the United Nations System

AD	Administrative Office
AO	Area Office
BO	Branch Office
B. Rec.	Branch Office of Regional Economic Commission
CM	Chief of Mission
CO	Correspondent
CR	Country Representative
EDI	Economic Development Institute of the IBRD
FC	Field Coordinator
FO	Field or Country Office
FOAO	Field Office Area Office
FS	Field Staff
GC	UNICEF Greeting Card Office de Janiero
HQ	Headquarters
HR	Honorary Representative Casablanca
IBE	International Bureau of Education
IC	Information Centre
ICATVT	International Centre for Advanced Technical and Vocational Training
ICJ	International Court of Justice
ICTP	International Centre for Theoretical Physics
IDFA	Industrial Development Field Adviser
IEDP	Institute for Economic Development Planning
IIEP	International Institute for Educational Planning
IILS	International Institute for Labour Studies
IMFI	International Monetary Fund Institute
Inf. Ctr.	Information Centre
IS	Information Service
JO	Joint Office
LMR	Laboratory of Marine Radioactivity
LO	Liaison Office
MO	Marketing Office
PAC	UNICEF Packing and Assembly Centre
R	Office of the UNDP Representative
RCBDA	Regional Centre for Book Development in Asia
RCM	Regional Chief of Mission
REG	Office of Regional Representative

Reg. Econ. Comm.	Regional Economic Commission
RISD	Research Institute for Social Development
RLO	Regional Liaison Office
RM	Resident Mission
RO	Regional Office
RR	Office of the UNDP Resident Representative
SAA	Senior Agricultural Adviser
SBO	Sub-Branch Office
SDRI	Social Defence Research Institute
SFO	Sub-Field Office
SO	Science Office
SR	Special Representative
SUB	Sub-Office Associated with a Regional Office
UNSCEAR	United Nations Scientific Committee on the Effects of Atomic Radiation
WR	WHO Representative
ZO	Zone Office

Location of offices of Members
(technical assistance missions, United Nations political missions and

Cities (Listed alphabetically)	Inf. Ctr.	Reg. Econ. Comm.	UNDP	UNFPA	UNICEF	UNHCR	UNRWA	UNCTAD	UNEP	UNIDO
						United Nations				
Abidjan (Ivory Coast)			RR		AO RO					IDFA
Abu Dhabi (United Arab Emirates)					AO					
Accra (Ghana)	IC		RR							IDFA
Addis Ababa (Ethiopia)	IS	ECA	RR		AO	RLO				IDFA
Aden (Democratic Yemen)			RR							
Aleppo (Syrian Arab Rep.)							FOAO			
Alexandria (Egypt)										
Algiers (Algeria)	IC		RR		AO	CO				
Amman (Jordan)			RR				FO FOAO			
Ankara (Turkey)			RR		FO	BO				IDFA⁴
Apia (Western Samoa)			REG FC							
Arusha /Tanzania)			R							
Asuncion (Paraguay)	IC		RR							
Athens (Greece)	IC		RR			BO				
Baghdad (Iraq)	IC		RR							
Baiqaa (Jordan)							FOAO			
Bamako (Mali)			RR							
Bangkok (Thailand)	IS	ECAFE	REG FC		AO RO	RO			REG	IDFA
Bangui (Central African Republic)			RR							
Banjul (Gambia)			RR							
Beirut (Lebanon)	IS	ECWA	RR	FC	AO RO	RO	HQ FO		REG	IDFA¹⁴
Belgrade (Yugoslavia)	IC		RR			CO				
Belize (British Honduras)										
Berne (Switzerland)										
Bogota (Colombia)	IC	SUB	RR		AO					IDFA
Bombay (India)			SFO		SUB					
Bonn (Federal Republic of Germany)					JO⁷	BO				
Brasilia (Brazil)			RR		FO					IDFA
Brazzaville (Congo)			RR		AO					
Bridgetown (Barbados)										
Brussels (Belgium)						BO				
Bucharest (Romania)	IC		R							
Budapest (Hungary)										
Buenos Aires (Argentina)	IC	B.Rec.⁴	RR			RO				IDFA
Bujumbura (Burundi)	IC		RR			BO				
Bukavu (Zaire)						SBO				
Cairo (Egypt)	IC		RR	FC	AO	BO	AD			IDFA
Calabar (Nigeria)										
Calcutta			SFO		SUB					

of the United Nations Family
temporary relief offices – e.g. in Bangladesh and S. Vietnam – not included)

UNITAR and other Institutes[1]	UN/FAO/WFP[2]	ILO	FAO[3]	UNESCO	WHO	IBRD/IDA/IFC	IMF	ICAO	ITU	UPU	WMO	IMCO	IAEA	Total
	FS		SAA/FO		WR	RCM								8
														1
	FS		RO SAA/FO		WR	RM								8
	FS	RO	SAA/FO[24] LO	LO[8] CR	LO WR	RM								15
	FS		SAA/FO		WR									4
	FS													2
					RO									1
	FS	AO	SAA/FO		WR									8
	FS		SAA/FO											5
	FS		SAA/FO		WR									7
	FS		SAA/FO[25]		LO									5
														1
	FS		SAA/FO		WR									5
														3
	FS		SAA/FO		WR									5
														1
	FS		FO[4]											3
IEDP		RO	SAA/FO RO	RO[6] RO[9]	LO WR	RCM		RO						18
	FS				WR									3
	FS													2
	FS	AO		RO	LO									15
		CO												4
					WR									1
										HQ				1
	FS		SAA/FO[21]		WR	RM								9
														2
		BO												3
			SAA/FO	CM	ZO									6
	FS		FO		RO									5
					WR									1
		LO												2
														2
		CO												1
		AO	SAA/FO		ZO									8
	FS		FO		WR									6
														1
	FS	AO	SAA/FO RO	SO	LO			RO						14
	FS													1
														2

Appendix 4

Cities (Listed) alphabetically)	Inf. Ctr.	Reg. Econ. Comm.	UNDP	UNFPA	UNICEF	UNHCR	UNRWA	UNCTAD	UNEP	UNIDO
Caracas (Venezuela)			RR							
Casablanca (Morocco)						HR				
Chandigarh (India)					SUB					
Colombo (Sri Lanka)	IC		RR	FC	AO					IDFA⁴
Conakry (Guinea)			RR							
Copenhagen (Denmark)	IC				PAC					
Cotonou (Dahomey)			RR							
Dacca (Bangladesh)			RR		FO					
Dakar (Senegal)	IC		RR	FC	AO	RO				IDFA
Damascus (Syrian Arab Republic)			RR				FOAO FO			
Dar Es Salaam (Tanzania)	IC		RR			BO				
Dera'a (Syrian Arab Republic)							FOAO			
Doha (Qatar)			SUB							
Dubai (United Arab Emirates)										
El Paso (United States)										
Entebbe (Uganda)										
Enugu (Nigeria)										
Freetown (Sierra Leone)			RR							
Gaborone (Botswana)			RR			BO				
Gaza (Egypt)							FO			
Geneva (Switzerland)	RO	IS ECE	REG		AO RO	HQ	LO	HQ¹³	REG LO	
Georgetown (Guyana)			RR							
Guatemala City (Guatemala)			RR		AO					IDFA
Hague, The (Netherlands)	ICJ					BO				
Hama (Syrian Arab Republic)							BO			
Havana (Cuba)			R⁴							
Hazmieh (Lebanon)							FOAO			
Hebron (Jordan)							FOAO			
Homs (Syrian Arab Republic)							FOAO			
Irbeid (Jordan)							FOAO			
Islamabad (Pakistan)	IC		RR		FO					IDFA⁴
Istanbul (Turkey)										
Jayapura (Indonesia)			SFO							
Jakarta (Indonesia)			RR	FC	FO					IDFA
Jeddah (Saudi Arabia)			SFO							
Jericho (Jordan)							BO			
Jerusalem (Israel/Jordan)			RR			CO	FO			
Juba (Sudan)			SFO							
Kabul (Afghanistan)	IC		RR		FO					
Kaduna (Nigeria)			SFO							
Kampala (Uganda)			RR		LO	BO				
Karachi (Pakistan)			SFO							
Katmandu (Nepal)	IC		RR		AO					

of the United Nations Family
temporary relief offices – e.g. in Bangladesh and S. Vietnam – not included)

UNITAR and other Institutes[1]	UN/FAO/WFP[2]	ILO	FAO[3]	UNESCO	WHO	IBRD/IDA/IFC	IMF	ICAO	ITU	UPU	WMO	IMCO	IAEA	Total
	FS		SAA/FO		ZO									4
														1
														1
	FS		SAA/FO		WR									8
	FS				WR[28]									3
					RO									3
	FS		SAA/FO[26]		WR									4
		AO	SAA/FO[4]		WR	RM								6
IEDP	FS	AO	SAA/FO[17]	RO	WR				RO					13
	FS		SAA/FO											5
	FS	AO	SAA/FO		WR	RM								8
														1
														1
					WR									1
					FO									1
					WR									1
	FS													1
	FS		SAA/FO[29]											3
	FS													3
														1
BO RISD IILS	LO	HQ[19]	AD	IBE	HQ		LO		HQ			HQ[11]	LO	23
	FS				WR									3
			FO		ZO									5
														2
														1
			FO	RO[9]	WR									4
														1
														1
														1
														1
	FS	AO	SAA/FO		WR	RM								9
		AO												1
														1
	FS	AO	SAA/FO	SO[9]	WR	SR								10
			SFO											2
														1
														3
														1
	FS		SAA/FO		WR	RM								7
														1
	FS		SAA/FO											5
	FS			RCBDA										3
	FS		SAA/FO		WR	RM								7

Location of offices of Members
(technical assistance missions, United Nations political missions and

Cities (Listed alphabetically)	Inf. Ctr.	Reg. Econ. Comm.	UNDP	UNFPA	UNICEF	UNHCR	UNRWA	UNCTAD	UNEP	UNIDO
Khartoum (Sudan)	IC		RR		FO	BO				
Kigali (Rwanda)			RR			BO				
Kingston (Jamaica)			RR	FC						
Kinshasa (Zaire)	IC	SUB	RR			RO				IDFA
Kuala Lumpur (Malaysia)			REG	FC						
Kuwait (Kuwait)			RR							IDFA
Lagos (Nigeria)	IC		RR	FC	AO RO					IDFA[4]
Lahore (Pakistan)										
La Paz (Bolivia)	IC		RR							
Lattakia (Syrian Arab Republic)							BO			
Libreville (Gabon)			RR							
Lima (Peru)	IC		RR		AO					IDFA
Lomé (Togo)	IC		RR							
London (United Kingdom)	IC				JO[5]	BO				
Lucknow (India)					SUB					
Lusaka (Zambia)	IC[4]	SUB	REG		AO	BO				IDFA
Luxembourg (Luxembourg)						CO				
Madras (India)					SUB					
Madrid (Spain)						CO				
Malabo (Equatorial Guinea)			RR							
Managua (Nicaragua)			RR							
Manama (Bahrain)			SUB							
Manila (Philippines)	IC		RR	FC	AO					IDFA
Maseru (Lesotho)	IC[4]		RR							
Mbabane (Swaziland)			RR							
Mexico City (Mexico)	IC	B.Rec.	RR	FC	AO					IDFA
Mogadiscio (Somalia)			RR							
Monaco-Villa (Monaco)										
Monrovia (Liberia)	IC		RR							
Montevideo (Uruguay)		SUB	RR							
Montreal (Canada)										
Moscow (USSR)	IC		R							
Muscat (Oman)			SUB							
Nablus (Jordan)							FOAO			
Nairobi (Kenya)	IC[4]		RR	FC	AO RO	BO			HQ REG	IDFA
Nassau (Bahamas)						CO				
Ndjamena (Chad)			RR							
New Delhi (India)	IC		RR		AO RO	BO				IDFA
New York (United States)	HQ		HQ	HQ	HQ	RO	LO	LO	LO	LO
Niamey (Niger)		SUB	RR							IDFA[4]
Nicosia (Cyprus)			RR							
Nouakchott (Mauritania)			RR							
Nurnberg (Fed. Rep. of Germany)						SBO				

of the United Nations Family
temporary relief offices – e.g. in Bangladesh and S. Vietnam – not included)

UNITAR and other Institutes[1]	UN/FAO/WFP[2]	ILO	FAO[3]	UNESCO	WHO	IBRD/IDA/IFC	IMF	ICAO	ITU	UPU	WMO	IMCO	IAEA	Total
	FS		SAA/FO		WR	RM								8
	FS													3
	FS				WR									4
	FS	CR	SAA/FO		WR	RM								10
	FS		SAA/FO[18]		WR									5
		CR												3
	FS	AO	SAA/FO	CM	WR	RM								12
	FS													1
	FS		SAA/FO		WR									5
														1
	FS		FO											3
	FS	RO	SAA/FO		ZO			RO						9
	FS				WR									4
		BO				SUB						HQ		6
														1
	FS	AO	SAA/FO[20]		WR	RM								11
														1
														1
														1
														1
	FS		FO		WR									4
														1
	FS	AO	SAA/FO		RO									9
	FS				WR									4
	FS		SAA/FO[16]											3
	FS	AO	SAA/FO	CM	ZO			RO						12
	FS		SAA/FO		WR									4
													LMR	1
	FS				WR									4
			SAA/FO	SO[9]	WR									5
								HQ						1
		BO												3
														1
														1
			SAA/FO	SO	WR	RCM								13
														1
	FS		SAA/FO											3
	FS	AO	SAA/FO	SO[9]	RO	RM								13
					WR									
HQ	LO	LO	LO	LO	LO	SUB / MO	LO						LO	19
	FS		SAA/FO		WR									6
	FS													2
	FS		FO[4]											3
														1

Location of offices of Members
(technical assistance missions, United Nations political missions and

Cities (Listed alphabetically)	Inf. Ctr.	Reg. Econ. Comm.	UNDP	UNFPA	UNICEF	UNHCR	UNRWA	UNCTAD	UNEP	UNIDO
Ottawa (Canada)						CO				
Ouagadougou (Upper Volta)			RR							
Palembang (Indonesia)										
Panama City (Panama)			RR							
Paramaribo (Surinam)										
Paris (France)	IC					BO				
Phnom-Penh (Khmer Republic)			RR		FO					
Port-Au-Prince (Haiti)			RR							
Port Louis (Mauritius)			RR							
Port Moresby (Papua New Guinea)	IC		RR							
Port of Spain (Trinidad and Tobago)	IC	SUB	REG							IDFA
Prague (Czechoslovakia)	IC									
Quito (Ecuador)			RR							
Rabat (Morocco)	IC		RR							IDFA
Ramallah (Jordan)							FOAO			
Rangoon (Burma)	IC		RR		FO					
Rio de Janeiro (Brazil)	IC	B.Rec.	SFO		GC					
Riyadh (Saudi Arabia)	IC		RR							
Rome (Italy)	IC				JO¹²	BO				
Saida (Lebanon)							FOAO			
Saigon (Republic of Viet-Nam)			RR		FO					
Salvador (Brazil)										
Sana'a (Yemen)			RR							
San Jose (Costa Rica)			RR							
San Salvador (El Salvador)	IC		RR	FC						
Santiago (Chile)	IS	ECLA	RR	FC	RO				REG	IDFA
Santo Domingo (Dominican Republic)			RR							
Seoul (Republic of Korea)			RR	FC	FO					
Singapore (Singapore)										
Sofia (Bulgaria)										
Surakarta (Indonesia)										
Suva (Fiji)			SUB							
Sydney (Australia)	IC				JO⁷					
Taiz (Yemen)			SFO							
Tananarive (Madagascar)	IC		RR							
Tangier (Morocco)		SUB								
Tegucigalpa (Honduras)			R							
Teheran (Iran)	IC		RR	FC	FO					
Tokyo (Japan)	IC				JO¹²	CO⁴				
Traiskirchen (Austria)						SBO				
Trieste (Italy)										

of the United Nations Family
temporary relief offices – e.g.in Bangladesh and S. Vietnam – not included)

UNITAR and other Institutes[1]	UN/FAO/WFP[2]	ILO	FAO[3]	UNESCO	WHO	IBRD/IDA/IFC	IMF	ICAO	ITU	UPU	WMO	IMCO	IAEA	Total
		BO												2
	FS		FO[4]		WR									4
	FS													1
					WR									2
					WR									1
IIEP	LO	BO		HQ		SUB SR	RO	RO						10
			FO		WR									4
	FS				WR									3
	FS													2
														2
	FS	AO	SAA/FO[22]		WR									8
														1
	FS		SAA/FO		WR									4
	FS		SAA/FO		WR									6
														1
					WR									4
	FS	BO			ZO									7
			SAA/FO											2
SDRI	HQ	BO	RO											8
			HQ											1
					WR									3
	FS													1
	FS		SAA/FO		WR									4
		AO	FO		WR									4
	FS		SAA/FO[23]		WR									6
IEDP	FS	LO	SAA/FO	RO[9]	WR									14
			RO											
	FS		SAA/FO[15]		WR									4
	FS		SAA/FO		WR									6
					WR									1
		CO												1
	FS													1
					WR									2
														2
														1
	FS		SAA/FO[27]		WR									5
														1
			FO		WR									3
	FS	CR	SAA/FO											7
		BO				SR								5
														1
													ICTP[10]	1

Location of offices of members
(technical assistance missions, United Nations political missions and

Cities (Listed alphabetically)	United Nations									
	Inf. Ctr.	Reg. Econ. Comm.	UNDP	UNFPA	UNICEF	UNHCR	UNRWA	UNCTAD	UNEP	UNIDO
Tripoli (Lebanon)							BO			
Tripoli (Libyan Arab Republic)			RR							
Tunis (Tunisia)	IC		RR	FC		HR				
Turin (Italy)										
Tyre (Lebanon)							BO			
Ulan Bator (Mongolia)			RR							
Venice (Italy)										
Vienna (Austria)	BO³⁰ IS						BO			HQ
Vientiane (Laos)			RR		FO					
Warsaw (Poland)										
Washington, D.C. (United States)	IC	B.Rec.	LO							
Yaoundé (Cameroon)	IC		RR							IDFA
Zomba (Malawi)			RR							
Total – 1974	4	55	16	115	19	56	40	26	2	8	31
Total – 1973	3	52	14	115	19	54	46	26	2	8	30
Total – 1972	3	51	14	115	7	47	49	20	2	0	28
Total – 1971	3	51	14	111	2	45	50	20	2	0	24
Total – 1970	3	50	14	108	1	48	44	20	2	0	22

of the United Nations Family
temporary relief office – e.g. in Bangladesh and S. Vietnam – not included)

UNITAR and other Institutes[1]	UN/FAO/WFP[2]	ILO	FAO[3]	UNESCO	WHO	IBRD/IDA/IFC	IMF	ICAO	ITU	UPU	WMO	IMCO	IAEA	Total
					WR									1
														2
	FS		SAA/FO		WR									7
ICATVT														1
														1
					WR									2
				LO										1
					LO								HQ	6
					WR									3
		CO												1
IMFI		BO	LO		RO	HQ	HQ							10
EDI														
	FS	AO	SAA/FO	RCM	WR									8
	FS													2
12	85	41	80	21	91	24	4	7	1	1	1	1	5	746
12	82	41	75	20	90	21	4	7	1	1	1	1	5	730
12	81	41	74	20	90	21	4	7	1	1	1	1	5	695
12	81	42	73	32	86	19	4	7	1	1	1	1	6	688
12	77	43	73	46	86	14	4	7	1	1	1	1	6	684

Appendix 5
Chart of the United Nations System*

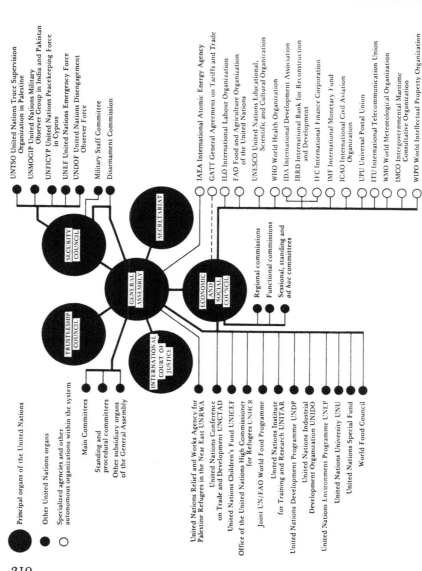

Principal organs of the United Nations

Other United Nations organs

Specialized agencies and other autonomous organizations within the system

Main Committees

Standing and procedural committees

Other subsidiary organs of the General Assembly

SECURITY COUNCIL

SECRETARIAT

GENERAL ASSEMBLY

TRUSTEESHIP COUNCIL

ECONOMIC AND SOCIAL COUNCIL

INTERNATIONAL COURT OF JUSTICE

UNTSO United Nations Truce Supervision Organization in Palestine
UNMOGIP United Nations Military Observer Group in India and Pakistan
UNFICYP United Nations Peacekeeping Force in Cyprus
UNEF United Nations Emergency Force
UNDOF United Nations Disengagement Observer Force
Military Staff Committee
Disarmament Commission

IAEA International Atomic Energy Agency
GATT General Agreement on Tariffs and Trade
ILO International Labour Organization
FAO Food and Agriculture Organization of the United Nations
UNESCO United Nations Educational, Scientific and Cultural Organization
WHO World Health Organization
IDA International Development Association
IBRD International Bank for Reconstruction and Development
IFC International Finance Corporation
IMF International Monetary Fund
ICAO International Civil Aviation Organization
UPU Universal Postal Union
ITU International Telecommunication Union
WMO World Meteorological Organization
IMCO Intergovernmental Maritime Consultative Organization
WIPO World Intellectual Property Organization

Regional commissions
Functional commissions
Sessional, standing and ad hoc committees

United Nations Relief and Works Agency for Palestine Refugees in the Near East UNRWA
United Nations Conference on Trade and Development UNCTAD
United Nations Children's Fund UNICEF
Office of the United Nations High Commissioner for Refugees UNHCR
Joint UN/FAO World Food Programme
United Nations Institute for Training and Research UNITAR
United Nations Development Programme UNDP
United Nations Industrial Development Organization UNIDO
United Nations Environment Programme UNEP
United Nations University UNU
United Nations Special Fund
World Food Council

* Taken from United Nations publication – Sales No. E.75.1.13.

210

Appendix 6

A new UN structure for global economic cooperation[1]
– list of conclusions and recommendations of the
group of experts, prepared by the Secretariat

I. WHY RESTRUCTURING?

1. In its thirtieth anniversary year the United Nations has reached a turning point. In one direction lies the prospect of new capacity to cope with the central issues facing mankind in the decisive last quarter of the twentieth century. In the other direction lies the danger of a decline in the effectiveness of the United Nations. Which direction the Organization takes will be significantly influenced by the decisions on policy and structural questions which its Member States take in the months and years ahead. A world without a strong United Nations, in the opinion of the Group, is inconceivable. It is in the interest of every Member of the United Nations to make the Organization a more effective instrument for the strengthening of international peace and security and for international economic and social cooperation. (paras. 1 and 2.)

2. The proposals of the Group of Experts for structural change are designed to enable the United Nations System to:

(a) Deal with international economic and social problems in a more effective and comprehensive manner, with better coordination throughout the United Nations System as a whole;

(b) Harmonize, as far as possible, the views and approaches of Member countries towards these problems;

(c) Contribute to a significant improvement in the transfer of real resources and technology to developing countries;

(d) Promote economic cooperation between States, including those with different social systems;

(e) Increase the capacity of the United Nations System to provide essential services for all its Members;

(f) Improve the management of United Nations resources available for assistance to the developing countries so as to maximize the benefit to these countries;

(g) Respond effectively to new opportunities, problems and challenges arising from changing requirements of world economic cooperation;

(h) Foster better utilization of the capacities of developing countries for economic and technical cooperation among themselves;

(i) Make the United Nations a more effective instrument for the establishment of a new, more rational and just international economic order (para. 14).

3. While the members of the Group may place a somewhat different emphasis on the factors mentioned below, they are in agreement that the following represent major problem areas where structural improvements will be necessary if the United Nations System is to realize its potentialities as an instrument for development and international economic cooperation: (1) fragmentation of effort, (2) decision making, (3) methods of work, (4) levels and type of representation, (5) the artificial separation of planning and operations, (6) the quality of the international staff, (7) functions not yet adequately performed in the institutional structure, (8) problems of universality of membership, and (9) regional structures (paras. 15–25).

4. The Group of Experts had neither the time nor the resources to develop fully detailed answers to the nine basic structural problems identified above. What is has sought to do in its report is to provide, in broad outline, a picture of what a restructured United Nations System might look like, and a number of practical first steps to implement that institutional design. The Group has confined itself to recommending reforms that can be initiated by the General Assembly itself and which do not require amendment of the Charter. The Group recognizes that many of the proposals made in its report will require some time for their full discussion and implementation, yet it believes that some of them can and should be set in motion by the General Assembly this year to provide a clear signal to the world that the urgently needed process of institutional revitalization has in fact begun. Without that, talk of structural reform will lack real credibility (para. 26).

5. The Group is proposing major changes in the central structures of the United Nations. Its proposals call for new approaches to the handling of economic items in the General Assembly, a major reform in the Economic and Social Council and its subsidiary bodies, and new consultative procedures to encourage agreed solutions leading to speedy implementation by Governments. They also call for the creation of a new post of Director-General for Development and International Economic Cooperation to provide leadership to the central Secretariat and the entire United Nations system, and for the consolidation of funds for technical cooperation and pre-investment activities in a United Nations Development Authority (UNDA), headed by an Administrator who would serve as a deputy to the Director-General (para. 27).

6. In moving towards the institutional design put forward in the report, it will be essential to ensure that, at every stage in the reform process, the enlightened self-interest of Member States in development and international cooperation will be promoted rather than sacrificed. Decisions taken to strengthen the central institutions are inevitably linked to decisions in some key sectoral areas (para. 28).

7. For example, some members of the Group feel that the appointment of a Director-General for Development and International Economic Cooperation, as envisaged in the report, and the agreement that he should be a national from a developing country when the Secretary-General is from a developed country, should be conditioned upon the gradual in-

corporation into the central Secretariat of those portions of the UNCTAD secretariat that are not dealing with sectoral trade questions. For other members of the Group, however, the creation of UNCTAD reflected the widespread feeling that the then existing structure of the Economic and Social Council was not serving the international community and especially the developing countries sufficiently well. These members feel that the incorporation into the central structure of those portions of the UNCTAD secretariat not dealing with trade questions, and especially those concerned with development financing and international monetary issues, should only take place when developing countries are satisfied that the new central structure is able to deal adequately with such questions. In their view, progress in the field of monetary reform, especially revisions in the distribution of voting rights under the weighted voting system of the World Bank and the International Monetary Fund, is an essential prerequisite. The same principle applies to the incorporation of the intergovernmental organs of UNCTAD into the revitalized central structure. These members feel, moreover, that pending the development of an adequate institutional framework for dealing comprehensively with trade questions – an ITO or other device – it would not be realistic to expect any such incorporation of either the Secretariat or the intergovernmental components of UNCTAD into the central system (para. 29).

8. To take account of the above concerns, the Group recommends that in its first biennial period the Economic and Social Council should not establish negotiating groups of the kind outlined in Chapter II, section D to deal with subjects under consideration in UNCTAD. At the end of this initial two-year period there should be a review to decide whether the central structures are working sufficiently well to warrant further progress in the direction of strengthening the central institutions. The Group further agrees that during this transitional period, the decision-making process of UNCTAD should be improved by the application of the consultative procedures proposed in the report (para. 30).

9. Similarly, with respect to the subject of operational activities, in Chapter II, section F, some members of the Group feel that the eventual consolidation of the various existing funds into the new UNDA and the designation of the Administrator of UNDA as deputy to the Director-General for Development and International Economic Cooperation must be dependent upon the negotiation of satisfactory arrangements regarding the composition of the new Operations Board and the division of responsibility between that Board and the Council and the UNDA Administrator, as well as a satisfactory definition of the status of the Administrator. The Group, therefore, recommends that these views be accepted as part of the general understanding governing the implementation of the proposals regarding the new UNDA, while noting its expectation that such concerns can be taken care of in negotiations within a two-year period (para. 31).

10. The Group envisages a process of institutional restructuring which could be initiated immediately by the seventh special session of the General Assembly and unfold over a five-year transitional period, during which the many difficult questions involved could be resolved to the

satisfaction of all the Members. At every stage during the five-year period the General Assembly could examine the measures needed to implement the restructuring with a view to ensuring a fair balance of advantages to different groups of Member States, and all the measures would be reviewed at the end of the five-year period to ensure that the restructuring in the centre and the sectoral areas was mutually compatible and regarded as satisfactory by the membership as a whole (para. 32).

II. CENTRAL STRUCTURES FOR GLOBAL POLICY MAKING, PROGRAMMING AND PLANNING AND OPERATIONAL ACTIVITIES

1. *General Assembly*

1.1 Whenever issues of global significance need urgent and separate consideration, special sessions of the General Assembly, on the pattern of the sixth and seventh special sessions, or special sessions of the proposed 'Development Committee' (see recommendations 1.3–1.6), should, after careful preparation, be convened rather than *ad hoc* world conferences (para. 37 (a)).

1.2 There should not be a fixed periodicity for any global conferences; a decision as to the best timing and approach and the most suitable arrangements for the consideration of a given issue should be taken by the Assembly, on a case-by-case basis, in the light of developments. For this purpose, the possibility of convening special sessions of the General Assembly or special sessions of the proposed Development Committee should be explored[2] (para. 37 (b)).

1.3 The Second Committee of the General Assembly should be renamed the Committee on Development and International Economic Cooperation (to be known as the 'Development Committee'). Consideration should be given to transferring from the Third Committee to the Second Committee, on a case-by-case basis, those items on social development that might more appropriately be dealt with in the Second Committee, bearing in mind the need to avoid overloading the Second Committee's agenda (para. 39 (a)).

1.4 The agenda of this Committee should be organized around meaningful clusters of issues (rather than be based on a mechanical consolidation of some of the items that traditionally appear on the agenda of the Second and Third Committees), reflecting an integrated approach to the economic and social aspects of development (para. 39 (b)).

1.5 Some days during the meeting of this Committee should be organized for discussions and decision making at senior or ministerial level on key issues that are ready for decision (para. 39 (c)).

1.6 The Economic and Social Council should be consulted in the elaboration of the Committee's agenda and should be asked to prepare its discussions and submit draft recommendations for action by the Committee (para. 39 (d)).

1.7 The Third Committee should be renamed the Committee on Social Problems, Human Rights and Humanitarian Activities (para. 39 (e)).

2. *Economic and Social Council*

2.1 The General Assembly at its forthcoming special session should re-affirm the Council's central role with respect to global policy formulation and implementation and the setting of priorities for the System as a whole (para. 44).

2.2 The Council should organize its programme on a biennial basis, with its calendar subdivided into frequent subject-oriented sets of short sessions spread throughout the calendar year (except during the General Assembly period). These sessions would take place in New York, Geneva or in other cities, such as Nairobi, depending on the subject-matter and the location of the relevant secretariat units. A typical calendar of the Council under these arrangements would be as follows:

(a) An initial substantive session (presumably in January of the first year) devoted to the identification, in the light of the General Assembly's debates and decisions and an analysis and assessment of the economic and social situation, of the themes and issue areas to be included in the Council's programme of work and the preparation on that basis of the Council's calendar;

(b) Short subject-oriented sessions devoted to policy making in respect of the major issue areas identified as requiring policy decision would then follow throughout the two years; the programme for these sessions should be set so as to ensure that all sectors at present covered by the Council's subsidiary machinery, such as population, environment, natural resources, science and technology, social development, human settlements etc., would all be discussed either in their present form or in some appropriate regrouping, over the two-year cycle;

(c) The calendar would also include, every year, a one-week ministerial session (which might be held during the last week of June) devoted to an over-all policy review, focusing mainly on world economic questions, including trade, monetary and financing issues related to development, and to the preparation, on the basis of the results of the preceding meetings, of a policy statement to be submitted to the General Assembly for its consideration and adoption;

(d) This ministerial session would be followed each year by two sessions of about two weeks each, to be held preferably during the month of July, to carry out in succession: (i) a review, in alternate years, of programme budgets, and medium-term plans, respectively, of the entire United Nations System,[3] and (ii) a review of the operational activities of the system, including, in particular, the activities of the United Nations Development Authority proposed below (see recommendation 6.3 below) (para. 46).

2.3 The Council should establish small negotiating groups to deal with key economic issues identified by it as requiring further negotiations with a view to bringing about agreed solutions (see in this connexion recommendation 4.1 below) (para. 49).

2.4 The General Assembly should recommend to Member States that they take all the steps necessary to ensure the systematic attendance of higher-level and more specialized Government representatives at the Council's meetings, it being understood that the composition of such delegations would be governed by the specific subject-matter to be considered at any given session (para. 51).

2.5 The United Nations should provide travel expenses for a number of delegations from capitals to meetings of the Council, along the lines of the present practices in respect of the General Assembly and the meetings of the functional commissions of the Council (para. 50).

2.6 The executive heads of the specialized agencies and programmes concerned should be urged to participate as actively as possible in the Council's review of issues impinging upon their fields of responsibility (para. 52).

2.7 The Council should assume direct responsibility for the work now performed by its existing subsidiary bodies. As a result, the permanent commissions and committees of the Council would be discontinued, except for the following bodies: the regional commissions; the Statistical Commission; the Commission on Narcotic Drugs; the Committee for Development Planning; the Commission on Transnational Corporations; and the Commission on Human Rights. The Council should, over a two-year cycle, address itself to all of the sectors now covered by its subsidiary machinery, either in their present form or in some appropriate regrouping (para. 54).

2.8 The Council should be assisted by a subsidiary body in connexion with its responsibility with regard to the programme budgets and medium-term plans of organizations and their coordination (see recommendations 5.7–5.8 below) (para. 55).

2.9 As already provided for in the Council's rules of procedure, any country not a member of the Council which was especially interested in a particular sectoral issue should be permitted to participate in the relevant discussion with all rights of membership, except the right to vote (para. 57).

2.10 Since the discontinuance of a number of subsidiary bodies dealing with sectoral areas could create considerably greater pressure for representation in the Council, the General Assembly and the Council should consider the suggestions mentioned in paragraph 58, and other possibilities, with a view to meeting this problem (para. 58–59).

2.11 Countries not members of the Council should be eligible to participate in the Council's negotiating groups with the same rights as members (in this connexion, see recommendations 4.1 and 4.2 below) (para. 60).

2.12 The Council should assume direct responsibility for the work now performed by the Committee on Natural Resources, the Committee on Science and Technology for Development, the Committee on Review and Appraisal, the Committee on Crime Prevention and Control, the Population Commission, the Commission for Social Development, the Commission on the Status of Women, and the Committee on Housing, Building and Planning, all of which would cease to exist (para. 61 (a)).

2.13 The Committee on the Application of Science and Technology to Development should cease to exist. Instead, to provide the United Nations in general and the Economic and Social Council in particular with ready access to the resources of the world scientific community, small *ad hoc* groups of scientists should be convened on a case-by-case basis to study specific problems and formulate recommendations which would then be taken into account by the Council in the formulation of relevant policies.[4]

The establishment of such groups, which would be based on rosters of scientists representing a wide range of scientific disciplines, would provide the Council with the necessary flexibility to deal, as appropriate, with diverse and constantly changing issues (para. 61 (b)).

2.14 A science adviser to the Secretary-General should be appointed. He should be an individual of international eminence and recognized competence, to serve as a link between the Secretary-General and the world scientific community. His main function would be to provide timely advice to the Secretary-General to help him anticipate the impact of advances in science and technology and identify the options that their application presents, especially for the benefit of the developing countries (para. 61 (b)).

2.15 The Council should assume direct responsibility, through the device of subject-oriented sessions as described above, for the policy functions in respect of environmental issues at present being carried out by the Governing Council of UNEP. Inasmuch as responsibility for managing the UNEP Fund would be assumed by the proposed Operations Board responsible for all pre-investment funds (see recommendation 6.4), the Governing Council of UNEP would be discontinued. The environment secretariat would remain in Nairobi, subject to the authority of the Director-General for Development and International Economic Cooperation (para. 61 (c)).

3. *Secretariat support facilities*

3.1 In recommending the following changes in the central Secretariat, the Group of Experts anticipates that there would be no increase in staffing costs; indeed, these changes may result in substantial savings that could be utilized for operational purposes (para. 69).

Reorientation of the Department of Economic and Social Affairs

3.2 A necessary first step towards strengthening the analytical capabilities of the Secretariat and enabling it to concentrate its efforts on the task of providing support, on an interdisciplinary basis, for the policy-making function of the Council, is to divest the Department of Economic and Social Affairs of its sectoral technical functions in the economic and social field and, particularly, of its sectoral operational responsibilities (para. 70).

Appendix 6

Director-General for Development and International Economic Cooperation

3.3 Within the United Nations Secretariat, a new post of Director-General for Development and International Economic Cooperation should be established. This official would be directly responsible to the Secretary-General, would serve as *primus inter pares* among the heads of United Nations organizations and agencies dealing with economic and social affairs and would be in charge of directing all activities at present being carried out by the Department of Economic and Social Affairs and the various United Nations offices and programmes with respect to research, policy-making support, inter-agency coordination and operational activities. The autonomous position of the specialized agencies would, of course, not be affected, but the new Director-General would seek to promote improved system-wide cooperation. He would chair the proposed Advisory Committee on Economic Cooperation and Development mentioned below (recommendation 3.8). He would need to be assisted in this task by two Deputy Directors-General, one for Research and Policy, and the other to serve as Administrator of the new United Nations Development Authority. Under these arrangements, the existing post of Under-Secretary-General for Economic and Social Affairs would cease to exist (para. 71).

3.4 The Director-General should be appointed by the Secretary-General and confirmed by the General Assembly. Careful procedures would need to be established for the process of selection of the candidate, to ensure that the individual chosen enjoys the confidence of all groups of countries. The implementation of this and related proposals should be carried out in a manner that ensures the fullest understanding and co-operation of the specialized agencies as this is a necessary basis for the successful operation of the system envisaged here (para. 73).

3.5 The post of Director-General should be assigned to a national of a developing country, at least during those years when the post of Secretary-General is occupied by a national of a developed country. If the post of Secretary-General were occupied by a national of a developing country, this arrangement would have to be reviewed. (It should be understood that the reference to developed and developing countries is to be interpreted as embracing countries with different social systems.) The post of Administrator of the new United Nations Development Authority and that of Deputy Director-General for Research and Policy could then be allocated, respectively, to a national of a developed country and a national of a developing country (para. 74).

3.6 The Director-General should be elected for his five-year term at the same time as the Secretary-General is elected for his five-year term. However, if the proposals in the Group's report are accepted, the Director-General could be appointed on an interim basis in time for his appointment to be confirmed by the General Assembly at its thirtieth session (para. 74).

3.7 As it builds its capacity for global intersectoral analysis, the Director-General's staff should progressively be able to function as an early-warning system geared to providing timely and effective advice to the intergovernmental organs on major emerging developments in the economic sphere requiring their urgent action. In order to play this role effectively, this secretariat should have at its disposal a flexible mechanism for drawing upon the expertise and knowledge of existing international organizations, national Governments and the private sector generally (para. 75).

Advisory Committee on Economic Cooperation and Development
3.8 A new inter-agency mechanism, to be known as the Advisory Committee on Economic Cooperation and Development, should be established, under the chairmanship of the new Director-General for Development and International Economic Cooperation. The Managing Director of IMF, the President of the World Bank, the Secretary-General of UNCTAD, the Executive Director of UNIDO, the Directors-General of the ILO, FAO, UNESCO and WHO, the Executive Secretaries of the regional commissions, the Deputy Director-General for Research and Policy and the Administrator of the new United Nations Development Authority would be *ex officio* members of this Committee. The Director-General of GATT would also be invited to join the Committee,[5] and the executive heads of other United Nations agencies and programmes would be invited, as necessary, to attend. The main task of the Committee would be to review the world economic and social situation and bring to the attention of high-level meetings of the Economic and Social Council, together with its own assessment and recommendations, all issues which, in its view, require international decisions and actions. Whenever possible, alternative policy options should be developed for submission to the Council, either by the Committee as a whole or by any of its members (paras. 77–78).

Joint research, planning and programming staff
3.9 A small 'joint unit' should be established within the new Director-General's Office to be composed of high-level staff seconded by the various organizations of the system – for a longer or shorter duration depending on central requirements – and such other highly qualified officials as may be required by the Director-General. This joint staff, whose members would be responsible to the new Director-General and would not, therefore, formally represent the agencies to which they belong, would have the following functions:
  (a) To serve as a centre for global policy analysis and assessment, in support of the work of the Advisory Committee and the Economic and Social Council; and
  (b) To serve as a system-wide planning bureau for the elaboration, on the basis of general policies and priorities laid down by the Council, of short- and medium-term plans to serve as guidelines for the programmes of individual organizations. It would also develop budgetary proposals for joint programmes in close collaboration and consultation with the Department of Administration and Management of the United Nations Secretariat and the relevant organs and offices of the specialized agencies (paras. 80–82).

Appendix 6

Deputy Director-General for Research and Policy

3.10 The staff under the Deputy Director-General for Research and Policy should be structured along intersectoral lines and should be so organized as to ensure that expertise on major aspects of development and international economic cooperation is available to it. This staff would have the responsibility of digesting and analysing material and inputs coming to the centre from the various sectoral components of the system and of preparing on that basis concise documentation for action by the Economic and Social Council (para. 83).

Administrator of the United Nations Development Authority

3.11 To ensure harmony between planning and operations, it would be useful to establish a post of Administrator of the United Nations Development Authority, who would be responsible for the functions now being carried out by the Administrator of UNDP and the executive heads of other United Nations voluntary programmes and funds for technical assistance and pre-investment activities (excluding, for the time being, the Executive Director of UNICEF (see recommendation 6.1)). In addition, this official would also serve as a Deputy to the Director-General for Development and International Economic Cooperation. It is recognized that the eventual consolidation of United Nations funds in the new UNDA and the designation of the Administrator of UNDA as Deputy to the Director-General for Development and International Economic Cooperation must be dependent on the negotiation of satisfactory arrangements with regard to the composition of the new Operations Board and the division of responsibility between the Board and the Economic and Social Council and the Administrator of UNDA, as well as a satisfactory definition of the status of the Administrator. It is expected that these negotiations could be concluded within a two-year period (para. 84).

Coordination arrangements

3.12 The Inter-Agency Consultative Board (IACB) of UNDP and the Environment Coordination Board (ECB) should be merged with ACC. However, the Programme Working Group and the Meeting of Environmental 'Focal Points', the two subsidiary bodies that now back up IACB and ECB, should be maintained and function as subsidiary bodies of ACC (paras. 87–88).

3.13 In order to avoid duplication, ACC should be kept regularly informed of the work of the new Advisory Committee on Economic Cooperation and Development (see recommendation 3.8 above) (para. 89).

3.14 With respect to the responsibilities at present assigned by ACC to its Preparatory Committee, the executive heads should be invited to carry out these responsibilities themselves, or if those responsibilities have to be delegated to another body, that they be represented on that body by their deputies who would have full authority to act on their behalf (para. 90).

3.15 Steps should be taken for a progressive reorientation of the work of the subsidiary bodies of ACC towards joint programming and planning. The progress made in this direction, and the obstacles faced, should be regularly and fully reported to the intergovernmental organs concerned (para. 91).

Personnel practices and policies

3.16 Member States and those who bear the principal responsibility for the management of the international civil service should rededicate themselves to the Charter requirements concerning the recruitment of staff (para. 93 (a)).

3.17 Competitive examinations for United Nations service should be held and recruitment requirements with regard to academic and other formal qualifications should reflect the diversity of cultural and socio-economic settings in the different regions of the world. Countries in a subregion or region should be permitted, on the basis of mutual agreement, to pool the number of secretariat posts allocated to them for purposes of satisfying the requirements of equitable geographical distribution (para. 93 (b)).

3.18 A programme of 'pre-recruitment training' should be undertaken to assist developing countries, particularly the least developed among them, in the training of candidates for posts subject to geographical distribution. While the main purpose of such an operation should be to train candidates for United Nations service, the programme should also envisage training for national civil service since developing countries, especially the least developed, cannot be expected to send their best technicians unless the programme, at the same time that it provides training for service in the United Nations System, helps to satisfy national needs for skilled personnel (para. 93 (c)).

3.19 Steps should be taken to increase the proportion of women in the professional category, especially at the senior level (para. 93 (d)).

3.20 A United Nations Fellows Programme should be established to bring to the United Nations System young people of superior ability from all regions of the world (para. 93 (e)).

3.21 To upgrade the skills of United Nations staff members, bring them up to date on new developments in their fields, improve their morale and enhance prospects for career development, the following measures should be taken:

(a) Consideration should be given to reviving the Staff College project as part of the development of new and improved training facilities. The Staff College would not only provide common training to officials coming from different agencies but would also give them the opportunity to exchange experiences and establish personal relationships of lasting professional value once they return to their respective posts throughout the United Nations System. It would thus help generate a system-wide sense of common identity that would make a singular contribution to the cohesion of the United Nations family of agencies;

(b) In view of the rapid pace of change in the various areas of United Nations interest and action, staff members should be encouraged to take sabbaticals in universities or institutes of advanced study to refresh and enhance their knowledge and skills;

(c) Staff rules concerning retirement should be applied more rigorously;

(d) Personnel rules and practices, particularly in respect of language allowances for professional staff pursuant to General Assembly Resolution 2480 B (xxiii), should be set and applied to avoid any discrimination against staff whose mother language is not one of the official languages of the United Nations;

(e) Measures should be taken to improve the United Nations System of career development, including greater staff mobility within and between different United Nations agencies;

(f) The promotion process should do more to reward ability and initiative, and administrators should show more willingness to eliminate unproductive staff;

(g) There should be better and more frequent communication between high-level and lower-level staff since the latter are often not adequately informed about the work of the Organization and this adversely affects their morale (para. 94).

3.22 The United Nations agencies should move towards a unified personnel system, including a unified system of salaries, grading, conditions of service and recruitment. The International Civil Service Commission should be given additional powers and responsibilities to enable it to achieve the objective of a unified personnel system as stated (para. 95).

3.23 In order for the United Nations to be able to secure the services of highly skilled specialists, it should have the flexibility to resort to fixed-term appointments as necessary (para. 96 (a)).

3.24 The search for talent should not be limited to foreign ministries and United Nations missions. An effort should also be made to recruit outstandingly qualified persons from the academic and scientific communities and from private corporations or state enterprises (para. 96 (b)).

3.25 Careful balance should be achieved in recruitment policy between the requirements for specialists in their respective fields and the employment of high-level generalists with particular experience in field activity who are in a position to understand the multidisciplinary and intersectoral aspects of development and international economic cooperation (para. 96 (c)).

4. *Consultative procedures*

4.1 Consultative procedures would normally be initiated at any early stage in the discussion of a given subject and before the stage of the passing of resolutions, but the procedures could also be initiated at the end of a process of debate or even after a decision where this seemed to be appropriate. It would be for the Economic and Social Council, if the recommendations in this section were accepted, to work out these consultative arrangements in appropriate rules of procedure which would specify, among other things, the kinds of subjects on which consultative procedures could take place (para. 98).

4.2 The following arrangements are recommended for a system of negotiating groups under the restructured General Assembly and Economic and Social Council:

(a) At the request of the General Assembly or the Economic and Social Council, or upon the motion of one tenth of the members of either body, a small negotiating group would be constituted by the Council to seek agreement on a specific action proposal or related action proposals in the field of development and international economic co-operation.[6] Negotiating groups would be of manageable size, normally between 10 and 30,[7] and would include countries principally interested in the subject-matter whether or not they were members of the Council. During the initial two-year period, negotiating groups would only be constituted by majority vote of the General Assembly or the Council;

(b) Negotiating groups would normally be created at the beginning of the Council's biennial calendar, although they could be created at other times when the need arises. These groups would operate for periods of one or two years, subject to renewal as determined by the Assembly or the Council. The Council would be kept informed by the negotiating groups of the progress being made by them. During the two-year period, the General Assembly and the Council would be free to consider subjects under discussion in the groups and to vote resolutions thereon, but in deciding upon whether to vote a particular resolution, the General Assembly and the Council would take into account the progress of the negotiations;

(c) Each negotiating group would function under the guidance of a full-time chairman with the assistance, as necessary, of a small representative bureau of vice-chairmen, all of whom would be proposed by the Secretary-General and confirmed by the General Assembly or the Council, depending on where the proposal for the group originated. The full-time chairman would serve for the duration of the group;

(d) Each negotiating group would operate on the basis of unanimity. When a negotiating group reached agreement, it would report to the Council, which would adopt the agreement, refer the matter back to the negotiating group for further consideration, or take such other action as it deemed appropriate. Upon approval by the Council, the agreement would be passed to the General Assembly, which could approve the agreement, refer the matter back to the group, or take some other action;

(e) The Council should consider possible arrangements designed to ensure the implementation of policy decisions taken by the General Assembly or the Council after use of the consultative procedures. The aim of these arrangements would be to promote the necessary action by United Nations Members within the time horizon required. Action would include the negotiation of formal international agreements, where appropriate, and consideration should be given to instituting arrangements to ensure that such agreements were effectively implemented (para. 103).

5. *Planning, programming and budgeting*

5.1 The appropriate intergovernmental bodies and secretariat units charged with programming and budgeting should develop a thematic approach to priority setting through such devices as the establishment of intersectoral programmes, to the degree that this is compatible with the managerial considerations underlying the incremental approach which is at present the dominant one in the United Nations and some agencies (para. 114).

At the inter-agency level

5.2 The United Nations and the specialized agencies should take immediate steps to adopt *comparable* (not necessarily uniform) programme-budget presentations and a common methodology of programme classification and description of content. Regular reports should be submitted to the competent intergovernmental organs indicating the progress made in this direction and identifying possible constraints (para. 116).

5.3 Appropriate steps should be taken throughout the United Nations System to synchronize budget cycles and to set time-tables for budget preparation, review and approval that will permit the General Assembly and the Economic and Social Council to review the budgets of the specialized agencies prior to their adoption (para. 117).

5.4 To provide Member Governments and United Nations organizations with a clearer picture of the activities carried out by the Organization, irrespective of their source of funding, whether assessed or voluntary, the following steps should be taken: (a) the United Nations and the agencies should provide to the extent possible full and compatible information on extrabudgetary resources in their programme budgets; (b) country programming periods should be harmonized with agency medium-term planning periods; (c) the UNDP and other funds, which it has been proposed to consolidate, should prepare 'project budgets' for the same period as the agency budget periods; and (d) UNICEF's programme cycles and methodologies, as far as its development-related projects are concerned, should be harmonized with those of the new UNDA and the relevant agencies (paras. 118–120).

5.5 The results of prior consultations on medium-term plans should be regularly reported to the Economic and Social Council (through CPC) and to the governing bodies of the agencies in question, and a joint inter-agency planning unit should be established for the purpose of preparing system-wide medium-term plans (para. 123).

5.6 The results of prior consultations on the work programmes should be reported to the Economic and Social Council (through CPC) and to the governing bodies of the agencies in question, and the United Nations and the agencies should utilize the system of programme budgeting to develop their cooperation in related programme areas into joint programming (para. 127).

At the intergovernmental level

5.7 To assist the Council in the performance of the expanded functions envisaged for it in the fields of programming and planning, CPC should be strengthened to make it a more effective body for reviewing programmes and determining priorities and, thus, for achieving a coherent and deliberately chosen balance among the wide-ranging activities of the subordinate bodies of the United Nations. For this purpose, CPC needs higher and more expert representation and should be able to devote far more time than at present (several weeks) to this important and complex task (para. 130 (a)).

5.8 As a long-term goal, the United Nations should work towards a single body to advise the Economic and Social Council as well as the General Assembly with respect to the review, approval and evaluation of both programmes and budgets. This could be a small body representative of the different groups of Member States composed of highly qualified individuals nominated by Governments but serving in their personal capacity. The ACABQ, whose small membership of 13 adequately balances the groups of developed countries, developing countries and socialist countries, might eventually be transformed into such a body. Alternatively, the membership of CPC might be adjusted to make it the small, balanced group necessary for this task. A first step towards the establishment of a single programme and budget body might be to promote more frequent and effective consultations between CPC and ACABQ (para. 130 (b)).

5.9 A mechanism should be established for continuing supervision and evaluation of programme implementation for the purpose of furnishing the competent intergovernmental organs with information on programme management and execution and on the progress made towards achieving programme objectives. Towards this end, a small body of independent experts, functioning on a full-time basis, should be created. Alternatively, the Joint Inspection Unit should be transformed into such a body (para. 132).

At the secretariat level

5.10 High-level machinery should be strengthened for centralized policy direction with respect to programming and budgeting in the United Nations itself. The high-level programme and budget review machinery established by the Secretary-General should be further developed with a view to the rationalization of the United Nations programming and budgeting process (para. 133).

5.11 As proposed in recommendation 3.9 above, the joint staff to be created within the Office of the new Director-General for Development and International Economic Cooperation should serve, *inter alia*, as a system-wide planning bureau for the elaboration, on the basis of the general policies and priorities laid down by the Economic and Social

Council, of short- and medium-term plans to serve as guidelines for the programmes of individual organizations. In addition, it should have the function of developing budgetary proposals for joint programmes in close collaboration and consultation with the Department of Administration and Management of the United Nations Secretariat and the relevant organs and offices of the specialized agencies (para. 133).

6. *Operational activities*

Consolidation of operational activities and funds
6.1 All United Nations funds for technical assistance and pre-investment activities should be consolidated for the purpose of more effective policy making, administration and management into a new United Nations Development Authority. Certain small funds for capital investment should also be consolidated, as hereinafter specified, in UNDA. For the time being, UNICEF is not included in this consolidation. This move could, however, be considered at some future stage, taking into account the unique character of UNICEF's role within the system. With respect to trust funds established by individual donors, their future disposition would be subject to further study and negotiation among interested parties (para. 141).

Maintenance of separate identity of funds
6.2 In the consolidation of funds under a single administrative and management structure, the separate identity of the funds would be maintained so that donors would continue to have the right to earmark contributions for particular purposes, a right which the Group believes will encourage a higher level of total contributions. Therefore, under the consolidated administration, management and policy-making structure being proposed, separate accounts should be kept for identified programmes and existing practices for earmarking funds to particular programmes should be permitted to continue (para. 142).

Integration of intergovernmental policy-making organs
6.3 There should be a single governing body responsible for reviewing the operational activities of the United Nations system as a whole and providing over-all policy guidance within the context of global development strategies. The Economic and Social Council is the appropriate body to perform this policy-making function since it is fitting that global policy making on operational activities be part of the responsibilities of the body charged with the task of formulating global development policies. This arrangement would not only promote the integration of global policy and operations but would also avoid the duplication of discussions that debates in the various governing bodies and the subsequent Council review of reports of the voluntary programmes and funds entail. For this purpose, the Economic and Social Council should include in its programme of work an annual session devoted to a global review of operational activities (see in this connexion recommendation 2.2) (para. 143).

Integration of management bodies

6.4 There should be a consolidation, as early as possible and under appropriate administrative arrangements, of intergovernmental structures such as the UNDP Governing Council, the UNEP Governing Council, the United Nations/FAO Intergovernmental Committee of the World Food Programme, and the Board of Governors of the Special Fund, and these bodies should be replaced by a single Operations Board which would be responsible for the conduct of the general operations of UNDA and would exercise all the powers delegated to it by the Economic and Social Council. The mandate of the Operations Board would extend to all operational funds currently administered by the United Nations, UNDP (including the Capital Development Fund, the United Nations Volunteers programme and the United Nations Revolving Fund for Natural Resources), UNFPA, UNEP (including the United Nations Habitat Human Settlements Foundation), WFP and the Special Fund. Its membership should be relatively small (18–27) and equitably balanced between net donors and net recipient countries. There should also be appropriate representation of countries with different social systems. It would be in a position to function on a year-round basis, as necessary, and would not be confined to members of the Economic and Social Council. It could establish subgroups to deal with subjects not directly related to economic and social development, such as a subgroup for disaster relief and emergency assistance, and a subgroup for drug abuse control or other activities. The Board and its subgroups would be in close contact with the Administrator to assist in management functions (paras. 144–145).

Integration at the secretariat level

6.5 In the consolidation of funds under the proposed United Nations Development Authority, the separate identities of certain administrative units should be maintained, notably in the case of population, environment and other areas where this would facilitate fund raising or operations (para. 146 (ii)).

6.6 The present Department of Economic and Social Affairs, which would become part of the secretariat under the authority of the Deputy Director-General for Research and Policy, should be relieved of the responsibilities at present performed by the Office of Technical Cooperation, which would be transferred to UNDA, when established. The sectoral/technical functions of ESA should be progressively transferred to other parts of the system as soon as satisfactory arrangements can be worked out, with the understanding that certain technical functions would remain at the centre. The secretariat units performing functions cutting across sectoral areas, such as statistics and public administration, would continue to provide, as appropriate, the necessary substantive support services (para. 146 (iii)).

6.7 The eventual consolidation of funds into the new UNDA and the designation of the Administrator of UNDA as Deputy to the Director-General for Development and International Economic Cooperation must be dependent upon the negotiation of satisfactory arrangements with respect to the composition of the Operations Board and the division of responsibility between the Board and the Economic and Social Council and the UNDA Administrator, as well as a satisfactory definition of the status of the Administrator. It is expected that these negotiations could be concluded within a two-year period (para. 148).

Execution of projects
6.8 Management decisions with respect to the execution of projects should be governed by considerations as to which means of implementation are the most economical and effective so that savings in administrative costs may be made available for development purposes. The long-term requirements of recipient countries, particularly with regard to institution building and the development of national expertise, must also be fully borne in mind. Recipient countries should be given greater flexibility with respect to the execution of field projects. Towards this end, the administering authority should study the best method of implementation in close consultation with the recipient country, taking into account the latter's capabilities. Responsibility for the execution of projects need not be automatically assigned to the specialized agencies, but could be entrusted to: the recipient Government itself; institutions in the recipient country; appropriate consultants, universities, contracting agencies or firms etc.; institutions of other developed or developing countries; the new United Nations Development Authority; regional commissions (particularly for regional and subregional projects) (para. 150).

Information systems
6.9 The new UNDA should have access to a coordinated information system ensuring (a) the effective and coordinated collection and evaluation of data by the various agencies and branches concerned, and (b) the compatibility and reliability of data to be used by decision makers at the national and international levels. To this end, the greatest degree of co-operation between the national and international agencies concerned will be required (para. 152).

Evaluation
6.10 An independent system of evaluation and monitoring of projects should be set up by UNDA, in cooperation with other United Nations agencies, to ensure that at the critical stages of project operations a process of independent evaluation should take place benefiting from all relevant intellectual inputs, including those of the government authorities concerned, the executing agency directly responsible and other agencies whose contribution can be relevant to the proper evaluation of the project. This independent system should also call on outside advice. It would present its report to the Administrator of UNDA (para. 153).

Supporting systems for project implementation
6.11 The UNDA should initiate a general review of procedures covering the recruitment of experts, the procurement of equipment and sub-

contracting arrangements at all levels, with the assistance of all agencies operating in the field, using the advice of the World Bank, UNICEF and, if possible, the regional commissions, the regional banks and national assistance agencies. The aim of this review would be, *inter alia*, to ensure that field projects receive the necessary logistical support taking full advantage of local supplies and equipment as well as local potential in the fields of transportation, communications and other relevant aspects which may also be made use of in connexion with projects in other countries of the region. In this connexion, full use should be made of the experience accumulated by the United Nations Field Service in the operation of transport, communications and maintenance systems. The Field Service's experience has, so far, been used to support peace-keeping activities; its potential could, however, also be utilized in appropriate circumstances to support development activities (para. 154).

Role of the resident representative

6.12 The resident representatives, who play a key coordinating role at the country level, should represent the whole United Nations system within a country in the economic sphere. There should be full implementation of the Consensus adopted by the Governing Council of UNDP in the summer of 1970 and later in the year by the General Assembly, which, *inter alia*, provides that the resident representative should have ultimate authority on behalf of the Administrator for all aspects of the programme at the country level and should, 'subject to the agreement of the organizations concerned, be the central coordinating authority on their behalf for the other development assistance programmes of the United Nations system' (General Assembly resolution 2688 (xxv))(para. 155).

Relations with IBRD and other agencies

6.13 The new UNDA should establish the closest possible working relations with the World Bank. Moreover, the recommended merger of the other voluntary funds with the new UNDA will make it possible for the country programmes to cover a broader range of operations, including those in the fields of population, environment and so on. Therefore, the country programmes of UNDA and the World Bank should, in the future, be coordinated and harmonized (para. 157).

6.14 There should be the fullest possible exchange of information, experience, ideas and personnel between the United Nations and the Bank. Towards this end (a) there should be the closest possible contacts between headquarters staff in the new UNDA and in the World Bank; (b) in field operations, UNDA should, in suitable cases, engage staff from other agencies, including IBRD, on an individual basis; (c) whenever possible, UNDA/IBRD/IMF country missions should be organized jointly (para. 158).

Coordination at the national level for policy-making and operational activities

6.15 It is advisable that Member States establish within their Governments, arrangements for high-level coordination and review of multilateral affairs and operations, where they have not already done so (para. 161).

7. *Regional structures*

7.1 Structural changes will be necessary in the regional commissions, at both the intergovernmental level and the secretariat level, to align them with the structural pattern proposed for the centre. It is recognized that there may be significant differences in the requirements of the various regions in this respect: developing regions, such as Asia, Africa and Latin America, may require a structure, and may need to adopt policy objectives somewhat different from those of ECE, most of whose members are developed countries with different political conditions (paras. 164–165).

7.2 On the operational side, the regional commissions should play a more active role in identifying, initiating, formulating and executing regional and subregional programmes and projects (para. 168 (a)).

7.3 Subject to the observance of agreed criteria and standards, decentralization of activities to the regional commissions should include all responsibilities relating to their substantive and administrative support services. In addition, the International Civil Service Commission should be asked to consider the feasibility of greater decentralization to the regional commissions with respect to the recruitment of staff (para. 168 (b)).

7.4 Since all sectoral and regional studies on the economic situation should be made to converge in the Economic and Social Council, the regional commissions should perform their fact-finding task not only in connexion with their regional responsibility but in such a way as to contribute to the Council's global assessment. It would be necessary, therefore, for the commissions to single out in their fact-finding processes those elements that have significance beyond the regions and which are, as a result, of particular relevance to the centre (para. 168 (c)).

7.5 In performing their policy-making functions, the regional commissions should make a distinction between strictly regional matters and those that extend beyond the region or apply to more than one region. In the latter case, the proposals from the commissions should be designed to assist the Council in the performance of its global policy-making function. In their policy making, the regional commissions should be guided by the policies laid down by the Council (para. 168 (d)).

7.6 The economic commissions should promote and intensify regional economic cooperation that best corresponds to the needs and interests of the regional community as well as those of the global community (para. 168 (e)).

8. *Cooperation among developing countries*

8.1 The United Nations system should be geared to undertake more specific measures to accelerate cooperation among developing countries in trade, industry and agriculture, as well as in other related fields of development. Therefore, the General Assembly at its seventh special session should give consideration to initiating a programme of action in respect of cooperation among developing countries and also set up joint machinery for follow-up action (paras. 171 and 174).

III. STRUCTURES FOR SECTORAL ACTIVITIES

9. *Trade*

9.1 The following issues should be carefully examined in appropriate forums as a matter of priority:

(a) The possibility of bringing GATT into closer association, on a formal basis, with United Nations central organs, and the possibility of strengthening GATT/UNCTAD relations;

(b) The strengthening of GATT in various ways. The following possibilities for strengthening GATT were particularly emphasized by members from developed market economy countries:

  (i) The negotiation of a new code of trade liberalization which would be administered by an inner group of countries adhering to the code, possibly under special procedures. The arrangements under which the existing GATT is administered on a one nation one vote basis would not be altered. The higher level of obligations in the new code of trade liberalization might be made available via the most favoured nation clause to GATT Contracting Parties not parties to the code;

  (ii) The negotiation of new rules on export controls and access to supplies;

  (iii) The negotiation of a new uniform 'escape clause' provision, covering the exceptional resort to import restrictions;

  (iv) Elimination of the 'grandfather clause' in GATT, permitting Contracting Parties to maintain pre-1947 import restrictions otherwise inconsistent with GATT rules;

  (v) Improved procedures for advance notification, consultation, the submission of complaints (possibly by private parties as well as Governments), the settlement of disputes by independent panels of experts, and arrangements to deny the benefits of GATT to Contracting Parties which act inconsistently with the Agreement in ways not sanctioned by the Contracting Parties as a group;

(c) The strengthening of UNCTAD in various ways. Members from developing countries strongly favoured equipping UNCTAD with the elements necessary for its gradual transformation into a comprehensive international trade organization;

(d) Measures to eliminate voluntary agreements, such as the Long-term Cotton Textile Agreement, which permit quantitative restrictions in derogation of traditional GATT norms, and the establishment of new rules limiting resort to quantitative restrictions;

(e) The possibility of establishing an international trade organization which, in effect, would incorporate UNCTAD and GATT into a single organization with two chambers, one concerned with broad policy and the other with trade negotiations, but using a common secretariat;

(f) The possibility of establishing an umbrella commodity organization standing by itself or as a 'third chamber' in a new international trade organization;

(g) In defining the mandate of any new international trade organization that might ultimately come into existence, consideration would have to be given to the question of whether it should deal not only with trade issues but also with other issues such as restrictive business practices, transfer of technology, private investment, and transnational enterprises (paras. 177 and 179 (a)).

9.2 GATT and the United Nations should enter into a mutually satisfactory agreement providing for a formal relationship, including exchange of information and closer administrative collaboration (para. 179 (b)).

9.3 As a longer-term objective, there should be an evolution towards the creation of an international trade organization to deal with trade issues in a comprehensive manner (para. 179 (c)).

9.4 Any structural change in the field of trade should not be allowed to interfere with the multilateral trade negotiations now being carried out under GATT auspices (para. 180).

10. *International monetary reform*[8]

10.1 The following issues should be carefully examined in appropriate forums as a matter of priority:

(a) Recycling of petrodollars through IMF to help both developed and developing countries deal with balance-of-payments problems related to the higher costs of energy, food, fertilizer and other imports;

(b) Ways of rectifying the imbalance between countries that has characterized the process of international liquidity creation over the past four years, both between developed and developing countries, on the one hand, and within these two groups of countries, on the other;

(c) The need for a symmetrical adjustment mechanism, with a degree of international surveillance of the adjustment process, including exchange rates and macro-economic policies;

(d) Better international management of global liquidity, with SDR becoming the principal reserve asset and the role of gold and reserve currencies being reduced;

(e) The need for interim steps in the direction of longer-term reform, including the possibility of establishing a gold substitution account in the International Monetary Fund which would permit the substitution of monetary gold stocks for SDR and the redistribution of some parts of the resulting book-keeping profits to the developing countries;

(f) Measures to enable developing countries, particularly those most seriously affected, to adjust to a higher level of international prices in a manner consistent with their development needs, possibly through the establishment of facilities within the International Monetary Fund; in this context, the trust fund category of proposals would require consideration as one possibility;

(g) Measures to enable developing countries to have indirect access to Fund resources in ways unrelated to their quotas, through IMF support for international funds, e.g., in agriculture;

(h) The examination of voting power in the Fund, including the question of the power of veto on decision making by a single member; more generally, the possible increase of the share of developing countries to the range of 45–50 per cent of the total, with a substantially greater access of developing countries to IMF credit;

(i) Consideration of changes in the staffing of the Fund to provide for a greater role for developing countries in senior positions and of arrangements to enable career members of the Fund staff to have the experience of working in developing countries, perhaps through suitable links with UNDP's technical assistance programmes (paras. 181 and 182 (a)).

10.2 The distribution of voting rights under the weighted voting system in the International Monetary Fund should be revised to reflect the new balance of economic power and the legitimate interest of developing countries in a greater voice in the operation of that institution (para. 182 (b)).

11. *Development financing*[9]

11.1 The following issues should be carefully examined in appropriate forums as a matter of priority:

(a) The possibility of establishing a 'third window' in the World Bank, and of enlarging its resources beyond the $1 billion currently under discussion;

(b) Improving procedures to alleviate the debt problem of developing countries on terms consistent with their long-term development;

(c) Ways of canalizing investments of OPEC countries to other developing countries under suitable bilateral or multilateral auspices. This may also include appropriate forms of triangular cooperation between developed countries, OPEC countries and other developing countries. Consideration should be given to: (i) appropriate guarantee mechanisms for such investments; (ii) the acceptance of a suitable code of conduct governing the transfer of technology associated with such investment; and (iii) principles governing the mixture between debt and equity in investments which take place on a joint venture basis;

(d) The examination of voting power in the World Bank, including the question of the power of veto on decision-making by a single member; more generally, the possible increase of the share of developing countries to that of parity with developed countries;

(e) Consideration of changes in the staffing of the World Bank to provide for a greater role for developing countries in senior positions, and of arrangements to enable career members of the Bank staff to have the experience of working in developing countries, perhaps through suitable links with UNDP's technical assistance programmes;

(f) The possibility of cooperation between OECD/DAC and OPEC countries in the exchange of information on aid programmes;

(g) Measures to encourage more effective development efforts by the aid recipients (paras. 183 and 184 (a)).

11.2 The distribution of voting rights under the weighted voting system in the World Bank should be revised to reflect the new balance of economic power and the legitimate interest of developing countries in a greater voice in the operations of that institution (para. 184 (b)).

11.3 The 'third window' in the World Bank should be established (para. 184 (c)).

12. *Industrialization*

12.1 UNIDO should assume the task of examining global trends concerning supply and demand in the various industrial and related sectors with a view to the better exchange of information on sectoral economic policies (para. 190).

IV. MEANS OF IMPLEMENTATION

13. *Committee on the structure of the United Nations System*

13.1 The Secretary-General should appoint a committee on the structure of the United Nations system, to study and report regularly to the General Assembly on the progress of the restructuring effort (para. 194).

13.2 If it is decided to implement the institutional design proposed in the report, it will be desirable that actions by the General Assembly or other organs of the United Nations System be consistent with the recommended structural reforms. Some continuing arrangement would, therefore, be necessary during the period of restructuring for evaluating proposals that may be made to ensure that they are consistent with this design. Accordingly, all institutional proposals, including proposals for the holding of special conferences, should be referred to the committee mentioned above for an advisory opinion before being decided upon by the General Assembly or other intergovernmental body (para. 195).

Notes

Introduction

1. C. Wilfred Jenks, *The International Labour Organisation in the U.N. Family*. UNITAR Lecture Series, 3 (1971), p. 45.
2. For a description of the integrated organization by the United Nations of the civilian operations in the Congo, see *Annual Report of the Secretary-General on the Work of the Organization, 16 June 1960 to 15 June 1961 (Official Records of the General Assembly, Sixteenth Session, Supplement No. 1* (A/4800)), pp. 47–55. The technical assistance activities of all the United Nations organizations were placed under a Chief of Civilian Operations who reported to the Secretary-General and was advised by a Consultative Group consisting of the heads of the groups of experts made available by the organizations concerned.
3. UNITAR has undertaken a series of studies on the relationships between the United Nations and non-United Nations regional organizations. The studies already published include: A. H. Robertson, *The Relations between the Council of Europe and the United Nations*, UNITAR, Regional Study No. 1 (1972); and Sir Peter Smithers, *Governmental Control: A Prerequisite for Effective Relations between the United Nations and Non-United Nations Regional Organizations*. UNITAR, Conference Report No. 3 (1973).
4. Document DP/5, 2 Vols., 1969. See also Mahdi Elmandjra, *The United Nations System: An Analysis* (London, Faber and Faber, and Hamden, Conn., Archon Books (1973)); and 'An account of the operational and research activities of the United Nations system in the field of economic and social development' (E/4744, Vols. I and II, 1969).
5. *Official Records of the Economic and Social Council, Eighteenth Session*, 798th meeting, para. 19.
6. See his address entitled 'The Development of a Constitutional Framework for International Co-operation' delivered at the University of Chicago on 1 May 1960, reproduced in *Dag Hammarskjöld: Servant of Peace*, ed. by Wilder Foote (Harper and Row, New York), p. 257. For another interesting indication of Hammarskjöld's views on United Nations–agency relations, see his letter dated 15 March 1960 to the United States Secretary of State, Christian Herter, quoted in Brian Urquhart, *Hammarskjöld* (New York, Knopf, 1973), p. 325.
7. *Five-year Perspective, 1960–1964*. Consolidated report on the appraisals of the scope, trend and costs of the programmes of the United Nations, the ILO, FAO, UNESCO, WHO, WMO and IAEA in the economic, social and human rights fields (United Nations publication, Sales No. 60.IV.14).
8. 'Enlarged Committee for Programme and Coordination; final report (E/4748).
9. *Partners in Development: Report of the Commission on International Development* (New York, Praeger, 1969).

1. Relationship problems inherent in the decentralized United Nations System

1.   The passages that follow are largely based on the writer's recollection of and notes on the San Francisco Conference. Many of the considerations and arguments referred to, however, can be found in C. Wilfred Jenks, 'Co-ordination in international organisation; an introductory survey' in *British Yearbook of International Law*, 1951 (London, Oxford University Press, 1952).

2.   Including the work of the League of Nations High Commissioner for Refugees (originally the Nansen Office), the Settlement of the Assyrians of Iraq and the Programme of Assistance to China, 1933–1939.

3.   The need for coordination within the League of Nations itself was first officially referred to in 1938, when the League Council set up a Coordinating Committee, as recommended in the report of a Committee it had appointed to consider the 'Structure and Functions of the Economic and Financial Organization of the League of Nations'. The report explained its recommendation on the ground that 'the Organization is more concerned than heretofore with questions which lie on the border-land of social and of economic policy'. League of Nations, *Official Journal*, 19th Year, Nos. 5–6 (May–June 1938), 101st session of the Council, Annex 1712, p. 553.

4.   While Article 63 authorizes the Council to coordinate the activities of the specialized agencies, Article 58 states that 'the Organization' *shall* make recommendations for the coordination of their 'policies and activities'. This has generally been taken to mean that the coordination of policies involves the General Assembly and not just the Council. For views and practices regarding the respective roles of the two principal organs under Article 58, see *Repertory of Practice of United Nations Organs*, Vol. III, *Articles 55–72 of the Charter* (United Nations publication, Sales No. 55.V.2, Vol. III), pp. 127–151.

5.   In addition to the Articles referred to above, the main provisions of the Charter bearing directly on coordination and the relations between the United Nations and the specialized agencies include Articles 17 (3), 59, 64, 66 and 70, but a much broader range of provisions are relevant to the concept and purposes of, and the issue of order and coherence in, the United Nations System. Beginning with the Preamble, these include Article 1 on Purposes and Principles, Articles 10 and 13 on the Functions and Powers of the General Assembly, Article 22 on General Assembly Procedure, and Articles 55 and 56 on International Economic and Social Co-operation.

6.   For almost all practical purposes, the IAEA acts and is treated like a specialized agency. For the sake of brevity, it is normally included in the term 'specialized agencies' throughout this study.

7.   *Official Records of the Economic and Social Council, Fifty-fifth Session, Supplement No. 1* (E/5400), 'Decisions', p. 33.

8.   For a discussion of the special features of these agreements, see Edward S. Mason and Robert E. Asher, *The World Bank Since Bretton Woods* (Washington, D.C., The Brookings Institute, 1973), pp. 54–60.

9.   See 'First report of the Secretary-General's Committee on Coordination to the Economic and Social Council' (E/614, 1948), Annex VI.

10.   *Official Records of the General Assembly, Seventh Session, Supplement No. 3* (A/2172), Introduction, p. x.

11.   A. Loveday, 'Suggestions for the reform of the United Nations economic and social machinery', *International Organization* (Boston, Mass.), Vol. VII, No. 3, August 1953, p. 326.

12. The ILO Andean Indian project, which involved a 'special groups' approach, was later merged with general rural development programmes in the countries concerned.

13. See E/3107 and E/4844.

14. 'The ACC. . . has tried to ensure that the Council's decisions were such as could be accepted and implemented by the governing organs of the agencies, to promote the necessary action by those organs (which, while very willing to co-operate with the United Nations, have been sensitive to any impairment of their autonomy) and to facilitate coordination of policies at the national level through the close contact of its members with the key officials of the different ministries handling the affairs of their respective agencies'. Martin Hill, 'The Administrative Committee on Coordination', *The Evolution of International Organizations*, ed. Evan Luard (London, Thames and Hudson, 1966).

15. Several countries have, however, been extremely sensitive to any United Nations Secretariat action thattight seem to affect Governments' unique policy-making authority. The agency staffs usually have a freer hand to take initiatives and positions.

2. Developments that have affected inter-agency relationships and coordination

1. But note that, especially in the case of the highly technical agencies, a substantial proportion of their work remains 'self-contained'.

2. The Secretary-General's letter to the President of the Council transmitting his proposals for the Expanded Programme included the following observation: 'It was – and remains – my view that in the interest of coordinated action the most appropriate way of financing the programme would be through the establishment of a single common fund into which all special contributions from Governments would be paid and out of which allocations would be made to the several international organizations to meet, subject to such broad policies as might be laid down by the Economic and Social Council and the General Assembly, the varying needs of Governments for technical assistance as they arose. The majority of my colleagues from the specialized agencies were not able to subscribe to this position.' (Official Records of the General Assembly, Fourth Session, Supplement No. 3 (A/972), para. 61).

3. A third, the Economic Commission for Latin America (ECLA) was created in 1948, a fourth, the Economic Commission for Africa (ECA) in 1958, and a fifth, the Economic Commission for West Asia (ECWA), in 1973. Prior to the establishment of ECWA, a United Nations Economic and Social Office in Beirut (UNESOB) had been built up by stages to serve the area and perform some of the functions of a commission. The title of ECAFE was changed in 1974 to Economic and Social Commission for Asia and the Pacific (ESCAP).

4. 'Fourth report of the Administrative Committee on Coordination to the Economic and Social Council' (E/1076).

5. See Council Resolution 823 (xxxii).

6. Forthcoming studies of the United Nations Institute for Training and Research will deal with the measures taken for the same purpose by certain regional economic commissions and non-United Nations bodies.

7. Council Resolution 1756 (LIV), para. 2.

8. This situation was corrected in due course: the Council was enlarged from 18 to 27 members in 1963, and then to 54 members in 1973.

9.   The non-aligned movement took form at the Belgrade meeting of heads of 'non-aligned' countries in 1961 and was influential in shaping the resolution, adopted by the General Assembly the following year, which led to the calling of the first UN Conference on Trade and Development (UNCTAD) in 1964. The objectives of the non-aligned movement and the interests of the developing countries in general have since tended more and more to converge. Nevertheless, the distinction remains valid and necessary. At the 1962 session of the General Assembly, where informal discussions took place on questions of trade and development within different broad groups, the group of developing countries numbered 77. That number has stuck as a title, although there are now more than 100 members of the group.

10. For a comprehensive and authoritative account of the thinking and the negotiations leading to the establishment of UNCTAD, see Diego Cordovez, 'The making of UNCTAD' in *Journal of World Trade Law* (London), Vol. 1, No. 3, May–June 1967, pp. 243–328. His book entitled *UNCTAD and Development Diplomacy: From Confrontation to Strategy*, published by the same journal in 1971 contains, *inter alia*, a thorough analysis of the relations between UNCTAD and GATT.

11. General Assembly Resolution 1995 (xix), para. 3 (d).

12. General Assembly Resolution 2152 (xxi), para. 27.

13. *Official Records of the General Assembly, Twenty-first Session, Supplement No. 5* (A/6305), Foreword by the Secretary-General, para. 20.

14. Note, for example, the reports of the Industrial Development Board on the work of its sixth and seventh session (1972 and 1973).

15. 'Question of the establishment of a comprehensive international trade organization', Report of the Secretary-General of UNCTAD. Doc. TD/B/535 of 30 December 1974.

16. See especially the request of the Industrial Development Board to the General Assembly at its Twenty-eighth Session, contained in the Board's report on the work of its Seventh Session (ibid., paras. 127–133).

17. Sometimes all funds constituted by voluntary contributions are categorized as 'trust funds', a formal definition of which has been given as follows by the Advisory Committee on Administrative and Budgetary Questions: 'A "trust fund" in United Nations terminology is an account set up for specific activities outside of the United Nations regular budget accounts... The Secretary-General is custodian of resources received for specific purposes which are consistent with the policies, aims and activities of the Organization and which do not directly or indirectly involve additional financial liability for the United Nations, except in those cases where the consent of the appropriate intergovernmental body has been obtained.' (A/8840/Add.1). More usually, however, the term is not applied to the funds established directly under General Assembly decisions but reserved for those set up by the Secretary-General under the second part of the definition just quoted.

18. See Joint Inspection Unit: Report on Trust Funds of the United Nations, by the Advisory Committee on Administrative and Budgetary Questions, A/8840/Add.1, transmitting comments by the Secretary-General and the Administrator of UNDP; A/8840/Add.2, 1972; and the annual UN Financial Reports and documents.

19. For a recent authoritative statement regarding the relationship between UNDP and the participating organizations, and between the resident representatives and the organizations' country representatives, see 'Sectoral

support and advice for resident representatives; report of the
Administrator' (DP/19, September 1973).

20. See discussion of 'Programme Integration as an output of systemic
co-ordination' in Mahdi Elmandjra, *op. cit.*, pp. 194–202.

21. General Assembly Resolution 2029 (xx), para. 6.

22. See 'Draft statute of the UNDP for consideration by the Governing
Council' (DP/22).

23. The current UNDP administrative budget provides for an Administrator at
the level equivalent to the head of a major specialized agency, three
Deputy Administrators (including the Executive Director of UNFPA) with
the rank of Under-Secretary-General of the United Nations (USG), and
seven Assistant Administrators with the rank of Assistant Secretary-General
(ASG). UNICEF has only one official of USG level, its Executive Director,
and none at all at the ASG level. The same modest structure prevails in
UNCTAD and UNIDO as well as in the Office of the High Commissioner
for Refugees. ESA has, in addition to one USG, two ASG posts.

24. In 1973, for example, while ACABQ found itself unable to recommend the
creation of new Assistant Secretary-General posts on the United Nations
budget for the Head of the Centre for Development Planning, Projections
and Policies, and the Deputy Executive Heads of UNCTAD, UNIDO and
UNHCR, the Governing Council of UNDP approved a proposal that the
post of Executive Director of the United Nations Fund for Population
Activities be raised to the Under-Secretary-General level. ACABQ
reported at the same time that the offer of the United Nations Secretariat to
help prepare the draft financial rules and regulations for that Fund had not
been accepted, and recommended that the Governing Council defer
consideration of those draft rules and regulations 'until the Secretary-General
has been given an opportunity to state his views thereon'. (DP/18, 25
September 1973).

25. So far, Central Africa, West Africa, East Africa and southern Africa, the
Caribbean and the South Pacific. A note on the purpose and character of
these teams was submitted by ACC to the Council in the Thirty-sixth
Report (E/4840 and Add.1).

3. *The content of coordination activities*

1. On the differences between the staff rules and regulations of the various
agencies and the United Nations, and generally on the subject of this
section, see Theodore Meron 'Administrative and Budgetary Coordination
by the General Assembly' in 'United Nations Administration of Economic
and Social Programmes' (Columbia University Press, 1966), p. 37. Note
that the level of emoluments for the professional grades in the common
system is 15–25% lower than that prevailing in the Bank and the Fund.
Another important point, generally overlooked, is that the UN Secretariat
is, in relation to the staffs of the other major specialized agencies, a depressed
service. Whereas the present Directors-General of ILO, FAO, UNESCO
and WHO, and the immediate predecessors as well as many of their top
officials, have all served as staff members of their organizations, the election
of a staff member of the UN Secretariat as Secretary-General would be
well-nigh unthinkable, and out of the thirty-odd UN officials with the grade
of Under- or Assistant-Secretary-General, all but one was brought in from
national services. Except in the rarest of cases, the top grade available in the
UN to a career official is that of Director.

2. The two actions which resulted from initiatives taken at different times by the *Ad Hoc* Committee, led to not a little confusion and overlap.

3. See especially the report by Mr Maurice Bertrand, of the Joint Inspection Unit, entitled 'Programming and budgets in the United Nations family of organizations' (A/7968, April 1970).

4. See 'Form of presentation of the United Nations budget and the duration of the budget cycle; report of ACABQ to the General Assembly at its twenty-seventh session' (A/8739), para. 57.

5. Note the presentation by some of the major agencies of expenditures from extra-budgetary funds so as to show their relationship with programmes funded by the regular budget; also the emphasis laid by CPC and ACABQ in their reports on the proposed United Nations programme and budget for 1974–1975 on the importance of systematically presenting in future programme budgets full information about the uses made as well as the sources of extra-budgetary funds.

6. The Preparatory Commission of the United Nations reported to the first session of the General Assembly as follows: 'The salary and allowances of the Secretary-General should be such as to enable a man of eminence and high attainment to accept and fulfil with dignity the high responsibility of the post. Similar considerations apply to the other principal higher officers. The Assistant Secretaries-General should be ensured a status at least equivalent to that of the heads of the specialized agencies.' (PC/20, Chap. VIII, Sec. 2, para. 67). The last sentence may have been unrealistic when it was written: in any event, it quickly became a dead letter. The governing organs of the agencies – and not only the major ones – have fixed the remunerations of their chief executive officers at a level approaching that of the United Nations Secretary-General or well above that of the top appointed officials of the United Nations. The major agencies now have deputy executive heads remunerated at a level somewhat above that of the United Nations Under-Secretaries-General – now the top echelon in the United Nations. The Assistant Directors-General of the major agencies have been assimilated to Assistant Secretaries-General of the United Nations.

7. E/4744. So called because the General Assembly had asked for a 'clear and comprehensive picture of the existing operational and research activities of the United Nations family of organizations...' The actual title of the document however, is 'An account of the operational and research activities of the United Nations system in the field of economic and social development'.

8. Including general development planning and policy; the strengthening of institutions and governmental services; the development of human resources, including education and training; social development, welfare and living conditions; development of natural resources; scientific resources and the application of science and technology to development; transport, communications and related services; statistics and other information data.

9. In its annual report for 1972–1973 (E/5289, Part I, para. 101), ACC stated that 'there continues to be a growing need for more efficient co-ordination of activities in the field of marine science and its applications' and suggested that the subject, to which the United Nations Conference on the Law of the Sea, as well as the United Nations Committee on the Peaceful Uses of the Sea-Bed and the Ocean Floor, lent urgency, should be 'included among the topics for in-depth consideration by the Council in 1974, or in 1975'. The Council took up the idea and, at its request, a detailed report on

coordination in this area was submitted to the Council by the
Secretary-General in 1975.

10. See 'Report on medium-term planning in the United Nations system' by
Maurice Bertrand, Joint Inspection Unit (JIU/REP/74/1, 1974).

11. Council Resolution 1756 (LIV), para. 3.

12. See Chapter 2 above.

13. 'Regional cooperation: study on regional structures; report of the
Secretary-General' (E/5127, 1972).

14. On the special difficulties of the Economic Commission for Africa, see
James S. Magee, *ECA and the Paradox of African Co-operation* (New York,
Carnegie Endowment for International Peace, 1970).

15. See especially 'Coordination at the country level: report of the
Secretary-General'. (E/4336, 1967), and the Capacity Study.

16. These missions, to Iran, Ecuador, Thailand, Chile and Tunisia, were
organized by the Secretary-General under Council Resolutions 1042
(XXXVII) and 1092 (XXXIX).

17. JIU/REP/684; circulated to the Council in document E/4698 and
Corr.1.

18. Temporarily so called. The old title was soon resumed.

19. General Assembly Resolution 2688 (xxv), Annex, para. 63.

20. See Chapter 2, the section on the impact of UNDP.

4. *Intergovernmental organs responsible for coordination*

1. General Assembly Resolution 3199 (XXVIII), para. 4.

2. Council Decision 1 (LVI), para. 2 (i).

3. General Assembly Resolution 3172 (XXVIII), para. 1.

4. See Chapter 3.

5. General Assembly Resolution 2188 (XXI), para. 2.

6. This is true even in the case of the World Bank whose decision to establish
IDA in 1960 was largely influenced by General Assembly pressure for a
SUNFED (Special United Nations Fund for Economic Develop-
ment).

7. Although the proposal was fully considered in ACC before it was finally
formulated, the Governing Body of the ILO sent a tripartite delegation to
New York in order to ensure that the programme autonomy of the ILO
would not be affected.

8. United Nations publication, Sales No. 60.IV.14.

9. Council Resolution 694 (XXVI), Annex, para. 14.

10. Council Resolution 798 (XXX).

11. Council Resolution 920 (XXXIV).

12. Council Resolution 992 (XXXVI), para. 2.

13. Council Resolution 1090, G (XXXIX), para. 5.

14. UN and agency representatives have always been ready to withdraw when
particularly sensitive matters are being discussed.

15. Council Resolution 1768 (LIV).

16. E/5259.

17. *Official Records of the Economic and Social Council, Fifty-fourth Session,*
Supplement No. 7 (E/5273).

18. E/5259, para. 18 (c) and *General Assembly Official Records, Twenty-eighth
Session,* Supplement No. 7 (A/9007).

19. Minor lapses, however, are always likely to occur. For example, at a time of
natural disaster, everybody able to make a contribution wants to do so.

5. *The Administrative Committee on Coordination*

1. For the critical importance of executive leadership as a determinant of the growth in scope and authority of international organization, see Robert W. Cox: *The Executive Head: An Essay on Leadership in International Organization.* International Organization, Vol. xxiii, Issue No. 2, Spring 1969.

2. UN Document PC/20.

3. Council Resolution 13 (iii).

4. See Introduction. One notable incident was a public criticism in the Council by the then Director-General of FAO, Dr B. R. Sen, of Hammarskjöld's proposal for setting up an international administrative service to assist developing countries directly as civil servants and not just as advisers. There had just been a meeting of ACC and Hammarskjöld felt any objection to his proposal should have been raised privately there. That was in 1958; 2 years later, he himself was criticized by some ACC members for the address he gave in Chicago, a few days after an ACC meeting, urging a *constitutional* framework for international cooperation through the UN to replace the weak *institutional* links existing between the UN and the specialized agencies. (See Foote *op. cit.*, pp. 251 et seq.).

5. For twenty years, Mr Philippe de Seynes, with whom the author worked especially closely.

6. Martin Hill, 'The Administrative Committee on Co-ordination', *op. cit.*, pp. 107–108.

7. E/4668. See below.

8. A rare instance of such disagreement being reported in the early years occurred in 1949 (GA official records, Fourth Session, Supplement 3 (A/972) p. 16) when the Secretary-General recorded his disagreement with his colleagues in connexion with the plan worked out through ACC for an expanded programme of technical assistance. (See Chapter 2, footnote 2.)

9. The following hand-written exchange between the writer and Hammarskjöld took place during the Council's discussion of Coordination matters in July 1957:
   M.H. The beginning of Schürmann's [Ambassador Carl Schürmann, representative of the Netherlands] speech, when you were out of the room, contained a lengthy criticism of ACC's evasive, smug and misleading reporting!
   D.H. What do they expect?
   M.H. They and the U.K. want differences of opinion, and the real problems that are not being overcome, to be brought out.
   D.H. This would mean on the whole U.N. *versus* Agencies (with the Council on our side).

10. 'Report on the meeting of the Council's officers and Chairman of the Coordination Committee with the Administrative Committee on Coordination, held on 20 July 1964' (E/3957), para. 6.

11. E/4668, para. 16.

12. For example, the words 'key policy issues' became 'key political issues' in the Russian translation of the report.

13. E/4755, para. 7.

14. In the joint meeting, the representative of France maintained that the proposed change would adversely affect the coordinating role of the Economic and Social Council. Since the Office was in part concerned with coordinating matters of substance, he felt that its activities should be supervised by the Department of Economic and Social Affairs.

15. Council Resolution 1547 (XLIX).
16. Council Resolution 1643 (LI), para. 9.
17. Martin Hill, 'The Administrative Committee on Co-ordination', *op. cit.*, p. 129.
18. Both quotations are from C. Wilfred Jenks, *The International Labour Organization in the U.N. Family*, UNITAR Lecture Series 3 (1971), pp. 40 and 41.
19. *Ibid.*

6. *The Secretary-General and the secretariats of the United Nations and the agencies*

1. See his article entitled, 'Pour une réforme du Conseil économique et social' in *Politique étrangère* (Paris, August–December 1951).
2. See Chapter 1.
3. Council Resolution 1174 (XLVI).
4. 'Thirty-third report of the Administrative Committee on Co-ordination' (E/4337), para. 24. Such a suggestion must be distinguished from that of the Group of Experts on the Structure of the United Nations System for a small joint research, planning and programming staff within the office of the proposed Director-General for Development and International Economic Cooperation.
5. E/4755, para. 8. For other aspects of this discussion, see Chapter 5.

7. *Some current constraints on order and coordination in the system*

1. Under the International Opium Convention of 1925, the League of Nations established, for purposes of narcotics control, a group of independent experts, the Permanent Central Opium Board, with its own staff, separate from the League's Committee and Section of Narcotic Drugs. The separation was maintained after the United Nations took over. A move, launched by ACABQ, is under way to look into these separate staff arrangements with a view to avoiding duplication.
2. The discrepancy between the top structure of UNDP and ESA has already been noted in Chapter 2. The discrepancy between ESA and the ILO (whose Director-General is flanked by two Deputy Directors-General and six Assistant Directors-General), or FAO (with one Deputy Director-General and six assistant Directors-General at Headquarters) is no less striking.
3. See *Proposed Programme Budget for the Biennium 1974–1975 (Official Records of the General Assembly, Twenty-eighth Session, Supplement No. 6* (A/9006)), 'Foreword of the Secretary-General'.
4. The role of UNCTAD in a new United Nations structure for global economic cooperation. TD/B/573.

8. *The context and the perspective*

1. A/6343; approved by the General Assembly in Resolution 2150 (XXI).
2. E/4748, para. 6.

9. *The role of the Economic and Social Council*

1. For an interesting discussion of how UNIDO has been exercising and should exercise its coordinating role in industrial development matters, see the report of the Industrial Development Board on the work of its sixth session

(*Official Records of the General Assembly, Twenty-seventh Session, Supplement No. 16* (A/8716)), paragraphs 104–110.

2. The following comment on a draft of this study made by the then Secretary-General of UNCTAD, Mr Manuel Perez-Guerrero, in February 1974 is of particular relevance:
    > 'Perhaps the experience gained with respect to UNCTAD and UNIDO might show how to ensure autonomy and coordination within a centralized political, organizational and budgetary setting. In this connection, the case of UNCTAD may be worth particular attention since our competence is not of the sectoral type. We are concerned with so many of the major policy issues with which the Council is occupied and preoccupied that sometimes the Council and UNCTAD are presented as competing organs. In fact, the Council has too broad a horizon to scan to be able to devote to international economic relations the attention given to them by UNCTAD. In turn, however broad the terms of reference of UNCTAD might be, the scope of our activities cannot compare with the over-all perspective of the Council.'

3. On this and many other aspects of the Council's difficulties, see Walter Rice Sharp, *The United Nations Economic and Social Council* (New York, Columbia University Press, 1969).
4. 'Basic programme of work of the Council for 1974' (E/5437). See also corresponding document for 1976 (E/5753).
5. Council Resolution 1768 (LIV).
6. One of the earliest such suggestions came from Professor Henri Laugier, the first United Nations Assistant Secretary-General for Social Affairs, in his article 'Pour une réforme du Conseil économique et social', in *Politique étrangère* (Paris, August–December 1951). A recent one can be found in *The United Nations in the 1970's; A Report of a National Policy Panel established by the United Nations Association of the United States of America* (New York, 1971).
7. See ACABQ's first report on the proposed programme budget for 1974–1975 (*Official Records of the General Assembly, Twenty-eighth Session, Supplement No. 8* (A/9008)).

10. *Other aspects of UN–agency relationships*

1. Rule 80 of the Rules of Procedure of the Council.
2. See Chapter 5.
3. Council Resolution 1643 (LI), para. 7.
4. See 'Report of the Secretary-General on action taken in pursuance of the agreements between the United Nations and the specialized agencies' (*Official Records of the Economic and Social Council, Fourth Year, Ninth Session, Supplement No. 17* (E/1317)).
5. See Introduction.
6. See Chapter 3: programme coordination, above.

11. *The functioning of the Administrative Committee on Coordination*

1. *Op. cit.*, paragraph 78.
2. This appears to be also the primary view of ACC itself. Document E/5704, paragraph 11.

12. *Some structural and organizational issues*

1. Many of the subjects discussed in this chapter have been the subject of far-reaching recommendations by the Group of Experts on the Structure of the United Nations System, which reported in 1975. The author is in broad agreement with these recommendations, but has preferrred to maintain in this study, with minor revisions, the more modest suggestions that he put forward in the earlier UNITAR draft.

2. See 'The Future Role of UNDP in World Development in the Context of the Preparations for the Seventh Special Session of the General Assembly', Report of the Administrator; Document DP/114, March 1975.

3. See Chapter 3.

4. This idea was adumbrated in the Capacity Study, Vol. II, Chapter 7, paras. 148 and 149. A precedent exists for the use of the title of Director-General in the area of the United Nations economic and social work. There was a Director-General of the United Nations Technical Assistance Administration until the UNTAA was made an integral part of the Department for Economic and Social Affairs in 1959.

5. Questions relating to natural resources are now so close to the centre of national and international economic policy that it may seem desirable for the Council and ESA to retain policy responsibilities in that area even if they relinquish their control over operations.

6. A Study of the Capacity of the United Nations Development System, (United Nations publication, Sales No. E.70.I.10, Vol. II), pp. 301–328.

7. See the reports of the Secretary-General concerning the organization of the Department of Economic and Social Affairs contained in documents A/C.5/1380 and Corr.1, A/C.5/1430 and A/C.5/1506.

8. 'Organization of the Secretariat – Office for Inter-Agency Affairs' (ST/SGB/131/Amend.21).

9. A recent example being the assignment to UNCTAD of responsibility for drafting the Charter of the Economic Rights and Duties of States – a task which would normally have fallen within the province of the Economic and Social Council.

13. *Expansion, adaptation, concentration and the responsibilities of the General Assembly*

1. A specific procedural recommendation for dealing with an agenda of this sort was contained in the report of the Pearson Commission, *Partners in Development* (New York, Praeger, 1969), Chapter XI, Section entitled, 'Towards improved international co-ordination', p. 227.

Postscript

1. Document A/10201.

2. ECOSOC Resolution 1911 (LVII).

3. E/5524 and Addenda.

4. E/5476 and Addenda.

5. Report of the Chairman of the Policy and Programme Coordination Committee and the Chairman of ACC on the joint meetings of the PPCC and ACC, July 1975 (E/5704).

Appendix 2. Principal organs of the United Nations (General Assembly, Economic and Social Council and Secretariat) with subsidiary organs directly concerned with economic and social cooperation and coordination (Status of Spring 1976)

1. Further details of their membership and terms of reference may be found in Document E/5453.
2. *Official Records of the Economic and Social Council, Fifty-fourth Session, Supplement No. 1* (E/5367), item 6, p. 39.

Appendix 3. Chart of agencies related to the United Nations

1. Reproduced from Press Release SA/213/Rev. 13.

Appendix 4. Regional and branch offices of organizations of the United Nations System

1. Includes membership of the Annual Meeting of the Institutes within the United Nations Family.
2. The Resident Representative of UNDP is the representative of the WFP in all recipient countries. Those offices where WFP has field staff in addition are indicated FS.
3. Field Offices for FAO indicate offices of FAO Country Representative; however, areas where these functions are delegated to a UNDP or other Agency Representative are not listed.
4. Planned to be opened or established.
5. Joint UNIC/UNDP/UNICEF Office.
6. Also, there is an UNESCO/ESCAP Science and Technology Joint Unit which operates in ESCAP premises.
7. Joint UNHCR/UNICEF Office.
8. Liaison Office with ECA and OAU.
9. Regional Offices also entrusted with Chief of Mission responsibilities.
10. Joint IAEA/UNESCO operation.
11. Includes seats of the Regional Offices for Africa and Latin America.
12. Joint UNIC/UNICEF Office.
13. Also the International Trade Centre UNCTAD/GATT.
14. Also joint UNIDO/ECWA Industry Unit.
15. Also covers Haiti.
16. Also covers Malawi and Lesotho.
17. Also covers The Gambia.
18. Also covers Brunei and Singapore.
19. Includes the seat of the Regional Office for Middle East and Europe.
20. Also covers Botswana.
21. Also covers Panama.
22. Covers Caribbean area.
23. Also covers British Honduras, Costa Rica, Guatemala, Honduras and Nicaragua.
24. Common premises between the United Nations Regional Economic Commission and the ECA/FAO Joint Agriculture Division.
25. Also covers Fiji Islands, Cook Islands, French Polynesia, Gilbert and Ellice Islands, New Hebrides, Niue, Papua New Guinea, Solomon Islands and Tonga.
26. Also covers Togo.
27. Also covers Mauritius and Seychelles Islands.
28. Also covers Maldives.

246

29. Also covers Liberia.
30. UNSCEAR Office to be established.

Appendix 6. A new UN structure for global economic cooperation – a list of conclusions and recommendations of the group of experts, prepared by the Secretariat

1. The present appendix does not form part of the report of the Group of Experts on the Structure of the United Nations System and, therefore, has no official status. It has been prepared by the Secretariat at the request of the Group of Experts for the convenience of the reader, it being understood that a full appreciation of the Group's recommendations requires that the report be read in its entirety.

2. The above recommendations, of course, have to be read subject to the understanding mentioned in paragraphs 7 and 8 above. It is understood that the fourth session of UNCTAD would take place as scheduled and that a decision on the fifth session would be made in connexion with the review of the transitional arrangements in the light of the effectiveness of the central institutions.

3. As explained in Chapter II, sect. E on Planning, programming and budgeting, the Council's review of the programme budget and medium-term plan of the United Nations proper would be undertaken with a view to adopting decisions thereon, whereas the Council's review of the plans, programmes and budgets of the specialized agencies would be for the purposes of coordination, bearing in mind the constitutional autonomy of the agencies.

4. The United Nations Scientific Committee on the Effects of Atomic Radiation, being a subsidiary body of the General Assembly, would not be affected. On the other hand, the United Nations Scientific Advisory Committee would be discontinued.

5. See recommendation 9.2 proposing that GATT and the United Nations enter into a mutually satisfactory agreement providing for a formal relationship, including exchange of information and closer administrative collaboration.

6. This follows the UNCTAD formula, and would require a minimum of 14 countries in the present General Assembly or six in the present Council. The precise definition of the type of proposals subject to consultative procedures would be defined by the Council in an appropriate rule of procedure.

7. The Group could be smaller than 10, of course, if the majority of members of the General Assembly or the Council so desired. Each group would be open to all countries with an interest in the subject-matter. However, in case the size of the group became unmanageable, it would be open to the Council to select the participants with a view to making the group as representative as possible and promoting agreement in the Council and the General Assembly.

8. Only those members of the Group from countries participating in the International Monetary Fund subscribe to the recommendations contained in this section.

9. Only those members of the Group from countries participating in the World Bank subscribe to the recommendations contained in this section.

Index

Organizations that are only mentioned in Appendices 1 and 2 are not included in the Index. Throughout the Index, for each letter of the alphabet, there are two sections each in alphabetic order, the first of acronyms, the second of other entries.

Index

FAO, 37, 40, 45, 68, 78, 146, 147, 150, 170; works with UNCTAD and UNIDO, 30; and World Food Programme, 33, 73; and agricultural education, 52; Mr Boerma's proposal on, 58; and World Food Conference, 158–60

Five Year Perspective, 1960–1964, 68

Frazao, Armando Sergio, 6

Fund for Population Activities, 33, 36; establishment of, 99

GATT, 14, 22, 45, 76, 159, 164, 171; and UNCTAD, 30–31, 146, 172

Gardner, Professor Richard, 162

General Assembly (G.A.), *passim* 5–26, 53; main references, 62–5, 144–51; creation of UN agencies by, 29–34; and administrative coordination, 43–51; and ECOSOC, 106–8, 111–14; and specialist agencies, 115–23

Guerrero, Dr Manuel Perez, 162

Hammarskjöld, Dag, 4, 75, 85, 123

Havana Conference, (1947–1948), 14

IACB, 26, 136

IAEA, 1, 20, 44, 45, 46, 49, 68, 73, 76, 79, 80, 146, 148; creation of, 14–15; overlap problems with, 21–2

IBRD, 14, 15, 17, 36, 91, 159–60, 170, 172; main reference, 39–42

ICAO, 14, 17, 45

IDA, 40, 165; *see also* Bank Group

IFC, 15, 40; *see also* Bank Group

ILPES, 59

IMF, *passim* 12–17, 60, 99, 120, 155, 160, 170, 171; and Special Drawing Rights, 156; creates oil facility, 164–5

ITU, *passim* 14–20, 43–47, 132, 146

International Centre for Theoretical Physics, 73

International Civil Service Advisory Board (ICSAB), creation of, 45, 87; *see also* International Civil Service Commission

International Civil Service Commission (ICSC), 45, 49, 122, 123, 131, 165; establishment of, 17; and development service, 39

International Development Strategy, 5, 7, 24, 158

International Labour Organization (ILO), 1, 11, 12, 13, 14, 23, 44, 45, 52, 68, 73, 78, 146, 170; siting of, 18; principal functions of, 20; and developing countries, 31–2

International Monetary Reform, 155

International Relief Organization (IRO), 14, 33

International Trade Organization (ITO), 14

International Union of Official Travel Organizations (IUOTO), 15

Interpol, 15

JIU, 55, 68, 77, 125, 150; formation of, 46–7, 85, 122

Jenks, Wilfred, 79, 82, 157

Kampala, FAO conference at, 58

Kassym, Al Noor, 162

Kingston Agreement, 164, 171

Kingston, Commonwealth Conference at, 163

Laugier, Professor Henri, 84

League of Nations, 11–12, 13, 25

Lie, Trygvie, 65, 75

Lima, UNIDO conference at, 160–63

Lomé, multinational conference at, 163

Maheu, René, 79, 85, 157–8

Morse, David, 65

New International Economic Order, 153–5

'New UN Structure for Global Economic Cooperation', 166–70

Non-Aligned Countries, Fourth Conference of, 7–8

OAS, 109

OAU, 109

OECD, 100, 109, 163

OIAA, *see* OIACC

OIAAC, 86, 122, 141, 171; and CPC, 65; main role of, 125; separates from ESA, 139

Organization of Petroleum Exporting. Countries (OPEC), 7

Orr, Lord Boyd, 158

Owen, David, 84

For EU product safety concerns, contact us at Calle de José Abascal, 56–1°,
28003 Madrid, Spain or eugpsr@cambridge.org.

www.ingramcontent.com/pod-product-compliance
Ingram Content Group UK Ltd.
Pitfield, Milton Keynes, MK11 3LW, UK
UKHW010037140625
459647UK00012BA/1443